ROUTLEDGE LIBRARY EDITIONS: MULTINATIONALS

Volume 8

FOREIGN MULTINATIONALS AND THE BRITISH ECONOMY

FOREIGN MULTINATIONALS AND THE BRITISH ECONOMY

Impact and Policy

STEPHEN YOUNG, NEIL HOOD AND
JAMES HAMILL

Routledge
Taylor & Francis Group

LONDON AND NEW YORK

First published in 1988 by Croom Helm Ltd

This edition first published in 2017
by Routledge
2 Park Square, Milton Park, Abingdon, Oxon OX14 4RN

and by Routledge
711 Third Avenue, New York, NY 10017

Routledge is an imprint of the Taylor & Francis Group, an informa business

British Library Cataloguing in Publication Data
A catalogue record for this book is available from the British Library

ISBN: 978-1-138-28116-5 (Set)
ISBN: 978-1-315-27111-8 (Set) (ebk)
ISBN: 978-1-138-24242-5 (Volume 8) (hbk)
ISBN: 978-1-315-27132-3 (Volume 8) (ebk)

Publisher's Note
The publisher has gone to great lengths to ensure the quality of this reprint but
points out that some imperfections in the original copies may be apparent.

Disclaimer
The publisher has made every effort to trace copyright holders and would welcome
correspondence from those they have been unable to trace.

Foreign Multinationals and the British Economy

IMPACT AND POLICY

Stephen Young, Neil Hood and James Hamill

CROOM HELM
London • New York • Sydney

© 1988 Stephen Young, Neil Hood and James Hamill
Croom Helm Ltd, Provident House,
Burrell Row, Beckenham, Kent BR3 1AT
Croom Helm Australia Ltd, 44–50 Waterloo R
North Ryde, 2113, New South Wales

Published in the USA by
Croom Helm
in association with Methuen, Inc.
29 West 35th Street
New York, NY 10001

British Library Cataloguing in Publication Data

Young, Stephen, *1944–*
    Foreign multinationals and the British
    economy.
    1. International business enterprises —
    Great Britain 2. Great Britain —
    Economic Conditions — 1945–
    I. Title   II. Hood, Neil   III. Hamill
    James
    338.8'8841 HD2845
    ISBN 0-7099-1285-4

Library of Congress Cataloging-in-Publication Data
  Young, Stephen, 1944–
    Foreign multinationals and the British economy : impact and policy
    / Stephen Young, Neil Hood, James Hamill.
       p.   cm.
    Bibliography:p.
    Includes index.
    ISBN 0-7099-1285-4
    1. International business enterprises — Great Britain.
2. Investments, Foreign — Great Britain. 3. International business
enterprises — Government policy — Great Britain. 4. Great Britain-
-Economic conditions — 1945–   I. Hood, Neil. II. Hamill, James.
III. Title.
HD2845.Y68 1988
338.8'8841 — dc 19   87-27573

It should be noted that Neil Hood's contribution
to this volume reflects his own personal opinions
and not those of the British government.

Filmset by Mayhew Typesetting, Bristol, England
Printed and bound in Great Britain by
Biddles Ltd, Guildford and King's Lynn

Contents

List of Tables

List of Figures

1

Introduction: The Issues

The aim of this book is to provide a benchmark review of inward investment in Britain in the late 1980s. The timing is appropriate in a number of ways. The country has experienced nearly a decade of the Thatcher experiment, increasingly affecting inward investment through events such as the 'Big Bang',[1] and yet the UK economy has shown only limited improvement. It is pertinent to ask: 'what part, if any, can foreign multinationals play in the restoration of British competitiveness and the regeneration of the British economy?' The international business environment within which inward investment is taking place has, moreover, changed very radically. While subject to much hype, from industrialists themselves (witness the 'world car'[2]) as well as from journalists and academics, it is still true that competition has become increasingly international, even global in scale, and this process may extend to a wider range of manufacturing and service sectors in the years to come. The role of the subsidiaries of multinationals in Britain within this global competitive framework needs to be considered and questioned, as indeed does the relevance of 'national' industrial policy. Ten years ago, two of the present authors wrote that the failure of the government's attempt to rescue Chrysler UK was due to a 'lack of understanding of the operations of multinational enterprises';[3] is the suggestion still not true in relation to British MNE policies?

Because of such changes in international business and the international environment too, it may not, in fact, be meaningful in future to analyse inward investment as a separate component of business activities: inward and outward direct investment are interrelated, and inward investment (itself perhaps more footloose) is only one of a number of means of undertaking business across national frontiers alongside other contractual forms such as licensing.

The role and impact of foreign MNEs in Britain has been the subject of a number of studies over the years. The work of Dunning, for example, has spanned nearly two decades, encompassing both the US direct investment phenomenon of the 1950s and 1960s and the Japanese investment issues of the 1980s.[4] Interest in the topic has ebbed and flowed: the optimistic findings of the report by Steuer and his colleagues for the Department of Trade and Industry in 1973 seemed to quieten the debate for some time;[5] but the reverberations associated with the oil price shock and the loss of competitiveness of some major American MNEs brought inward investment back closer to the centre of the stage, especially at the regional level in Britain. And in the 1980s there have been a succession of individual issues and controversies highlighted in the work of Brech and Sharp, Stopford and Turner and others.[6] The present volume aims to review the historical contribution of inward investment in Britain, and, from this to identify the major multinational issues of the present day and their link to Britain's competitive position in the world.

THE STATE OF BRITAIN AND BRITISH COMPETITIVENESS

It is almost unnecessarily trite to remark that since World War Two the British economy has witnessed a dramatic decline in relation to that of its principal competitors. Low productivity, low growth of *per capita* income and until the 1970s persistent balance of payments and exchange rate crises were characteristics of the British economy. The 1970s added frighteningly higher inflation, substantial intra-European industrial restructuring and severe unemployment to that list, while the unfavourable economic climate was a severe barrier to the growth of R & D and to innovation. Looking at the British economy in the mid to late 1980s, the fundamental problems still remained: in job terms especially the position had deteriorated further, with unemployment rising to historically high levels. On the other hand, inflation had been brought down to a rate below the OECD average, output was rising steadily and there was evidence of sharply improved productivity and corporate profitability, with even some signs of relative improvement *vis-à-vis* Britain's major competitors.[7]

Particularly worth emphasising because of the relationship to the multinational dimension is British trade performance. Traditionally the UK has been an importer of food and raw materials, but in 1983,

Figure 1.1: UK imports and exports of manufactures (by volume)

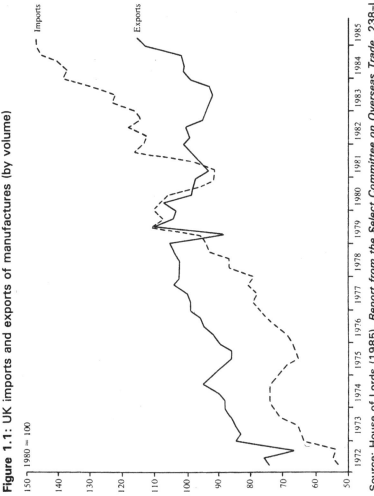

Source: House of Lords (1985), *Report from the Select Committee on Overseas Trade*, 238-I, Session 1984–5, HMSO, London, 30 July, Figure 2.2.

Table 1.1: Crude balance of trade (summary by class)

	Exports minus imports (£ millions)			Change in balance 1978–84
	1978	1983	1984	
Class 21 Extraction and preparation of metalliferous ores	− 619	− 764	− 801	− 182
Class 22 Metal manufacturing	− 236	− 528	− 181	55
Class 23 Extraction of minerals NES	− 252	− 269	− 79	173
Class 24 Non-metallic mineral products	289	196	165	− 124
Class 25 Chemical industry	1,192	1,582	1,682	490
Class 26 Man-made fibres production	82	54	73	− 9
Class 31 Metal goods NES	259	− 61	− 153	− 412
Class 32 Mechanical engineering	2,345	1,934	1,965	− 380
Class 33 Office machinery and data processing equipment	− 213	− 947	− 1,050	− 837
Class 34 Electrical and electronic engineering	697	− 1,036	− 1,398	− 2,095
Class 35 Motor vehicles and their parts	334	− 2,535	− 2,502	− 2,836
Class 36 Other transport equipment	521	1,150	1,279	758
Class 37 Instrument engineering	− 35	− 185	− 272	− 237
Classes 41/42 Food, drink and tobacco	− 1,947	− 2,591	− 3,301	− 1,354
Class 43 Textile industry	− 270	− 1,056	− 1,307	− 1,037
Class 44 Leather and leather goods	− 55	− 97	− 115	− 60
Class 45 Footwear and clothing industries	− 318	− 1,018	− 1,317	− 999
Class 46 Timber and wooden furniture	− 896	− 1,668	− 1,829	− 933
Class 47 Paper, printing and publishing	− 775	− 1,497	− 1,872	− 1,097
Class 48 Rubber and plastics processing	159	− 173	− 274	− 433
Class 49 Other manufacturing industries	− 139	− 444	− 491	− 352
Divns 2–4 Manufacturing industries (Rev definition)	124	− 9,948	− 11,765	− 11,889

Source: House of Lords (1985), *Report from the Select Committee on Overseas Trade*, 238–I, Session 1984–5, HMSO, London, 30 July, Table 2.4.

as the culmination of a trend that had been evident for a number of years, the UK recorded its first ever peacetime deficit in manufactured trade. The pattern is shown in Figure 1.1; clearly the developments since 1972 which are highlighted have contributed towards the decline in manufacturing output (both in absolute and in relative terms) which took place during the period. The poor export performance and increasing import penetration occurred in most industrial sectors, and balances of trade deteriorated against nearly all geographical trading areas. It is, nevertheless, worth drawing attention to Table 1.1 on changes in crude trade balances by industry class: between 1978 and 1984, the trade balance in both electrical and electronic engineering (class 34) and motor vehicles (class 35) deteriorated by between £2 and 3 billion; these sectors are dominated by foreign owned companies both as regards investment in the UK and UK trade.

The position on manufacturing trade balances does not reveal the whole balance of payments picture. Nor is manufacturing output and productivity the only contributor to GDP. Yet, the service industries cannot substitute for manufacturing, given that many services are dependent on manufacturing and it has been suggested that only 20 per cent of services are tradeable abroad. With the oil account in deficit before the end of the century, and income from overseas investment and inward capital investment flows unlikely to compensate fully, clearly manufacturing is crucial.

The declining state of Britain is thus fundamentally attributal to the lack of competitiveness of manufacturing industry, since success in selling goods at home and abroad is dependent on the competitiveness of the products. Competitiveness has numerous aspects — price, quality, design and process, delivery, reliability, selling efficiency and so on, together necessary to produce sustained growth in output levels. Price competitiveness is affected by a number of short run and long run components, including labour costs, investment, productivity and the exchange rate; the relative contribution of each of these two changes in UK competitiveness has varied over time — in the 1980s the improvement in relative productivity was supported by sterling depreciation, but competitiveness eroded by labour costs. Because of the work of the National Economic Development Council (NEDC) and the Economic Development Committees (EDCs) there is now a greater awareness of the significance of non-price factors, particularly quality and quality control, design, delivery and after sales service, but much remains to be done in implementing improvements. Digging deeper to identify the underlying causes of

Figure 1.2: Requirements for manufacturing competitiveness in Britain

	Macro	**Micro**
Hardware	1. Government fiscal and monetary policies and industrial policies — Macro policies favouring manufacturing and trade — Exchange rate stability — Low interest rates, especially for SMEs — Taxes and rates to favour manufacturing industry and investment — Supportive and integrated industrial policy — Support for innovation and export	2. Production capability — Level and quality of investment — Utilisation of investment — Creation of new technology
Software	3. Socio-economic environments — National attitudes — Educational system: attitudes, orientation, responsiveness, levels of expenditure — Regulation and deregulation	4. Corporate management[a] — Quality of management: in turn relating to range of managerial issues from corporate strategy to labour relations — Non-price-competitiveness factors, including quality, design, market research, delivery, after sales service — Import substitution and local sourcing — Export promotion

Note: a. Some of these factors may also be amenable to government policy intervention.
Sources: The matrix is derived from W.J. Abernathy, K.B. Clark, and A.M. Kantrow (1981), 'The new industrial competition', *Harvard Business Review*, September–October. The items within the matrix are drawn from House of Lords (1985), *Report from the Select Committee on Overseas Trade*, 236–I, Session 1984–5, HMSO, London, 30 July.

deteriorating competitiveness leads the observer first to the company and corporate management, and questions both of corporate strategy and specific matters such as the encouragement of marketing, the provision of finance, innovation and R & D, maker/user relationships and manpower and training; and thereafter to education, cultural and attitudinal factors. The fact that there is no panacea and that Britain's competitiveness problems are ubiquitous are perhaps the most important lessons learned in recent years.

A House of Lords Select Committee, appointed to consider the causes and implications of the deficit in the UK's balance of trade in manufactures reviewed many of the issues discussed above.[8] The conclusions have been summarised in Figure 1.2, distinguishing crudely between 'macro' and 'micro' issues, and 'hardware' (plant and equipment) and 'software' (people, corporate management). There is no question that stable and supportive fiscal and monetary policies provide an important framework within which firms compete. Nevertheless the key requirements for manufacturing competitiveness are associated with quadrants two and four, and these in turn are believed to be dependent upon attitudinal changes at all levels, an educational system which is responsive to the needs of industry and the revival of entrepreneurship (but it has to be asked whether some of these are real problems or not: for example, some foreign companies find their British workers as responsive and productive as anywhere in the world). The same problem areas could be analysed differently to distinguish between short run factors (North Sea oil and government financial and exchange rate policies); medium term factors such as demand considerations; and the long run variables of poor rates of investment and culture and attitudes.

It is within the theme of the restoration of British competitiveness that the position of inward investment and foreign multinationals needs to be considered. The broad issues associated with multi-nationality and the internationalisation of business are discussed in the next section. Before turning to this topic, it is interesting to look at the conclusions of the Select Committee on inward investment, competitiveness and the balance of payments. Essentially, four main points emerged:[9]

Inward investment flows and the balance of payments. To quote: 'there remains the theory that flows of inward capital investment could enable the country to sustain a permanent deficit in manufac-turing, but . . . there is no reason to suppose that investment in the United Kingdom will appeal to overseas investors on the scale that would be required. And over-reliance on inward investment is not desirable so long as development of strategies and innovation continue to be based overseas' (para. 95).

Operating characteristics of foreign firms. 'The Committee felt that many British firms had much to learn from foreign practices in the drive to be competitive . . . The factors are well known: attention to quality, good marketing, paying attention to the consumers' requirements, labour force motivation and cooperation, effective training, sufficient investment in R & D and up to date technology such as flexible manufacturing systems, etc. Many of these factors are transferable' (para. 124).

Sourcing policies of multinationals. Criticism was made of the import content of the manufactures of MNEs, especially in the motor and IT industries. It was accepted, nevertheless, that decisions on importing, as opposed to sourcing locally, were made because of high costs and poor industrial relations historically in the motor industry, and because of the failure of indigenous suppliers in the IT sector.

Government policy and MNEs. It was advised that pressure be brought to bear on MNEs to source more manufacturing in the UK. And in the case of new investors, 'Government should be less beguiled by the immediate employment opportunities they create and more concerned with the level of manufacturing and value added. They should be careful too in their encouragement of the import of foreign R & D to the detriment of development of new technologies by indigenous British firms. Britain's technical independence must not inadvertently be weakened' (para. 219).

The items above relate chiefly to quadrants two and four — the micro dimensions — in Figure 1.2. As the statements show, MNEs may make a positive contribution to Britain's competitiveness across these dimensions. On the other hand, the multinationals themselves may be hampered (as in local sourcing) by adverse features of the British economy deriving from quadrants one and three; the latter may also retard the transferability of superior management practices into the indigenous sector. Finally, centralised R & D at headquarters level within the MNEs is an offsetting negative factor in quadrant two. Already then some of the problems and contradictions associated with foreign multinationals can be seen.

MULTINATIONALS: THE GLOBAL ISSUES

Multinationals both react to and are a major driving force within the changing world economy. The shifting balance of economic power, market growth in developing and newly industrialising countries (NICs), the transition from old to new industries such as mecha-tronics (the interaction of mechanical engineering and electronics), informatics, fibre optics, biotechnology and so on, the revolution in information and communication systems — all have required a response from companies competing internationally. Differential rates of market growth, for instance, have affected the sales and manufacturing orientations of firms. The aspirations of the develop-ing countries have led to new forms of contractual arrangements in their dealings with MNEs. Multinationals, like all firms, have had to respond to product improvement and innovation, and failure to do this with sufficient skill or rapidity has led to disinvestment at home and abroad.

The same firms driving some of these developments have also been in the forefront of using them to create and sustain international competitiveness. Think of the experience curve-based cost reduction strategies in the semiconductor industry, which saw the discrete devices (transistors, diodes) of the 1960s, replaced by LSI ('large scale integration') chips; semiconductor assembly moving offshore to low wage, export processing zone sites in the NICs; and most recently some assembly being transferred back to the developed countries with innovations in robotic assembly. The international division of labour and the growth of intermediate product trade may not thus develop as far as many have predicted. The activities of MNEs, moreover, may be changing conventional notions regarding so called 'mature' industries. For example, the automobile industry is emerging as one of the largest users of electronic devices, and along with the aerospace industry is the principal operator of all the major elements of computer integrated manufacturing — robotics, flexible manufacturing systems, and computer-aided design.

The dynamics of the international economy clearly impact upon the role and activities of foreign multinationals in Britain and ultimately upon the competitiveness of the economy, and it is impor-tant, therefore, to highlight some of the major global issues of the present time.

The globalisation of business

While rolling easily off the tongue, it is not a straightforward matter to pinpoint exactly what terms such as 'global competition' and 'global strategy' actually mean. It is, nevertheless, true that in many industries, competition is now international rather than national; that manufacturing and marketing policies may be conceived on a regional if not a world scale; that despite the widening of sources of competition, the market may be dominated by a few global players; and that supporting and reinforcing these developments is the need to amortise investment in world-scale plants and R & D programmes, and in some product areas the growing standardisation of tastes.

From the present viewpoint, one of the most important conclusions to emerge from the globalisation thesis is that the market-servicing strategies of companies may vary widely. The typology of international strategies developed by Porter (Figure 1.3) is helpful in distinguishing between different types of policies according to the characteristics of the industry and the nature of competition:[10] where low cost manufacture and product quality are best achieved by production at home, then an export strategy will result; where transport costs are high, economies of scale low and national market differences exist, a market-by-market manufacturing policy may be required; contrast this with the pure global strategy of concentrating as many activities as possible in one or a few countries, and supplying the world from these closely coordinated operations. As an aside, with the divergence of policy to achieve the same end, the distinction between the multinational company and the more broadly defined international firm blurs considerably.

A number of points may be developed from the basic matrix in Figure 1.3:

Shifting strategies. Strategies will shift over time so as to maintain global competitive advantage.[11] It has been suggested that the assault of Japanese firms such as Sony, Casio, Seiko, Canon, Toyota and Honda has been a step wise process involving, firstly, a low labour cost based export strategy, with access to foreign markets through private labelling and collaborative ventures; secondly, investment in large scale plants and automation, though still involving exports; thirdly, heavy investment in worldwide distribution networks and global brands; most recently the movement of manufacturing and assembly operations to major developed countries in the face of protectionist pressures, while adhering to the principle of global strategies.

Transition to global competition. In a number of industries, the

Figure 1.3: Types of international strategies

	Geographically dispersed	Geographically concentrated	
High	High foreign investment with extensive coordination among subsidiaries	Purest global strategy	
Coordination of activities			Value activities
Low	Country-centred strategy by multinationals with a number of domestic firms operating in only one country	Export-based strategy with decentralised marketing	
	Geographically dispersed	Geographically concentrated	
	Configuration of activities		

Source: Porter, M.E. (1986), 'Changing patterns of international competition', *California Management Review*, 28(2), winter.

transition from country–centred to regional competition and then global competition has been observed, radically affecting the nature of production activity in foreign locations; and leading to close scrutiny of cost performance in alternative locations.

Non-dominant firm strategy. Smaller and non-dominant (home country) firms in global industries will require to seek protective market niches; but they may in addition be able to use market servicing flexibility, e.g. licensing and joint venture arrangements, to secure competitive advantage at least on a short run basis. Therefore quite a variety of forms of servicing international markets are likely to be apparent among these non-dominant competitors, and this may be one of the most obvious changes to be observed, given that the majority of companies fall into this category.

The European position. Linked to the technology discussion later, the majority of global companies are Japanese and American, posing major problems for the European firms in mounting an effective response. The European telecommunications industry is a case in point; and, more generally, where the European industry is protected, this may further delay the required reorientation of thinking among companies to move from national to international marketing.

11

Implications for the UK

As the location for foreign multinational subsidiaries, Britain is obviously affected by these developments, and the impact issues will be explored more fully in Chapter 5. Even so, there are a number of broad implications which seem to derive from the above discussion. In the *first* place where investments are taking place within a global competitive framework, *there may be a greater volume of investment in industries where domestic firms are already present.* In such cases, the issue of net benefit, taking into consideration the displacement of indigenous companies and their jobs and exports arises.

Secondly, presumably a consequence of the intensity of competition there will be *more footloose investment.* Certainly the possibility for production-switching by MNEs has been exaggerated in the past, given the fixed assets laid down and upheaval costs; but this may not necessarily be the case in the future when government support in terms of investment incentives, the availability of factory space in hi-tech parks etc. is taken into account. In any event, if product life cycles are short, then the time between major investment and locational decisions will also be shortening. Potential country locations may be scrutinised more rigorously too which brings in the country-specific attributes of the UK, as outlined in Figure 1.2.

Thirdly, the discussion of global strategies, and particularly the behaviour of the Japanese, throws *doubts on the inevitability of foreign manufacturing investment* as a stage in the internationalisation process. The argument has commonly been propounded that foreign manufacture is an important marketing tool; now it has been shown that heavy investment in branding and distribution is perhaps the key. Moreover, the stability of manufacturing investment made in response to protectionist pressures has to be questioned.

Fourth, a *dilemma* arises *for policy makers* in Britain. The country needs to be integrated into the global strategies of MNEs to ensure the competitiveness of the subsidiary operations. On the other hand, the subsidiaries so established may essentially be branch factories, with little autonomy and few linkages into the domestic economy. This topic of subsidiary strategies is developed in Chapter 5.

Finally, in the dynamic world of shifting policies, new sources of investment and new contractual forms, *the targeting strategies of the attraction agencies in the UK become much more difficult.* Is an American-owned assembly plant preferable to a Japanese marketing and distribution centre or an inward licence from West Germany?

Technology and the multinational

Alongside the growing internationalisation of business is a second key economic imperative — the new technologies. There is a whole range of these including information technology, fibre optics, advanced materials, biotechnology etc. All are at different stages in their development and application, and their impact on business and particularly the internationalisation of business is also rather uncertain at this point. This is especially true of biotechnology, for example, where early predictions of revolutionary breakthroughs have yet to be fulfilled, and most emphasis is placed here on technologies associated with electronics; although this does not simplify the problem of analysis since electronics technology is increasingly pervasive in its applications. In the area of information technology, innovations in micro electronics have allowed massive amounts of information to be processed more and more cheaply on smaller and user-friendly computers.[12] At the same time, other developments in telecommunications have permitted the worldwide transmission of this increased data availability, thereby revolutionising financial markets, facilitating the globalisation of newspapers and journals like *The Economist, The Financial Times, The Wall Street Journal, Time* and *Newsweek*, and bringing global product marketing a big step nearer.

At the industry level, information technology has been predicted to change the nature of products and services by its effect in shortening product life cycles, thus yielding a significant competitive advantage to firms which quickly adapt to new life cycle frequencies. Information technology may cause significant changes in some markets by raising computer literacy and thus increasing the demand for electronically based products and services. Information technology may, in addition, change the basic economics of some industries through applications like computerised warehousing and stock control and by altering the traditional trade-off between standardisation and flexibility.

At the level of the firm, the effects of information technology are determined by various competitive forces at work in the firm's environments:

Supplier relationships will be fundamentally altered; for instance, a firm which implements sophisticated quality control systems will increase pressure on materials and component suppliers to become more quality conscious themselves

Buyer relationships with firms will be affected as new products, services and distribution channels evolve within the industry

The substitution process in some industries will be accelerated by the use of computer-aided design and engineering systems by companies whose main strategy is to duplicate new products at low costs

In some industries, information technology will lower traditional entry barriers, and may erect new ones, so influencing the rate of new entry into the industry; as noted above, many distribution firms have implemented sophisticated warehousing and stock control systems but the sheer cost of these represents a considerable entry barrier

Information technology will also impact on industry structure by altering the rivalry basis amongst the member firms through the establishment of differential competitive positions.

This leads on to issues pertaining to strategy, and the technology-driven nature of strategy likely to emerge from the above. Among a number of such classifications, a distinction has been made between a leading-edge strategy, a wait-and-see strategy and a lagging-behind strategy.[13] The strategic choice of some of the smaller, hi-tech US firms fits the first of these categories, and the second is relevant to large American producers like IBM. In the third category are firms which have failed to gain a competitive edge in particular markets, perhaps despite heavy and continuous R & D programmes. It is necessary to be careful in any such classification. For instance, there are dangers in being mesmerised by the technology, when the real source of advantage may come from adding value at the customer level through marketing and distribution.[14] And, the commercial focus of R & D programmes is crucial, witness the success of DEC and Hewlett-Packard linked to the identification of applications and segments relatively ignored by IBM. Study of Japanese companies is instructive in this regard too, where success is based upon investing most heavily in R & D in pre-existing products and technologies and/or, investing only after specific products or technologies have been sufficiently well developed by other firms.[15]

There are close links between the international and technology dimensions of strategy: heavy R & D programmes demand large markets to amortise the investment; short product life cycles similarly mean rapid international marketing; the global competitors must take a position on the best R & D strategy to gain competitive advantage, as the non-dominant firms direct their research and development expenditures to product or market segments internationally where competition is less severe.

What then are likely to be the international business consequences of the new technologies? A range of topics can be explored:

Information technology: control and variety. Figure 1.4 highlights some of the information technology applications that would support either low cost or product differentiation strategies in firms.[16] If this is extended to multinational business, the main obvious implication is that of increased control, in a range of functional areas including planning, production, finance, personnel and marketing. This will certainly focus greater attention on cross-country performance, and *inter alia* may mean more centralisation; following on from this, IT should produce less need for functional specialists in overseas subsidiaries. It has been suggested, for example, that the engineering function will be returned to headquarters, with design blueprints, produced using computer-aided design (CAD) in the MNEs head office, being transmitted electronically to computer-aided manufacturing (CAM) factories abroad.[17]

At the manufacturing level, however, the four principal technologically based systems which are being implemented, viz. robotics, flexible manufacturing systems, CAD and CAM and computer-integrated manufacturing (CIM), are associated with smaller scale and greater variety. Economies of scale are being replaced by economies of scope, in which smaller factories and shorter production runs of any given design, along with easy and rapid shifts from one design to another, are key elements.[18] It would be wrong to underestimate the difficulties of implementing these systems and the great demands which are placed upon the software components. In the automobile industry much has been made of the changed fortunes of smaller and medium sized producers brought about by these advances in production technology, but the benefits do not yet seem very obvious at Austin Rover.

From the MNE perspective, the implication is of greater flexibility for subsidiaries in product design and product mix and, therefore, in adapting to local tastes, market conditions, etc. Here manufacturing systems link up with IT-induced flexibility and sophistication in marketing and sales (Figure 1.4) to provide the possibility for greater autonomy at subsidiary level.

There are, in addition, locational consequences as between

15

Figure 1.4: Information technology applications and generic strategies of firms

	GENERIC STRATEGIES	
	Low cost	Product differentiation
Product design and development	Product engineering systems Project control systems	R & D data bases Professional work stations Electronic mail CAD Custom engineering systems Integrated systems for manufacturing
Operations	Process engineering system Process control systems Labour control systems Inventory management systems Procurement systems Quality monitoring systems	CAM Quality assurance systems Systems for suppliers Quality monitoring systems
Marketing	Streamlined distribution systems Centralised control systems Econometric modelling systems	Sophisticated marketing systems Market data bases Graphic display systems Telemarketing systems Competition analysis systems Modelling systems Service-oriented distribution systems
Sales	Sales control systems Advertising monitoring systems Systems to consolidate sales function Strict incentive/monitoring systems	Differential pricing systems Office/field communications Customer/sales support systems Dealer support systems Customer order entry systems
Administration	Cost control systems Quantitative planning and budgeting systems Office automation for staff reduction	Office automation to integrate functions Environment scanning and non-quantitative planning systems Teleconferencing systems

Source: Parsons, G.L. (1983), 'Information technology, a new competitive weapon', *Sloan Management Review*, 25(1).

subsidiaries themselves. Robotics and automation more generally are reducing the significance of labour costs, meaning that the attractiveness of low wage countries is also reduced.

R & D programmes in multinational companies

Research and development in MNEs has typically been highly centralised, especially as regards basic research. However, some growing decentralisation of applied research and short term development work to the level of the foreign subsidiary has been observed among American MNEs. The likely impact of the new technologies on the location of R & D is not at all clear. One suggestion is that economies of scale eroded by CIM will have to be found elsewhere, with R & D as one likely candidate for concentration.[19] But this may principally refer to fundamental research: the logic of exploiting the product differentiation possibilities gained from IT in manufacturing and marketing is decentralised adaptation and modification-type R & D.

Relationships with suppliers in host countries

The R & D demands of new innovations are so great in some instances as to make the largest MNEs baulk at the prospect. This has led to greater outsourcing and an enhanced role for the procurement function within enterprises. Both centralised control over procurement and international search for potential suppliers are facilitated by IT, while tighter controls of in-process inventories are also feasible. These factors place increasing pressure on indigenous suppliers in host countries and give multinational supplying organisations a big advantage: aside from meeting the requirements of volume, price, quality and delivery, such companies are able to afford the R & D investment required to keep pace with product innovation at the customer level.

Implications for the UK

Like the ubiquitous nature of the technologies themselves, the ramifications for Britain could be wide ranging and far reaching and only some of the more obvious points are indicated here. *First*, at the broadest level, *trends* in both the internationalisation of business and *in technology* interact to *force an open British economy to be competitive* or be damned. This conclusion derives from the possibilities for international comparisons and the footloose nature of investment activity.

Second, and related, the *poor innovation performance* of the economy *places* a *heavy dependence on the importation of technology*, although not necessarily incorporated within the multinational. Alternative transfer modes such as licensing may represent another possibility, except that licensing is not normally associated with state of the art technology.

Third, the survival of multinational subsidiaries in Britain *requires that* the *factories are at the leading edge of technological advance*, not only in terms of product technology, but also production technology and production organisation. In relation to the latter, one of the lessons of the Japanese success is that the way people are organised and managed is a crucial dimension of competitiveness. As an associated point, it would be useful to undertake some categorisation of foreign-owned manufacturing units in Britain on the basis of technology incorporated into production. To a much greater extent than in the past, a distinction exists between hi-tech and low-tech branch plants (relating to manual versus automated assembly etc.).

Fourth, it is *by no means clear how* the product, process and management *technology* incorporated into inward investment *is transferable into the indigenous sector*. Are there mechanisms whereby an indigenous company which is technologically backward can catch up or leapfrog, using MNE subsidiaries as benchmarks?

Fifth, the discussions above indicated both centralisation pressures and decentralisation possibilities from technology. Referring to the latter, it has been remarked that 'old thinking about "custom" markets versus "mass" markets may well be obsolete. Big firms will be able to provide "custom" service, and small firms will be able to contemplate "mass" markets hitherto beyond their reach'.[20] *Multinationals should be in the position to permit their subsidiaries to explore specialised market segments and exploit these globally*, providing they do not damage the mass market of the parent. Hewlett-Packard could be viewed as a case in point in Britain: aside from its conventional role as a European manufacturing facility for products transferred from the USA, the UK company has a charter for the design and manufacture of test and measurement product and systems for the telecommunications markets of the world.

Sixth, the USA has seen its technological leadership challenged by the Japanese in a whole succession of sectors — electronic components, telecommunications and office machinery being the most recent. *This is relevant to inward investment promotional policies* which have been strongly targeted on the USA.

18

Seventh, and again a policy issue, *studies* of the location of high technology firms *have highlighted the labour-intensive nature of production operations*, with the companies employing a high percentage of technicians, engineers and scientists. Labour skills and labour availability dominate rankings of locational choice factors.[21] *This is of significance* both *for manpower policy* in the UK and the role of colleges and universities in providing the numbers of workers with the necessary skills, *and for incentive policies*.

Finally, given the contribution of inward investment to technology advance in the UK, there are issues to be discussed concerning the access of foreign MNEs to European and UK policy programmes such as the Alvey Directorate on Fifth Generation Computing, the 'European Strategic Programme for Research and Development in Information Technologies' (ESPRIT), the 'Forecasting and Assessment in Science and Technology' (FAST) and the European Research Coordination Agency (EUREKA) initiatives.

Other multinational dimensions

The internationalisation of business and the associated technological developments are not the only global level issues which impact on the UK and UK competitiveness through the medium of inward direct investment. They are, nevertheless, the main overriding themes, and other issues can be related to these twin imperatives of internationalisation and technology. For instance, the tide of deregulation flowing in the developed countries, under the influence of bold US and UK initiatives, is associated with both imperatives. Take the case of the liberalisation of financial services markets: improvements in IT have undermined the regulated structures which traditionally existed in individual national markets, and if predictions are correct, will allow the emergence of a handful of global security houses based in Japan, USA and Britain.[22] Failure by Britain to follow the lead of the United States and its two 'Big Bangs' — the approval of public ownership of New York Stock Exchange member firms and the abolition of fixed commission rates — would have further delayed the necessary global response by the UK financial community.

The twin imperatives are a driving force in another important phenomenon, which is the growing spread of collaborative agreements of various sorts between enterprises of different nationalities. In automobiles, there are over 200 joint ventures and collaborative agreements in existence in long term research, the development of components and/or new models, production and assembly, distribution etc.[23] While political factors in the form of support for national producers and protectionism have played a part, collaboration is also a (desperate and despairing?) response to the global threat posed by the Japanese automakers, from which even the mighty General Motors is not immune. In the IT industry itself, the technology imperative is having major repercussions: the development of digital exchanges requires R & D investments of the order of $1 billion, and therefore sales of $14–16 billion to amortise the cost; achieving such a level of sales depends crucially on penetrating *international* markets.[24] These huge costs along with the convergence of previously distinct technologies, have led to a merry-go-round of actual and abortive collaborations, mainly revolving around European enterprises and the European market. Deregulation is a factor too. Privatised British Telecom is beginning to open up its purchasing to include tenders from overseas, while the same firm is moving overseas through the acquisition of Mitel, a Canadian telecommunications supply company. The industry examples could be extended to include aerospace (Airbus and McDonnell Douglas) and aeroengines (Rolls Royce and GE) and so on.

The remaining major issues, including the changing forms of international involvement, the widening of global industries, and the expansion of developing-country based MNEs (Samsung, Hyundai — even Ecobank, Africa's first privately owned offshore bank)[25] will be discussed further in the next chapter.

CONCLUDING REMARKS

All of the issues highlighted above need to be brought down to the level of the UK and related specifically to inward investment. It is very clear, however, that there are potentially highly important implications as regards impact on the UK economy and UK competitiveness. It should also be apparent that the influences of foreign MNEs are rarely straightforward, but rather are commonly both long term and subtle, and, furthermore, are very open to political pressures. The globalisation and technology imperatives are significant in that they provide a strong *prima facie* argument in favour of the multinational in Britain. Without MNEs a good part of British industry could remain myopically insular; with MNEs there is at least an interaction with the real world, no matter how painful this may be.

It must be recognised that many of the issues discussed in this chapter are of very recent emergence: in essence they represent agendas for the future, with their full impact likely to be felt only in the last years of the 20th century. It will not, therefore, be possible in this book, which is inevitably based on historical evidence, to test many of the impacts postulated. The aim of this chapter has, however, been to provide a backcloth against which the evidence on multinational behaviour in the UK can be reviewed, and against which existing and possible new policy measures can be evaluated. It has also drawn attention to the significance of multinational strategy when considering UK impact and policy, and this theme will be pursued throughout the book.

NOTES

1. 'Big Bang' is the term used to describe the deregulation of the Stock Exchange which took place on 27 October 1986; fixed commissions were ended, the separation of broking and jobbing was abolished and dual capacity introduced. The significance of the Big Bang was that it allowed foreign firms to compete freely with British companies in all areas of the London stockmarket

2. Some years ago there was considerable interest in the so-called 'world car', epitomised by the Ford Escort and GM Cavalier (and equivalents elsewhere). In fact the world car never existed, because of legislative differences, tariff and non-tariff barriers, etc. and with changing technology the trend may now be towards product differentiation rather than standardisation

3. Young, S. and Hood, N. (1977), *Chrysler UK: a corporation in transition*, Praeger, New York

4. Dunning, J.H. (1958), *American investment in British manufacturing industry*, Allen and Unwin, London; and (1986), *Japanese participation in British industry*, Croom Helm, London

5. Steuer, M.D., Abell, P., Gennard, J., Perlman, M., Rees, R., Scott, B., and Wallis, K. (1973), *The impact of foreign direct investment on the United Kingdom*, HMSO, London

6. Brech, M. and Sharp, M. (1984), *Inward investment: policy options for the United Kingdom*, Chatham House papers 21, Routledge and Kegan Paul, London; Stopford, J.M. and Turner, L. (1985), *Britain and the multinationals*, John Wiley, Chichester

7. National Economic Development Council (1985), *British industrial performance: a comparative survey over recent years*, London; also, House of Lords (1985), *Report from the Select Committee on Overseas Trade*, 238-I, Session 1984-5, HMSO, London, 30 July

8. Ibid. The idea was suggested in Stopford, J.M. (1986), 'International competitiveness of European industry', in Macharzina, K. and Staehle, W.H. (eds), *European approaches to international management*, Walter de Gruyter, Berlin

9. House of Lords (1985), *Report from the Select Committee on Overseas Trade*

10. Porter, M.E. (1986), 'Changing patterns of international competition', *California Management Review*, 28(2), pp. 9–39

11. Hamel, G. and Prahalad, C.K. (1988), 'Creating global strategic capability', in Hood, N. and Valhne, J.-E. (eds), *Strategies in global competition*, Croom Helm, London

12. This section draws on the work of a Strathclyde Business School colleague, Mr J. Taggart

13. Macharzina, K. (1986), 'The European microelectronics industry and new technologies', in Macharzina and Staehle (eds), *European approaches to international management*

14. Blackwell, N. (1982), 'How to market technology', *Management Today*, December

15. Johnson, S.B. (1984), 'Comparing R & D strategies of Japanese and US firms', *Sloan Management Review*, 25(3), pp. 25–34

16. Parsons, G.L. (1983), 'Information technology: a new competitive weapon', *Sloan Management Review*, 25(1), pp. 3–13

17. *The Economist* (1986), 'Beyond factory robots', 5 July, p. 57

18. Jelinek, M. and Golhar, J.D. (1983), 'The interface between strategy and manufacturing technology', *Columbia Journal of World Business*, spring, pp. 26–36

19. *The Economist*, 'Beyond factory robots'

20. Jelinek and Golhar, 'The interface between strategy and manufacturing technology'

21. US Congress, Joint Economic Committee (1982), *Location of high technology firms and regional economic development*, US Government Printing Office, Washington, D.C.

22. *The Economist* (1986), 'Big Bang Brief', 20 September, pp. 80–1

23. Young, S. (1986), 'European car industry', in Macharzina and Staehle, *European approaches to international management*

24. Webber, D., Rhodes, M., Richardson, J.J. and Moon, J. (1986), 'Information technology and economic recovery in Western Europe: the role of the British, French and West German governments', *Policy Sciences*, September

25. *Multinational Business* (1986), 'Africa's first offshore bank', 1, pp. 32–4

2

Global Environment of International Business and the United Kingdom Position

A key point which emerged from Chapter 1 and which will be a recurring theme throughout this book is that in considering the activities of multinational enterprises Britain cannot be considered in a vacuum, either in impact or in policy terms. At its broadest, the world economic environment will be the major determinant of aggregate investment flows, for which Britain is a potential host along with other developed and, perhaps, developing nations. Britain's attractiveness as a host nation, moreover, will be linked to the evolution of the world and European economies as well as to its own domestic economic position and performance. Similarly, the role which foreign MNEs conceive for their British operations will be determined by similar factors as well as by competitive influences. From a policy perspective, British commitments to international and regional organisations will largely establish the framework and set the constraints within which independent policy initiatives may be pursued, while the national policy environment abroad may have some demonstration effect upon government strategy formulation in the UK.

Britain is not only affected by, but also affects the performance of the international economy, in part through the activities of its own multinationals (including two of the world's largest industrial companies in Royal Dutch Shell and British Petroleum), whose behaviour will in addition influence policy attitudes within international and other organisations.

It is appropriate, in the light of the above, to begin the discussion of foreign MNEs in the British economy with an overview of the global environment and changing characteristics of international business, the interdependencies of inward and outward investment within the UK, and the policy framework, with particular reference to intra-European competition for inward investment.

MULTINATIONALS AND THE INTERNATIONAL BUSINESS POSITION

Outward and inward direct investment patterns

To compare the emergence of multinational companies to their position today as enterprises owning and controlling some 90,000 affiliates around the world, it is necessary to go back over one hundred years.[1] Britain was by far the world's largest foreign investor, supplying and financing a large proportion of the world's early railway networks and supporting numerous governments through public bonds floated in London. As with French and German financial and industrial interests overseas, much of this took the form of portfolio investment. Still, these were the days of merchant adventurers and buccaneering entrepreneurs, and companies in merchanting, trading and shipping were very active in the countries of the British Empire. Some of these were 'multinational' by most definitions, and others moved into more direct operations abroad, e.g. merchanting into manufacturing, raw material sourcing into jute and cotton manufacture. During the years up to the end of World War Two, economic and political problems constrained all forms of investment by Europeans; foreign direct investment grew only modestly but was joined by Japanese corporate activity in Taiwan, Korea and Manchuria (Japanese colonies) and further afield into Malaya and Indonesia.

From its earliest days, American activity abroad was strongly oriented towards direct investment. As at 1850 at least 25 corporations were known to have established operations overseas, and by 1914 foreign direct investment amounted to $2.65 billion, 7 per cent of GNP. Resource requirements, especially oil, the costs of transporting manufactures to foreign markets and tariff and non-tariff barriers were all important determinants of overseas direct investment. These early activities included substantial involvement in Britain, and by the last quarter of the nineteenth century American enterprises had interests in both well established industries such as matches, boot and shoe machinery and tobacco, and new sectors, including electrical and photographic equipment.

While the fledgling American multinationals continued to expand healthily in the twentieth century until the 'great crash', it was the opportunities created by and the environment produced by World War Two, that led to the large surge of US direct investment abroad from about 1950. Corporate technological and managerial expertise joined with advantageous economic circumstances (the establishment of the dollar as the world currency at Bretton Woods and its subsequent overvaluation, import problems and limitations in Europe together with low labour costs), and favourable political conditions (the strong support of the US government, aided by tax concessions, investment risk insurance and treaties with foreign nations) to produce a unique concurrence in favour of multinational expansion.

It is arguably the case that the experiences of the American manufacturing multinationals during this time had a major influence on other firms — European, Japanese, even developing country and socialist enterprises. The advantages to be gained from more direct methods of international market servicing and particularly foreign direct investment, complementing more traditional forms such as exporting, could be clearly seen in the market shares built up overseas by companies as diverse as H.J. Heinz, Avon Cosmetics, Ford Motor Co, Johnson & Johnson, Kodak and others. The ability to serve and penetrate markets by operations within the market area itself has thus been a factor in foreign direct investment decisions. And at the present time, the foreign investment activities of small British hi-tech companies in American can be largely related to improved marketing and customer service. However, import restrictions have probably been the major locational determinant in investments from the middle of the nineteenth century through to the present day. For example, it was the threat of import tariffs that led Scottish textile firms such as J. & P. Coats and the Glasgow Linen Company to invest in the United States by the 1850s. Similarly, in recent years non-tariff barriers (import quotas in Europe) have been shown to be a key influence on investment by Japanese companies in Britain.

The recent trends in investment emerging from such factors, allied to broader dimensions associated with the changing competitiveness of the US, European and Japanese economies, changing cost and currency relationships, etc. are illustrated in Figures 2.1 and 2.2.

While international direct investment grew significantly in the 1950s, flows were still hampered by factors such as the non-convertibility of major currencies. With the gradual decrease of such barriers, the outflow of foreign investment increased continuously until 1979.[2] The upward trend in foreign capital flows was especially strong in the 1967–73 period, whereas some slowdown was apparent in the period since then, with actual falls in real terms

25

Figure 2.1: Direct investment flows from developed market economies (current prices and exchange rates)

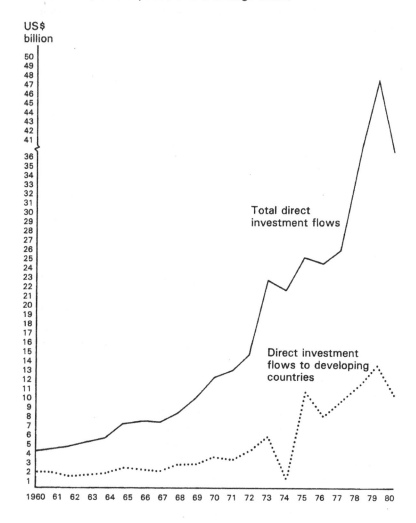

Sources: UN CTC (1983), *Salient features and trends in foreign direct investment*, New York; UN CTC (1983), *Transnational corporations in world development (third survey)*, New York.

Figure 2.2: Direct investment flows from developed market economies (1960 prices and exchange rates)

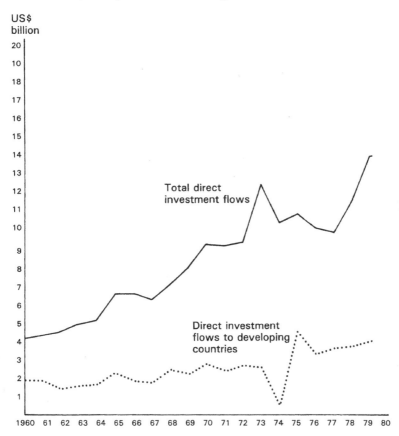

US$ billion

Sources: UN CTC (1983), *Salient features and trends in foreign direct investment,* New York; UN CTC (1983), *Transnational corporations in world development (third survey),* New York.

in some years. A number of factors contributed to the latter including the worldwide economic recession, currency instability, the 'new protectionism', and the regulatory position in particular countries and areas. Not all these factors were unfavourable to direct investment and some of the advantages of multinationality to companies lie in the ability to circumvent policy-induced distortions and imperfections. Of more significance was the fact that direct investment internationally has been less affected than domestic investment to major countries.[3]

27

This generally buoyant picture has been maintained within the context of a substantially changed source country balance in investment flows. The slowdown in the growth of American multinationals is in part a reflection of the weaker economic position of the US in terms of productivity and innovative performance, together with changing exchange rate and labour cost relationships internationally. At the specific corporate level, the highly publicised problems of some of the largest US enterprises, and the smaller number of 'new entrants' to the multinational arena is only partly offset by the strong international growth of the American electronics industry. In consequence the US share of outward direct investment flows from the major developed countries fell from over 60 per cent in the period 1961–67, to less than 30 per cent in the period 1974–9. Over the same periods, the European share increased from one third to over a half, while that of Japan rose from 2.4 per cent to 13.0 per cent.[4]

With the long term build up of the US direct capital stake abroad, America is still by far the largest home to multinational enterprises.[5] It is also the country with the highest share of the world's giant enterprises and globally-spread enterprises, in corporations such as General Motors, Ford, IBM, Du Pont and the oil majors Exxon, Mobil and Texaco. But, significantly, the number of non-US companies among the world's top 150 (strictly the top 12 in each of 13 industries) rose from 40 in 1959 to 83 in 1976, with Japanese enterprises in this group increasing from one to 20.[6] Philips, Unilever, ICI, Volkswagen, Mitsubishi and others thus provide a major challenge to their American counterparts in markets around the world; and the Japanese companies in particular have further strengthened their grip on the international economy in the years since 1976.

The comments on the historical background of foreign investment and its rapid growth in the post-war years have indicated that for US MNEs the European continent (along with Canada) was an irresistible, if sometimes rather unwelcoming, target. In 1985, 45.9 per cent of the United States worldwide stock of inward investment (and 47.3 per cent of that in manufacturing) was in Europe; this proportion was about double that of 25 years earlier.[7] For Continental European companies, historical trading relationships and interdependencies led again to a focus on foreign investment in Europe. Britain, so often the exception to its European neighbours, differed from this picture, with the Commonwealth countries traditionally taking the largest share of foreign investment. The increased role of the United States as a recipient of international direct investment flows during the 1970s, however, reflected the reorientation of British corporate goals and behaviour, and Continental MNEs too were attracted by the large, stable market, welcoming environment and competitive costs. With the growing interest of Japanese corporate investors in the United States also, the latter became the largest host nation for investment flows.

Figures 2.1 and 2.2 show that investment flows into developing countries have increased less rapidly than those into developed nations with, moreover, intermittently considerable fluctuations. For example, a drop of $1.1 billion was recorded in 1974 because of major divestments in the petroleum sector in the wake of nationalisations in OPEC countries. What is also worth observing is that the share of foreign direct investment in the flow of private financial resources to developing countries fell significantly between the 1960s and the 1970s, to be replaced by increased international bank lending, especially in the form of syndicated Eurocurrency credits. The debt problems of some developing countries have highlighted the dangers associated with this shifting balance, and have led *inter alia* to calls for the conversion of portfolio into direct assets.

Major new trends in international business activity

The above comments have focused on interchanges between developed countries and on the foreign direct investment component of international business. This is incomplete because it captures only part of the dynamics of the world economy and of international business within this. Considering first home and host country patterns, Dunning's 'investment development cycle', illustrated in Figure 2.3, is a useful way of highlighting macro relationships between GNP and foreign direct investment.[8] While the positioning of countries on the diagram represents only a snapshot as at 1971, it is easy to see the ways in which developments may take place in GNP, country comparative advantage and multinationality over time. The widening of sources of foreign direct investment is an obvious consequence of such patterns, and the state-trading countries of COMECON, OPEC nations and especially the newly industrialised countries (NICs) are a rapidly growing force overseas. The NIC multinationals are the most interesting phenomenon: the rapid growth and competitiveness of countries such as the Republic

29

Figure 2.3: Investment development cycle of countries

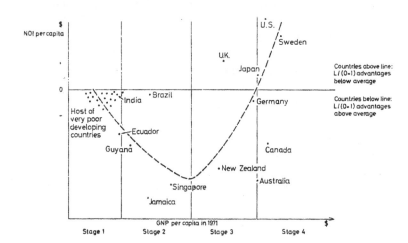

Source: J.H. Dunning (1981), *International production and the multinational enterprise,* Allen and Unwin, London.

of Korea, linked to the same protectionist pressures which proved the trigger for Japanese direct investment in the West, will undoubtedly mean that companies such as Hyundai, Samsung, Daewoo and Korea Oil etc. will soon become household names.

A second important pattern has concerned the sectoral balance of direct foreign investment. Extractive investment has declined as a proportion of total overseas direct investment by the main home countries, with a growth in manufacturing and in the service sector. Estimates by the UN indicate that at the beginning of the 1970s about one quarter of the world foreign direct investment stock was in services, whereas by the mid-1980s the figure had risen to 40 per cent.[9] The explanations relate to the requirement for foreign direct investment to deliver most services to overseas markets because they are non-tradeable; the expansion of trade and investment in goods which stimulates accompanying service investment; and a wide variety of other factors including the emergence of Eurocurrency markets, the rise of international lending, migrations of labour, the growth of tourism and advances in communications. So the growth of foreign direct investment in services must be seen in the broader context of the globalisation of the world economy as discussed in Chapter 1.

It was observed previously that some slowdown was apparent after 1973 in the overall expansion of direct foreign investment. This trend, however, has to be viewed in the context of other international business activities of MNEs, including changes in the forms of their participation abroad. There is no question that non-equity forms of participation as well as minority investments by these corporations overseas have been on the increase. Within the group of non-equity arrangements are a wide variety of forms of involvement — most obviously licensing, management contracts and turnkey operations — and these contractual forms are increasingly associated with buy-back deals and other types of counterpurchase agreement. At the same time, arrangements such as co-production, co-marketing and co-research ventures along with contract manufacturing, etc. are growing. These represent, in part, a continuing desire by host countries, especially in the developing world, to 'break up the package', encourage genuine technology transfer and indigenous industrial development. It is necessary to be slightly cautious before predicting that this trend will continue, because some developing countries' experiences with the 'new forms of investment' have not been very favourable.[10] Even so, alongside the 'pull' factors, there are 'push' factors from the corporate strategy side. Smaller and non-dominant firms within global industries may be able to use market servicing flexibility as a means of avoiding the competition of the industry leaders.[11] Furthermore, the shortening of product life cycles in some sectors is driving small-firm technological leaders towards strategies of licensing and joint ventures to capture the maximum return as quickly as possible. Other factors of significance, affecting even the largest enterprises, include the high costs of research and development, which are encouraging collaborative research efforts in aircraft, micro-electronics, including robotics, motor vehicles, pharmaceuticals, etc. The 'new forms of international involvement' are thus linked to a complex mixture of internal and external factors as illustrated in Figure 2.4.

More generally, direct investment through wholly-owned greenfield subsidiaries can no longer be regarded as the typical form of international business activity in developing countries. And even in developed nations, joint venture operations and entry or expansion through acquisitions is on the increase. After an era in which foreign direct investment expanded to complement exporting and become the principal method of involvement overseas for many companies, the next era may be one in which flexibility and pragmatism leads

Figure 2.4: New forms of international involvement

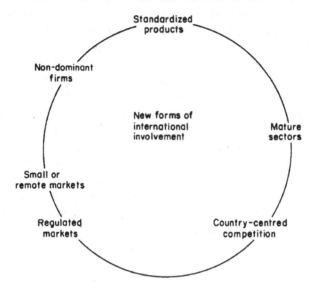

Source: S. Young (1987), 'Business strategy and the internationalization of business: recent approaches', *Managerial and Decision Economics*, 8, pp. 31–40.

to a whole variety of forms of ownership, management control and market supply. The data presented thus confirm many of the issues discussed in relation to the globalisation of business in Chapter 1. The consequences for the UK (p. 12) are worth emphasising too in terms of both impact and policy.

The policy environment internationally

The changes observed in international business patterns are closely aligned to changes in world economic and political conditions, and the national and international fiscal, monetary, trade and legal environments. As part of this complex intermeshing of the international and national, macro and micro elements, countries and international organisations have formulated strategies to deal specifically with the issue and perceived problems of the multi-national enterprise. While it is important to understand that demands for the control of multinational power have often been politically motivated, there have been genuinely economic reasons associated with regulatory efforts, relating to the impact of multinationals on the balance of payments, taxation, prices, the nature of economic development being promoted and so on. This section relates to the policy environment internationally, but clearly has important implications for UK policy, as discussed in Chapter 6.

It is possible to discern an evolutionary pattern in policies towards multinational companies. The period from 1950 to the mid-1960s has been regarded as the 'honeymoon period' between MNEs and host nations during which the benefits associated with the transfer of capital, management and technology were well recognised.[12] In Western Europe, American MNEs were welcomed for this resource package they brought with them and especially for their technology, incorporated in new products and processes, improved management techniques and organisation skills. In the developing countries, the role of the multinationals in tapping mineral resources was important, and similar benefits were seen in countries like Australia and Canada. Policies towards inward investment were usually fairly liberal, and although some countries did try to influence the nature and direction of investment, there were few constraints and cost/benefit analysis was rare.

In the second phase from the mid-1960s to the late-1970s the viewpoint from host countries and international organisations was much more critical — from honeymoon to separation. The Report of the Group of Eminent Persons in 1974,[13] while acknowledging the benefits from MNE operations, also identified the costs associated with the growing economic dominance of multinationals in high techology industries and in the ownership and control of vital raw materials. Changing views about the balance of economic impact, moreover, were paralleled by concerns about the political impacts of MNEs, emerging principally from the involvement of ITT in Chile. This period thus saw efforts being devoted to controlling MNEs at international, regional and national levels through the UN, OECD and ILO; in regional blocs such as the Andean Common Market and the EEC; and in host (and home) countries of a variety of shades of political opinion and levels of development. Most significance attaches to the host nation level of policy. For some countries the approach was to reject all association with MNEs through policies of nationalisation and expropriation; for others such as India, Mexico, Nigeria and Malaysia, fairly stringent equity-sharing controls were imposed along with restrictions on the sector of investor, performance requirements relating to local content or

33

export activity, etc. For others again, however, even during this period, export-oriented development strategies were associated with active attraction efforts. The significant number of countries offering incentives to multinationals as well as or rather than imposing performance requirements was shown clearly in the US Department of Commerce 1977 benchmark study.[14] In Europe, attitudes were ambiguous depending on country, extent of involvement with MNEs as home and host, government in power and the possibility of losing investment to neighbouring states.

The third and present phase from the late-1970s may be termed 'reconciliation'. Reflected in headlines such as: 'Big is not so bad after all',[15] the 1980s has seen a more balanced view towards multinationals. This is shown both in host country policies and in loss of interest in controlling MNEs through international codes of conduct.[16] In part, of course, the explanation lies in the fact that the recession has placed a premium on the investment capital of MNEs. In developing countries, there was a sharp shift from equity to debt finance in the 20 years to the mid-1980s, with foreign direct investment declining from 20 per cent of all capital flowing from industrialised to developing countries in the 1960s to around ten per cent. Debt-servicing problems with bank loans have thus been another factor changing attitudes. Even so, more welcoming reactions will not mean a return to the days of wholly-owned subsidiaries: joint ventures and other contractual forms are and will continue to be the norm. In Europe, the generally depressed economic environment and high unemployment have led to much increased competition between countries, both in terms of promotional activity and incentives offered, for the available internationally mobile projects.

It is clear that while policies have evolved, divergences between countries in terms of strategy towards multinationals are also very significant. Conclusions by Guisinger and Associates were that host countries successfully able to impose net disincentives (the balance of incentives and performance requirements) on MNEs were those with large domestic markets, limited market accessibility (meaning problems in serving the market by exports from the parent or subsidiaries located in neighbouring countries) and a level of development above some threshold minimum.[17] Large countries, such as India mentioned above, fall into this category. Where the host nation is seeking an export-oriented as opposed to a domestic-oriented MNE project, however, the position will be different: the need for the MNE to be internationally competitive will increase its bargaining power in negotiations with the host country. Where the domestic market is small, the host country strategy must be based on export orientation, and incentives will almost certainly be required as part of any inward investment policy package. The NICs of South East Asia fall into this group. Membership of a common market, such as the EEC, will also bias the package towards incentives, unless there are substantial cost differences between countries as production locations or unless agreement is reached between member states to limit incentives and/or impose performance requirements as an operating condition in all the states. This is an important conclusion with implications for the UK as a member of the European Community. Of policy significance also, from a domestic UK perspective, is the fact that Britain is the second most important home nation for outward foreign direct investment, as is illustrated in the following section.

INTERNATIONAL BUSINESS AND THE UNITED KINGDOM

The UK's outward and inward direct investment position

Britain has had a long association with international business whether in its direct foreign investment or other forms; and, in terms of their overall involvement in the economy, multinationals (British plus foreign) are more significant in Britain than in any other country in the world, with the possible exception of the United States. It is true that in the late nineteenth and early twentieth centuries, most of the outward investment took the portfolio form and at the present time too portfolio investment is growing faster than direct investment abroad. Nevertheless, many British companies have a long experience of and extensive commitment to overseas markets through direct investment. Nor are these solely manufacturing enterprises, for at the start of the twentieth century, 32 British overseas banks had a network of 2,104 branches, mainly in the colonies where they were able to exploit their familiarity with the colonial administrations and the dominant position of sterling as an international trading and reserve currency.[18] For manufacturing investment too the colonies proved easy pickings and the break up of the Empire did not eliminate this. As at 1962 over 70 per cent of the UK outward direct investment stock was located in the Commonwealth. The geographical reorientation of this only occurred from the late

1960s, as firms belatedly recognised the need to build, develop and hold their market position within the largest, richest and most advanced countries; and by so doing also reduce their commitment to the problematic UK economy. The United States has proved a particular attraction for British corporate investors in recent years, thus substantially eliminating the imbalance in transatlantic direct investment flows which had been overwhelmingly West-East for much of the present century.

The position at the start of the 1980s was that the United Kingdom accounted for 14.5 per cent of the total stock of direct foreign investment from the major countries of origin, still second to (albeit a long way behind) the United States (42.2 per cent) and followed by the Federal Republic of Germany, Netherlands and Japan (between seven and eight per cent). In terms of inward investment in the major recipient countries, the UK, with 10.2 per cent of the total, was vying with Canada for second place behind the United States (15.5 per cent).[19] Overall, the value of Britain's outward direct investment was just over 50 per cent greater than its inward investment in the early 1980s.

Regarding both outward and inward investment, the British position has been affected by the problems of the UK economic environment — low growth, the perceived volatility and short-term nature of government policy, even perhaps the depressing effect on perceptions of high unemployment. In relation to inward investment, the environment has affected the attractiveness of the UK as an investment location and perhaps also the nature of products and production processes that MNEs choose to locate in Britain. Consequently, the UK's share of inward investment has been declining. Conversely, faster growth and more stable markets outside the UK have stimulated outward investment, with British MNEs producing a higher proportion of their more sophisticated products in overseas countries where income levels are higher. After a long period during which the UK's share of outward investment fell, therefore, the country's share position began to improve from the late 1970s.

Sectoral and country breakdowns

The sectoral and country breakdowns of UK outward and inward investment stock are highlighted in Figures 2.5 and 2.6. The country profile confirms the points made earlier concerning the dominance of the United States historically as a source of inward investment, although the EEC is now also a significant source area. With the reorientation of outward direct investment away from the Common-wealth still a comparatively recent phenomenon, these two major areas account for a smaller proportion of outward than of inward investment. Despite the attention given to manufacturing industry, Figure 2.6 shows that this sector accounted for only two fifths of inward and a little over one third of outward direct investment in 1981. Other important sectors included oil, transport and communications, shipping and distribution. Although the point does not emerge clearly from the figures, given the level of aggregation, it should be noted that UK direct investment abroad is primarily concentrated in the less technology–intensive sectors (food, drink and tobacco, metal manufacture, textiles, paper, printing and publishing, etc.), whereas inward investment is chiefly located in the more technology-intensive sectors (mechanical and instrument engineering, electrical engineering, motor vehicles, etc.). This issue is discussed more fully in Chapter 3.

Outward and inward investment flows

Reviewing the trends in investment over the last two decades, Figures 2.7 and 2.8 show a widening gap between outward and inward investment. The size of this 'deficit' averaged around £80m per year in the period 1960–5 or about 0.3 per cent of GDP but rose to nearly £1,000m annually in the years 1975–80 (around 0.8 per cent of GDP). Some explanations for these patterns have already been suggested. Other factors at work during the latter part of the period included British entry into the EEC in 1973 and the abolition of exchange controls on outward direct investment in July 1979.

The elimination of trade barriers within the EEC should have facilitated exports by member countries without the requirement for direct investment. However, recent events have drawn attention to the innumerable non-tariff restrictions which still exist on intra-Community trade, suggesting that market penetration would be more effective through a local manufacturing presence. Available figures indicate that both outward and inward direct investment between Britain and the EEC may have been stimulated short term (the former seeming to respond earlier than the latter), but with little evidence of any sustained longer term increase in relation to foreign direct investment as a whole.

The abolition of exchange controls has probably been of more

Figure 2.5: UK direct investment position, country breakdown[a], 1981

Outward direct investment

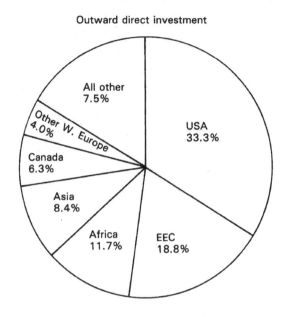

Inward direct investment

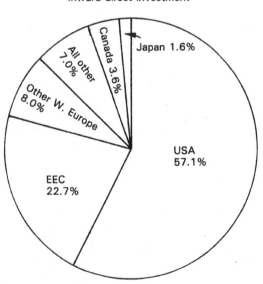

Note: a. Including oil, banks and insurance companies.
Sources: *Business Monitor, MA4*, 1981 supplement; *Bank of England quarterly bulletin*, June 1984.

Figure 2.6: UK direct investment position, sectoral breakdown[a], 1981

Outward direct investment

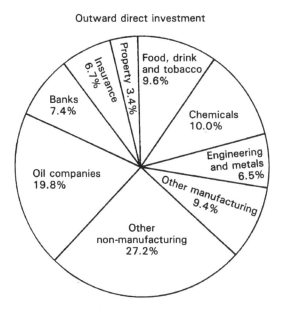

Inward direct investment

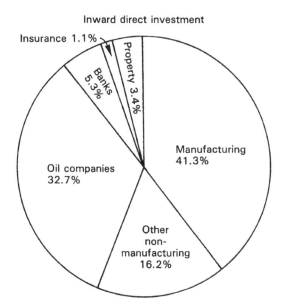

Note: a. Including oil, banks and insurance companies and property.
Sources: *Business Monitor, MA4*, 1981 supplement; *Bank of England quarterly bulletin*, June 1984.

39

Figure 2.7: Outward and inward direct investment flows

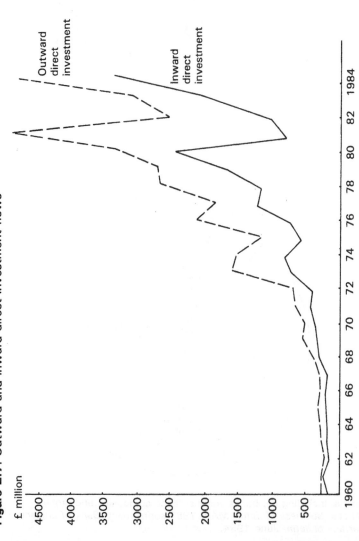

Sources: ESO, *UK balance of payments*, various issues; *Annual abstract of statistics.*

Figure 2.8: Ratio of direct investment to GDP

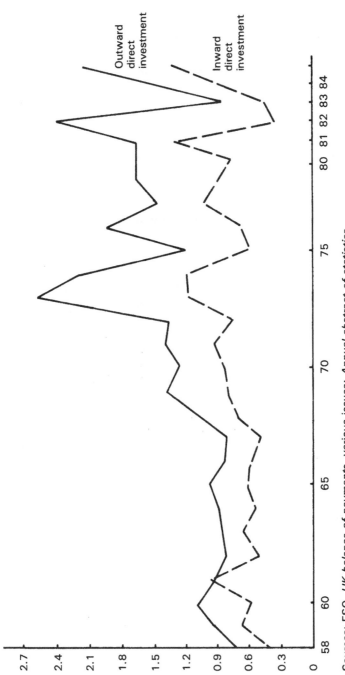

Per cent

Outward
direct
investment

Inward
direct
investment

Sources: ESO, *UK balance of payments*, various issues; *Annual abstract of statistics*.

significance, allied to the strength of sterling against the dollar in the late 70s and early 80s, and the cheapness of US stock prices. Such points highlight the fact that the concept of direct investment flows is essentially financial, so that the observed increase in net outward investment in part reflects the financial behaviour of corporate treasurers.[20] This is very apparent in the 1981 data for inward direct investment which fell sharply as compared with the previous year as a result of loans made by UK affiliates, mainly American motor vehicle firms, to their overseas parent corporations and a reduction in the amount of short-term finance provided to affiliates. Figures for subsequent years indicate a resumption of the high levels of inward (and outward) investment.[21]

Concluding remarks on outward and inward direct investment

The main purpose of this brief review of outward and inward direct investment has been to draw attention to the important British role in the multinational arena, to the parallels which clearly exist between the behaviour of British-based and foreign multinationals, and to the constraints which are imposed upon the formulation of inward investment policy by the large British capital stake overseas. When British and foreign MNE activity in the UK is taken together, it is apparent that there is a very high concentration of UK output and exports in the hands of multinationals, and that the potential problems associated with size and power may be associated with both groups of enterprises. The arguments that investment overseas creates jobs abroad instead of in the UK and that British MNEs have thereby played a large part in the deindustrialisation of Britain is commonly alleged, as is the claim that outward direct investment weakens the balance of payments. The fact that this book focuses on inward investing multinationals only should not detract from the importance which needs to be paid to the British giant enterprises.[22]

The United Kingdom and other international business forms

The point was made earlier in this chapter that substantial growth was taking place worldwide in non-conventional and non-equity forms of international business arrangements. It would be negligent, therefore, to conclude this review of international business and the United Kingdom without some comment on the broader picture as regards this country too.

Considering first the issue of ownership stakes in direct investment, the previous discussion revealed a decline in the importance of greenfield and wholly-owned subsidiaries worldwide. This is, however, mainly a developing country phenomenon. In fact, the proportion of wholly-owned subsidiaries in the UK has increased since the mid-1970s, a pattern which has been apparent for all investing countries. One interpretation of this is that with the recession conditions prevailing, one hundred per cent ownership was seen as necessary by the foreign MNEs to implement the policies required for survival and growth. There have been various well-publicised cases, where equity shares in foreign subsidiaries in Britain have been reduced, most obviously STC presently only 24 per cent owned by American ITT (since when STC has acquired ICL), but clearly the general trend is in the opposite direction.[23] Looking at outward investment by UK MNEs, it has been observed that in general the higher the *per capita* GNP of a country the lower the proportion of investment in the form of joint ventures.[24] And over time there has been a move away from joint ventures towards wholly-owned subsidiaries in developed countries as a whole; whereas, confirming the comment above, equity sharing with host country partners has become increasingly the norm in developing nations.

Available information on equity stakes in direct investment is very limited, and this weakness is even more apparent for non-equity contractual arrangements, such as licensing and franchising, management contracts and turnkey agreements. The extent of non-equity arrangements can only be estimated indirectly from data relating to UK royalty receipts and payments, where 'royalties' represent an umbrella measure of a whole range of different types of contractual agreements.[25]

Table 2.1 shows the structure of royalty receipts and payments with related and unrelated concerns by area and industry for 1984. The first point of note is the overwhelming proportion of royalty payments to related concerns, that is payments by foreign subsidiaries in Britain to their multinational parents, as compared to independent British companies licensing technology etc. from overseas enterprises. Reflecting this pattern, three quarters of all payments were directed to the United States; by comparison, the source of receipts was more varied, although still dominated by developed countries (81.1 per cent of total). Industry-wise,

Table 2.1: Structure of UK royalty receipts and payments in 1984[a]

By area	Total	Receipts Related concerns % of receipts	Unrelated concerns	Total	Payments Related concerns % of payments	Unrelated concerns
EEC	19.4	13.4	6.0	11.6	9.7	1.9
Other Europe	7.9	4.2	3.7	9.2	8.3	0.9
USA	32.8	19.5	13.3	74.6	66.5	8.1
Other developed countries	22.0	11.5	10.5	3.7	1.6	2.1
Rest of the world	17.9	10.6	7.3	0.9	0.3	0.6
World	100.0	59.2	40.8	100.0	86.5	13.5
By industry						
Food, drink and tobacco	9.0	6.5	2.5	6.7	5.5	1.2
Chemical and allied	27.9	17.4	10.5	16.0	14.3	1.7
Mechanical and instrument engineering	4.1	2.7	1.4	7.8	7.2	0.6
Electrical engineering	12.2	10.7	1.5	41.0	38.7	2.3
Motor vehicles	6.1	1.0	5.1	0.8	–	–
Paper, printing and publishing	9.7	8.0	1.7	2.3	1.0	1.3
Other manufacturing and non-manufacturing	31.0	12.9	18.1	25.4	19.8	6.4[b]
World	100.0	59.2	40.8	100.0	86.5	13.5
Value of royalty receipts and payments £ million	571.8	338.5	233.3	613.8	530.1	83.7

Notes: a Based on returns received; includes printed etc. royalties and technological and mineral royalties; excludes oil companies, banks and insurance companies.
  b Includes motor vehicle payments to related and unrelated concerns.
Source: *Business Monitor MA4*, 1984.

Figure 2.9: UK royalty receipts and payments (all businesses, excluding oil, banking and insurance)

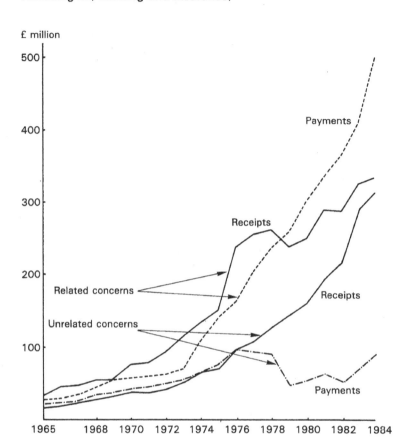

Source: *Business Monitor, M4 and MA4*, various issues.

electrical engineering, chemicals and non-manufacturing were the most important sectors for both receipts and payments.

It is interesting to observe the trends in receipts and payments over time as in Figure 2.9. The relative stability in payments to unrelated concerns (representing a fairly significant decline in real terms) is arguably a cause for concern. The declining competitiveness of the UK, in part due to technological backwardness, should lead to a big growth in the importation of technology through inward licensing agreements etc.

Using the figures for royalty receipts, Buckley and Davies estimated that production under licensing accounted for approximately ten per cent of the total overseas production of British companies in 1974.[26] The importance of non-equity agreements relative to British outward direct investment diminished in the period from 1972 to 1982, because of the declining importance of such agreements in developed countries. Paralleling the growth in joint ventures, however, non-equity agreements increased significantly in developing nations.

Non-equity arrangements are thus a significant international business phenomenon for Britain, alongside the more traditional direct investment route both outward and inward. But to date it would be wrong to conclude that these alternative forms of arrangement would suggest markedly new policy approaches for Britain in the international business field. Although not discussed at any length in this book, questions need to be raised as to whether inward direct investment is more desirable than, say, licensing as a means of obtaining technology from abroad. Of course, inward licensing itself requires an indigenous sector which is capable of utilising licensed technology effectively. The picture portrayed in Figure 2.9 suggests it either is not or British firms have been backward in looking overseas for new sources of products and processes. There have been some recent indications nevertheless of foreign companies taking the initiative in pushing licensing and other collaborative deals involving technology transfer and the supply of partly built-up equipment to British firms, and as at 1987 the Japanese were believed to have negotiated around a hundred such collaborative arrangements. Whether or not such deals are simply a first step towards outright ownership remains to be seen.

INWARD DIRECT INVESTMENT INTO THE UK AND THE COMPETITIVE POSITION

The growth of American manufacturing in the UK[27]

The American manufacturing presence in British industry dates from 1852, when Samuel Colt built a factory in London to manufacture revolvers, and soon after a vulcanised rubber factory was set up in Edinburgh by a New Jersey-based firm J. Ford and Company. What was to prove much more important was the establishment in 1867 of the first UK assembly operation of the Singer Company: soon extending into manufacture and consolidating smaller operations into a single site at Clydebank, near Glasgow, this factory was to become a huge employer of labour and the major world manufacturing base for sewing machines for the Singer Company.[28] To illustrate the variety, even in these early days, in the same year as Singer commenced operating, R. Hoe and Company of New York set up a British subsidiary in London to produce its newly-designed revolving printing press.

The early beginnings of multinatiqnality in Britain were largely associated with American corporations, and by 1900 it was estimated that over $10 million had been invested by the 75 US subsidiaries or jointly UK-US enterprises. Between 1901 and 1914 a further 70 operations were formed, with a widening of the sectors for inward investment to include patent medicine companies, food (including H.J. Heinz), engineering and machinery, and motor vehicles. In 1903 the first Ford car was sold in Britain and five years later The Ford Motor Co (Eng) Ltd started to assemble imported components at a factory at Trafford Park, Manchester, utilising large scale production methods to supply low priced standardised vehicles; by 1913 Ford was market leader in the UK with a 25 per cent share of output.

Between 1919 and 1929 new ventures and expansions continued apace, with growing import duties and quota restrictions having an important impact. This was, for example, a major factor in the purchase of Vauxhall Ltd by General Motors in 1927 and the entry of Goodyear and Firestone in the same year. Foreign direct investment in Britain expanded further during the depression years. Despite some withdrawals of capital and takeovers of American-originated firms, the Imperial Preference Tariff of 1932 and the increasing competition of British industry to US imports encouraged direct investment. As at 1940 there were 233 US firms operating branch units in the UK, new entrants in the immediately preceding years including Remington Rand Co, office equipment; Cincinnati Milling Machines, machine tools; The Hoover Company, domestic electrical appliances; Proctor and Gamble, soap products; and Champion Sparking Plugs Ltd.

The competitiveness and innovativeness of the US corporations throughout the years up to World War Two, derived in large part from the adventurous nature and inventive genius of its entrepreneurs, allied to characteristics of the economy such as a plentiful supply of capital, abundant land, ample and accessible energy resources and acute labour shortages. Liberal patent laws, high rewards for innovation, and tariff protection against imports, producing one of the largest free-trade areas in the world within the borders of the USA, were other variables in the equation. When allied to the huge economic stimulus provided by the war effort, American corporations entered the post-war period in a unique position to dominate the world economy.

The current position and characteristics of foreign enterprises in the UK

Nationality of ownership, employment and size

As at 1983 there were 838 US-owned manufacturing enterprises in the UK, operating 1,415 establishments and employing 459,500 people. As has been indicated, the recovery of the European economies and the rapid economic development of Japan and other countries has meant that multinational operations are now very widely spread by source nations. In 1983, therefore, the US MNEs in the United Kingdom were part (62.4 per cent in employment terms) of a foreign community of manufacturing enterprises numbering 1,589, with total employment of 736,000 people. Apart from the 362 EEC enterprises, there were significant numbers of firms from Switzerland, Sweden and Canada and smaller numbers from countries as far apart as Hong Kong, South Africa and Liechtenstein. The complete picture is summarised in Table 2.2 for a variety of indicators.

The characteristics of foreign subsidiaries in the UK are quite different from those in manufacturing as a whole as the following points indicate:

Much larger in employment. Average establishment employment was 312 in the overseas-owned sector in 1983 compared with 59 in all manufacturing

More multi-plant foreign enterprises. These further increased the size differential between overseas-owned and indigenous firms

Pay higher wages and salaries. In 1983, average wages and salaries for operatives were nearly 15 per cent higher in the foreign as compared with the indigenous sector

Much higher net output per head. On average, the value of net output per employee was 30 per cent greater in the foreign sector. When foreign enterprises are compared with the largest indigenous enterprises, moreover, there was still a productivity differential of 13 per cent[29]

Differences remain even when comparisons are made on an industry by industry basis. For example, in the important electrical and electronic engineering sector, productivity per head was 35 per cent higher among foreign firms; in mechanical engineering the differential in favour of MNE subsidiaries was 45 per cent. The sectoral characteristics of inward investing enterprises are shown in Table 2.3.

Information is not available on non-manufacturing industry in a comparable form. To study this important sector requires the use of direct investment data. Manufacturing industry accounted for just over 57 per cent of the direct investment stock in the UK in 1984, down somewhat from a level of 61 per cent at the end of the 1970s. The explanation for the change lies in part in the build up of North Sea oil-related assets. Oil exploration in the Scottish waters of the North Sea commenced in 1967 and production in 1975 and so inward investment dates back to these years; but a large new phase of exploration and drilling occurred in 1981 and 1982 and the oil companies' share of total investment stock peaked at almost one third in these years. With the decline in oil-related activity from the late 80s, the share of manufacturing investment along with banking, insurance and property will grow up to the end of the century.

Banking investment was, however, growing in importance from the end of the 1970s, as companies moved abroad to match the internationalisation of their customers. The North Sea factor emerges here again, for a desire to participate in oil activity has been important for the banks. Inward investment in insurance increased less rapidly up to the mid-1980s when, along with banking, a major stimulus was given by the UK's liberalisation of the financial services industry. Both American and Japanese companies took great advantage of the opportunities opening up to them. Taking the Japanese presence alone, it has been indicated that represented in the City of London by end 1986 were the offices of 23 mainstream banks, 20 offices of regional banks, 15 wholly-owned Japanese merchant banks, over 20 securities houses and around ten portfolio investment life insurance firms.[30] Included within this group was

49

Table 2.2: Characteristics of foreign manufacturing enterprises in the UK, by nationality, 1983

	Enterprises (number)	Establishments (number)	Employment (000)[a] Total	Employment (000)[a] Operatives	Employment (000)[a] Other[b]	Wages and salaries per head (£) Operatives	Wages and salaries per head (£) Other[b]	Gross output (£ million)	Net output (£ million)
EEC	362	560	108.5	67.0	41.5	7,362	9,802	5,738.5	2,021.7
of which									
Denmark	35	46	4.0	1.8	1.0	5,682	10.059	340.8	124.2
France	62	77	31.3	20.5	10.8	7,184	10,243	1,153.2	495.1
Germany	136	201	24.0	14.7	9.3	6,953	8,470	1,021.9	478.8
Irish Republic	21	51	7.5	5.7	1.8	6,130	8,402	317.7	101.3
Netherlands	79	146	36.6	19.8	16.8	7,388	9,632	2,250.7	727.4
Other EC	29	39	5.0	3.4	1.8	7,022	8,712	172.5	31.7
Australia	29	174	19.9	13.0	6.9	9,590	9,573	856.4	419.5
Canada	55	176	46.4	29.9	16.5	8,013	9,088	2,297.7	913.2
Japan	24	25	3.7	2.6	1.0	5,586	7,668	196.9	65.6
Sweden	70	120	17.1	11.4	5.6	7,014	8,657	686.3	260.9
Switzerland	91	151	38.7	24.7	14.0	6,354	8,753	1,657.9	626.5
USA	838	1,415	459.5	286.3	173.2	7,369	10,171	25,631.0	10,253.0
Rest of the world	77	183	22.8	19.8	7.9	6,558	8,712	869.2	410.1
All foreign enterprises	1,589	2,357	736.0	464.1	271.8	7,362	9,802	38,446.3	15,332.2
All enterprises in UK	86,003	102,445	5,078.8	3,445.4	1,603.4	6,417	8,669	189,200.1	80,804.0
Foreign as per cent of all enterprises in UK	1.8	2.3	14.5	13.5	16.9	114.7	113.0	20.3	19.0

Notes: a Average number employed during the year including full and part-time employees and working proprietors.
b Administrative, technical and clerical employees.
Source: *Business Monitor*, PA1002, 1983.

Table 2.3: Characteristics of foreign manufacturing enterprises in the UK by major sector[a], 1983

Sector[a]	Establishments (number)	Employment (000)			Wages and salaries per head (£)		Gross output (£ million)	Net output (£ million)
		Total	Operatives	Other	Operatives	Other		
Metal manufacturing (22)	103	23.7	17.0	6.7	8,284	9,415	1,919.6	525.0
Non-metallic mineral products (24)	174	13.7	9.3	4.4	6,793	8,870	580.1	295.2
Chemicals (25)	356	94.6	49.6	45.0	7,939	10,126	7,667.4	2,969.8
Metal goods n.e.s. (31)	201	28.6	19.8	8.8	6,777	8,927	1,080.6	457.1
Mechanical engineering (32)	566	130.5	73.2	57.2	7,439	9,625	4,859.2	2,365.1
Office machinery and data processing equipment (33)	34	12.7	3.8	8.9	7,876	10,769	973.6	361.9
Electrical and electronic engineering (34)	301	88.6	52.3	36.2	6,476	9,030	3,388.9	1,493.8
Motor vehicles and parts (35)	88	109.0	80.2	28.8	7,725	11,585	6,157.2	1,977.2
Instrument engineering (37)	116	18.8	10.3	8.5	6,300	9,442	601.6	283.7
Food, drink and tobacco (41/42)	146	71.0	52.9	18.0	6,788	10,194	5,938.6	2,008.4
Textile industry (43)	65	7.0	5.4	1.6	5,110	7,142	222.1	85.2
Paper and paper products; printing and publishing (47)	372	64.3	40.2	24.1	9,179	9,394	2,491.6	1,294.7
Processing of rubber and plastics (48)	151	42.2	27.1	15.2	7,253	9,925	1,485.7	719.0
Manufacturing[b]	2,917	736.0	464.1	271.8	7,362	9,802	38,433.1	15,532.2

Notes: *a* All sectors in which 1981 employment was 10,000 or more; bracketed figures indicate the revised 1980 Standard Industrial Classification divisions.

b Including sectors not specified separately.

Source: *Business Monitor*, PA1002, 1983.

the giant Nomura International which received its banking licence from the Bank of England in September 1986. As in the case of Nomura, which acquired the former Post Office headquarters in the City, some of these financial services investments have involved property investment too.

As a final comment, it should be noted that the sectoral pattern of capital flows into the UK indicates a continuing high level of investment in distribution. The importance of this lies in the fact that there is still for many companies a recognised evolution in their internationalisation, from exporting through to manufacture abroad. A high level of distribution investment may thus be a precursor to manufacturing activity.

The United Kingdom as a competitor for inward direct investment

The growth of inward direct investment into the United Kingdom has to be set alongside the evidence presented earlier in this chapter showing a declining share of global investment being directed to Britain. In some ways the latter is inevitable given the widening of source and host countries, and the fact that most of the major multinationals have had a longstanding presence in Britain and directed much of their early investment to this country. On the other hand there are disturbing features associated with the economic problems of the UK, which seem to have affected both the flow and character of investment in more recent years. At the same time the UK is facing much more competition from other European countries for the available internationally mobile direct investment.

To explore these issues in more detail it is necessary to begin by considering the motives for inward direct investment. Studies of locational determinants have shown that the dominant reasons for inward investment are market size and growth, with government financial aids being of lesser importance but still of some significance. It is necessary to emphasise that the investment decision will be based on the overall financial and strategic appraisals of firms in which a whole range of cost, market and competitive variables will be considered; the stress on market size and incentives emerges from survey studies in which businesses are asked to rank the most important factors in the decision, and other empirical work.[31] Other factors, including non-economic variables, cannot, furthermore, be dismissed, and historically for US enterprises and perhaps for Japanese firms today the use of the English language represents an important plus. The actual flow of investment is represented by new, first-time investing multinationals and by MNEs already established in Europe and considering expansion either at existing or new sites.

Flows of inward investment into the UK specifically will be a function of the overall level of investment by MNEs in Europe and thereafter by the UK's relative attractiveness (real or perceived) as a manufacturing base. In the light of the above comments, the latter in turn will depend principally upon the size and growth of the UK market and its potential as an export base for Europe and beyond, the financial assistance available in this country as compared with elsewhere and, finally, the ability of the country to market itself successfully as a desirable location.

It has already been shown that flows of manufacturing investment internationally are less buoyant than in earlier years, although continuing to outpace domestic investment. Within the total, the US share of outward flows dropped sharply in the 1970s, which is of more relevance to Britain given that the United States is the largest source of direct investment. It is not simply overall trends which are important in any event, but the share of this investment directed to Britain as against alternative locations. Considering US investment in manufacturing industry in the EEC, there is clear evidence of a diversion from Britain to the Common Market in the years immediately following the establishment of the Community and before Britain joined;[32] this period of significant decline in share ended around 1976, since when stability or only marginal falls have been recorded. As at 1985 the UK accounted for 30 per cent of US direct investment in the European Economic Community. The Republic of Ireland and West Germany are generally recognised as being the two main competitors to Britain for American investment and the shares of these three countries are highlighted in Figure 2.10.

The UK's position as a host country with respect to outward direct investment from EEC member countries is less optimistic.[33] Outward direct investment from this source increased rapidly during the 1970s and 1980s, but the main beneficiary of the rise has been the USA. For example, the USA received a massive 46 per cent of West German outward direct investment in the years 1976–80, in comparison with the UK's share of only 2½ per cent. In terms of West German manufacturing investment within the EEC, the UK was ranked behind Italy, Netherlands, Belgium and France. The UK

Figure 2.10: Shares of US foreign direct investment stock in manufacturing industry in the EEC

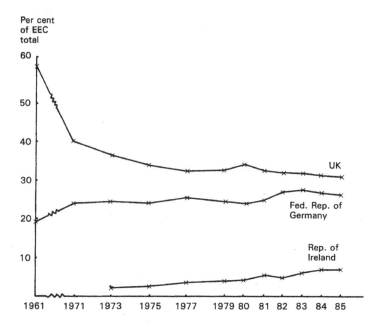

Source: US Department of Commerce, *Survey of current business*, various issues.

proportion of French outward direct investment was between 11 and 13 per cent in 1975–76 and rose as high as 16½ per cent in 1977. Although there were special factors at work in the latter year, some EEC-entry effect was also apparent. Subsequently, the UK share fell back to the 6–7 per cent level which was normal in earlier periods. Trends in the Netherlands direct investment position abroad are shown in Figure 2.11. The significance of the UK within the EEC is very apparent, but the biggest growth again has occurred in Dutch investment in the United States.

As a consequence of the above trend, much attention has been focused on Japan as a potential source of inward investment in the UK. Japan has come to the overseas manufacturing game quite late; a policy of domestically based development was vigorously applied by the Japanese government, and was reinforced by a strong yen and a production cost advantage in Japan. The rapid expansion

54

Figure 2.11: Netherlands direct investment position abroad

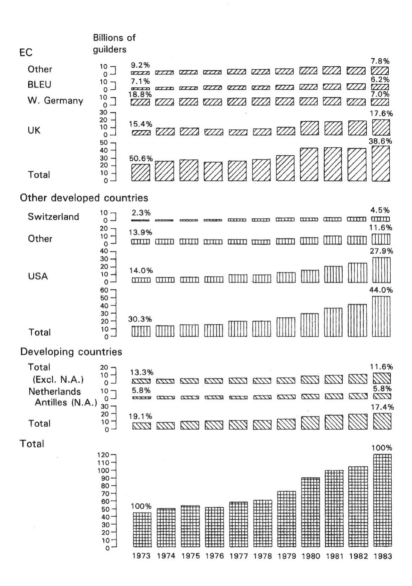

Source: Van Nieuwkerk, M. and Sparling, R.P. (1985), *The Netherlands international direct investment position*, Martinus Nijhoff, Dordrecht.

which took place in direct investment from the late 1960s focused first on the Asia Pacific region and then on North America, and even at present Europe still lags far behind these regions as priorities for investment. Within Europe, the UK is the biggest host to Japanese investment, representing 28½ per cent of the total over the period 1951–85. However, in common with American investment trends, Britain has been losing its predominant position steadily. For instance, taking 1984 and 1985 alone, the UK share was just under 18 per cent (the Netherlands by comparison accounted for 27½ per cent). In the growing list of Japanese investment announcements in the UK, it is important not to forget that other companies are investing elsewhere in Europe. Major electronics investment announcements made by Japanese companies in 1986 alone illustrate the point:[34]

Sony, Salzburg, compact discs
Matsushita Electric, Peine, Niedersachsen, West Germany, VCR components; South Wales, electronic typewriters and printers
Orion Electric, VCRs, South Wales
Hitachi, Lansberg, Bavaria, VCRs
TDK, Kaiserslauteren, West Germany, audio and video cassettes
NEC, Livingston, Scotland, semiconductors.

Notwithstanding these remarks Japan should offer big opportunities for Britain, although to exploit these the next few years must see increased and sustained promotional efforts.

Overall, the relative patterns of inward investment from the major source countries do not indicate very attractive prospects for the UK as a host nation, except with regard to Japan (as an outside bet) and Britain's traditional investment source, the United States. Competition for American investment is primarily from other European countries (although the NICs may be competitors for certain types of investment). Within the EEC constraints are placed on the financial incentives which may be offered to investors (an issue which is taken up again in Chapter 6 of this book), and aid ceilings are set which vary with the severity and type of regional problems. The importance of this in the present context is that the Republic of Ireland and Northern Ireland, as well as areas on the Continent such as the Mezzogiorno, have the ability to offer highly attractive incentive packages to prospective investors. Within this framework, the Irish Republic emerged as a very attractive location for inward investment and an important competitor to the UK, for US investment principally.

The attraction of inward investment became the key element of Ireland's industrial policy in 1958, when the import substitution and self-sufficiency policies of earlier years were replaced by an outward-looking strategy which aimed at creating an export-oriented industrial base through the attraction of inward investment. To achieve this aim, inward investors were offered numerous financial incentives including 100 per cent tax relief on incremental exports (in 1968, export profits tax relief was extended to 1990 for existing firms; then in 1981, for new investors, the system was replaced by a low rate of corporation tax following pressure from the EEC); depreciation allowances; capital grants towards the cost of fixed assets; training subsidies; and the provision of advance factories. Aside from the incentives, inward foreign direct investment was boosted by the signing of the Anglo-Irish Free Trade Area Agreement in 1965 and by Irish accession to the the EEC in 1973. In addition, an extensive promotional programme was adopted by the Industrial Development Authority (IDA) to encourage inward investment. In terms of the targeting of promotional campaigns, the use of American-style advertising campaigns and the general professionalism and intensity of its efforts, the success of the IDA was even grudgingly acknowledged and then copied in the UK.

Such policies were successful in attracting a large volume of inward investment into Ireland. The Republic's share of US manufacturing investment in the EEC increased from an insigificant amount in 1961 to 6½ per cent by 1985, representing a total US investment of $2.7 billion. By the early 1980s, there were approximately 800 foreign-owned firms operating in Ireland employing over 80,000 people, or one in three of the Irish manufacturing workforce. The US and the UK are the major source countries with respect to foreign direct investment in Ireland, accounting for more than two thirds of employment in overseas controlled firms. In terms of the value of investment, however, the US was by far the most important source, representing 70 per cent of the total value of inward direct investment in the early 1980s.[35]

There is little question that Ireland has been an attractive alternative to the United Kingdom for many potential inward investors. One study indicated that approximately 80 per cent of the affiliates studied had considered other locations before establishing in Ireland, with the UK being the most popular alternative location.[36] Other work has suggested that this competitiveness applied both to 'first-time' MNEs in Europe and also multinationals expanding their plant networks within Europe.[37] Certainly the number of new projects

Table 2.4: New foreign direct investment projects in the Republic of Ireland and Scotland, 1975–82

Year	Rep. of Ireland[a]		Scotland[b]	
	Number of projects	Job potential (000)	Number of projects	Job potential (000)
1975	24	9.9	13	2.4
1976	48	7.0	9	1.2
1977	72	10.3	6	0.2
1978	64	12.8	5	0.6
1979	90	13.5	10	1.2
1980	114	14.6	21	4.8
1981	102	15.4	10	3.9
1982	68	8.6	11	1.6
Total 1975–82	582	92.1	85	15.9

Notes: a New overseas projects approved by IDA, excluding projects originating in Great Britain.

b Category A Section 7 offers to non-UK companies for establishment of new plants in Scotland.

Source: Industry Department for Scotland (1984), *Overseas ownership in Scottish manufacturing industry*, briefing note 2, Edinburgh, March.

attracted to the Irish Republic has been very impressive, as Table 2.4 indicates. Approximately equivalent figures are presented for Scotland for comparison purposes, the reason being that of the UK regions, Ireland is believed to be particularly competitive to Scotland; and it is certainly true that both have targeted their promotional efforts heavily on US electronics corporations.

The 'job potential' figures quoted are unlikely to be achieved in practice. It was suggested in a report by the Telesis Consultancy Group[38] that only 30 per cent of the jobs approved by the IDA between 1970 and 1978 actually existed in companies in 1981. This is much lower than the figure for Scotland which suggests that actual jobs amount to about two thirds of those approved within five years. This same report and other work has been highly critical of the nature of the projects attracted to Ireland and the 'status' of the plants. Notwithstanding these facts, the Irish performance has been impressive, and has important implications for UK promotional and regional policy.

The main conclusion that emerges from this discussion is that the British position as a host for inward direct investment has become more vulnerable. This is in part due to the declining locational advantages of the UK. While the principal components of this are factors such as low growth, industrial relations problems, etc., the financial package offered to investors is also relevant. Given a country's package of locational advantages, furthermore, the way in which these are marketed by promotional agencies, such as the IDA, becomes relevant, especially when locational decision-making is by no means a totally rational process.

CONCLUDING REMARKS

The purpose of this chapter has been to set the scene for the more specific chapters on foreign multinationals in the UK economy which are to follow. Important issues have, nevertheless, been raised which have implications for both the impact of MNEs and policies towards multinationals. Among these at the international level are:

The slowdown in the growth of foreign direct investment worldwide

The changing source-country balance of foreign direct investment

Increase in non-equity arrangements and in ownership stakes within direct investment itself

Widely varying policy attitudes internationally, but with a strong bias towards net incentive packages within areas such as the European Community.

Not all these international trends are matched within foreign MNE operations in the UK. For example, wholly-owned subsidiaries are becoming more important within the UK and non-equity forms of arrangement are less important than in many other countries. Even so, an increasingly competitive environment for the attraction of inward investment is implied for the UK and confirmed by the activities of the IDA and regional development agencies in Continental Europe. This is especially important in an era when disadvantageous locational factors have reduced some of the former attractions of the UK as a host. The changing source-country balance of inward investment may have policy implications in terms of, say, the direction of attraction efforts, although this depends upon the contribution made to the UK economy by MNEs of different nationalities.

Britain's position as a major home as well as host to multinationals emerges forcefully in this chapter. Disturbingly, the same factors that have reduced the UK's attractiveness as a host, may be stimulating the internationalisation of British companies. If the latter is, as is alleged, leading to the export of jobs, then the economy will become increasingly reliant on the inward-investing MNEs. The slow growth and relative shrinkage of the UK market may, moreover, mean that both sets of multinationals are less likely to base new products and production methods in this country, with a type of cumulative disequilibrium being experienced.[39]

NOTES

1. United Nations Centre on Transnational Corporations (1983), *Transnational corporations in world development, third survey*, New York

2. UN CTC (1983), *Salient features and trends in foreign direct investments*, New York; UN CTC, *Transnational corporations*, p. 285

3. Organisation for Economic Cooperation and Development (1981), *Recent international direct investment trends*, Paris

4. Ibid. Data reproduced in Hood, N. and Young, S. (1983), *Multinational investment strategies in the British Isles*, HMSO, London, p. 7

5. UN CTC, *Salient features and trends*, Table 2

6. Franko, L.G. (1978), 'Multinationals: the end of US dominance', *Harvard Business Review*, November–December, pp. 93–101

7. US Department of Commerce, *Survey of current business*, various issues

8. Dunning, J.H. (1981), *International production and the multinational enterprise*, Allen and Unwin, London

9. Sauvant, K.P. (1986), 'Services, TDF and the Code', *The CTC Reporter*, 22, Autumn

10. See Oman, C. (1984), *New forms of international investment in developing countries*, OECD, Paris for a comprehensive review of the 'new forms'; and (1986), 'Changing international investment strategies in the North-South context', *The CTC Reporter*, 22, autumn for some cautionary remarks

11. Mascarenhas, B. (1986), 'International strategies of non-dominant firms', *Journal of International Business Studies*, spring, pp. 1–25

12. Dunning, J.H. (1974), 'The future of the multinational enterprise', *Lloyds Bank Review*, 113, July, pp. 15–32

13. United Nations Economic and Social Council (1974), *The impact of multinational corporations on the development process and on international relations: report of the Group of Eminent Persons*, New York

14. US Department of Commerce (1981), *The use of investment incentives and performance requirements by foreign governments*, Washington, D.C., October

15. *The Economist* (1983), 19 February, pp. 84–5; in the same vein but more soberly titled is Lall, S. (1984), 'Transnationals and the Third World:

changing perceptions', *National Westminster Bank Quarterly Review*, May, pp. 2–16

16. Hamilton, G. (1983), 'International codes of conduct for multi-nationals', *Multinational Business*, 3, pp. 1–10; for a wider discussion see Robinson, J. (1983), *Multinationals and political control*, Gower Press, London

17. Guisinger, S.E. and Associates (1985), *Investment incentives and performance requirements*, Praeger, New York

18. Yannopoulos, G.N. (1983), 'The growth of transnational banking', in M. Casson (ed.), *The growth of international business*, George Allen and Unwin, London, pp. 236–57

19. Stopford, J.M. and Dunning, J.H. (1983), *Multinationals: company performance and global trends*, Macmillan, London

20. A more detailed discussion on this point is in Beenstock, M. (1982), 'Finance and international direct investment in the United Kingdom', in Black, J. and Dunning, J.H. (eds), *International capital movements*, Macmillan, London, pp. 122–39

21. Central Statistical Office (1983), *UK balance of payments*, HMSO, London

22. A very interesting and provocative analysis of the activities of British MNEs is contained in Stopford, J.M. and Turner, L. (1985), *Britain and the multinationals*, John Wiley, Chichester; the approach taken is similar to that of the present volume in that the role and performance of British MNEs is evaluated within a framework of global competition. The authors are critical of the fact that 'far too many of the larger British firms have been content to settle among the followers behind the industry leader or to seek niches that may not prove defensible . . .' (p. 132). On the issue of jobs at home versus jobs abroad see also Shepherd, D., Silberston, A. and Strange, R. (1985), *British manufacturing investment overseas*, Methuen, London; or on a much more critical note Gaffikin, F. and Nickson, A. (1983), *Job crisis and the multinationals: deindustrialisation in the West Midlands*, Russell Press, Nottingham; the latter is one of a number of such studies looking at the job impact of MNEs from a regional perspective in the UK

23. Webber, D., Rhodes, M., Richardson, J.J. and Moon, J. (1986), 'Information technology and economic recovery in Western Europe: the role of the British, French and West German governments', *Policy Sciences*, September

24. Dunning, J.H. and Cantwell, J.A. (1982), *Joint ventures and non-equity foreign investment by British firms with particular reference to developing countries: an exploratory study*, University of Reading discussion papers in international investment and business studies 68, November

25. The data relate to licences, patents, trademarks, design, copyright, manufacturing rights, use of technical know-how, technical assistance, and royalties on printed matter, sound recording and performing rights. It should be noted that the data in Table 2.1 relate to information collected through a voluntary enquiry with no correction for non-responses, whereas the information in Figure 2.9 refers to all businesses

26. Buckley, P.J. and Davies, H. (1979), *The place of licensing in the theory and practice of foreign operations*, University of Reading discussion papers in international investment and business studies 47, November; see

also Hamill, J. (1985), *The internationalisation of British companies: a survey of research and developments*, Strathclyde International Business Unit working paper 85/8, University of Strathclyde

27. This section draws on Dunning, J.H. (1958), *American investment in British manufacturing industry*, Allen and Unwin, London, Chapter 1

28. Details are in Hood, N. and Young, S. (1982), *Multinationals in retreat: the Scottish experience*, Edinburgh University Press, pp. 42–60

29. The indigenous enterprises are represented by the non-overseas owned firms in the hundred largest private sector enterprises in the UK (defined by size of total sales and work done); see *Business Monitor*, PA1002, 1983, Table 17

30. *Financial Times Survey*, 'Japanese investment in Europe', 13 November 1986

31. Summarised in Hood and Young, *Multinational investment strategies*, pp. 91–7

32. Ibid., Table 8, p. 18

33. Ibid., pp. 26–46; this is the source for the data on European and Japanese foreign direct investment in the next two paragraphs, updated where necessary from *Monthly report of the Deutsche Bundesbank (Germany)* and *MITI* (Japan)

34. *FT Survey*, 'Japanese investment in Europe'

35. Fitzpatrick, J. (1982), 'Foreign investment in Ireland in the 1980s', *Multinational Business*, 4

36. Allied Irish Bank (1981), *Report on attitudes of overseas companies towards investment in Ireland*, Dublin

37. Hood and Young, *Multinational investment strategies*, Part 4, Chapter 5

38. Telesis Consultancy Group (1982), *A review of industrial policy*, National Economic and Social Council, Dublin

39. Panić, M. (1982), 'International direct investment in conditions of structural disequilibrium: UK experience since the 1960s', in Black and Dunning (eds), *International capital movements*, pp. 140–71

3

Impact of Inward Direct Investment on the United Kingdom

INTRODUCTION

The aim of this chapter is to consider the major economic issues relating to the impact of inward direct investment on the UK, reviewing official data sources and academic and other studies on the subject. The ultimate purpose is to establish some of the influences of inward-investing multinationals on UK competitiveness, thereby providing a basis for later consideration of sensible policies. This is the first of three chapters dealing with the impact of multinationals: the next chapter assesses the important regional dimensions of impact, and Chapter 5 considers the impact question within a corporate strategy framework (linking back to the Chapter 1 themes of globalisation and technology) as well as touching on industry and nationality of ownership dimensions.

Any attempt to evaluate MNE impact is fraught with difficulties. The problem of type of impact is surmounted by focusing only on economic effects, while accepting that there are other potentially important political, social and cultural influences. Even here there are problems at the margin relating, for instance, to the issue of sovereignty and autonomy. Secondly, difficulties emerge from the fact that MNE activities involve conflicts of interest. Some groups gain and some are likely to lose. This colours both the methodology used and the issues raised in analysing multinational activities. It also means that the outcome of any evaluation by particular groups may be pre-ordained.[1] Hopefully, any such tendencies here will be overcome by a sensible weighing of the evidence. Thirdly, the range of impact issues is extremely wide (technology transfer, trade and balance of payments, employment, etc.), with potentially negative effects in some areas being compensated by positive impacts in others, thus making it difficult to reach firm conclusions regarding overall impact on the economy. A related point is that inward direct investment can have important direct (first order) and indirect (second order) effects, both of which need to be examined.

Perhaps the most difficult problem to resolve is related to the nature of foreign direct investment in the UK itself. While it has already been seen that there are around 1,600 foreign enterprises in the United Kingdom, a mere 21 of them (all with net assets over £150 million) accounted for one third of total net assets in 1981.[2] These large MNEs are constantly in the public and media gaze, and therefore there are dangers of reverting to the anecdotal and trivial in using such companies as examples of positive or usually negative impact. On the other hand, their size, dominance of particular industries and influence on the performance of the multinational sector overall makes it impossible to ignore them.

This company-specific focus of attention goes back a long way. As early as 1911 the Singer Company came under attack for switching the production of sewing machines back to the USA during a strike at its British subsidiary.[3] In more recent times cases which have attracted attention include the Swiss-owned Hoffmann-La Roche regarding transfer pricing and excessive profits made on the sale of drugs to the National Health Service; IBM and its domination of the computer sector, where issues have arisen in the recent past concerning the embargo by the Reagan Administration on hi-tech exports to the Soviet Union and relating to foreign MNE access to UK and European financial programmes for developing the European computer industry; Ford and threats to withdraw from the UK because of industrial relations problems and low productivity (particularly at Halewood) in comparison with Continental plants; employment losses resulting from the closure or rundown of many long established American-owned subsidiaries; alleged production switching from the UK to France by Timex and from the Netherlands to the UK by Hyster; the pros and cons of the Nissan motor vehicle investment, and takeovers from abroad as with the Leyland Truck/Daf deal; the collapse of the De Lorean and the problems of the Lear Fan project in Northern Ireland and so on. Many of these cases have highlighted the possible negative effects of foreign ownership on the UK economy. At the same time, it is possible to quote many company-specific cases where foreign involvement has been highly beneficial.

To complete this opening section of the chapter, a few words are necessary on the framework to be employed in assessing economic impact. There have been a number of attempts to quantify the effects of foreign direct investment, covering either a macro-economic approach or applying social cost benefit analysis.[4] The former approach utilises mathematical models relating to the economy as a whole, and attempts to compare the with- and without-inward investment situations, possibly taking account of alternative ways of financing, and so on. Necessarily this quantification introduces a large element of abstraction and simplification, as well as facing problems at the empirical level because of gaps in data availability. An alternative methodology has involved a project-specific approach, utilising cost-benefit analysis to evaluate the balance of payments and income effects of multinational enterprises in host countries. The case for using social cost-benefit analysis is strong, but any results can only be regarded as partial. For example, the 'external' effects of MNEs on technology and industrial structure are omitted; the estimation of current shadow prices is difficult because of transfer pricing, the absence of free markets and the role of bargaining in pricing; and the 'alternative situation' is dealt with inadequately.

The approach taken here is in some ways less satisfactory than either of the above in that overall quantification at either macro-economic or project levels is not attempted. On the other hand, the approach of highlighting the area of impact associated with MNE operations does permit a wider view to be taken and is probably more useful from a policy perspective. When Chapters 3, 4 and 5 are taken together, furthermore, it should be possible to derive an understanding of the dynamics of multinational operations, and how MNEs interact with the UK environment to influence UK competitiveness positively or negatively. The problem of estimating what the employment, productivity, trade and technology position would have looked like without foreign direct investment regrettably still remains. Options include: raising capital and other resources domestically and establishing an indigenously-owned operation; borrowing money abroad; hiring engineers and managers directly or indirectly through a management contract; acquiring the know-how through a licensing arrangement; any partial combination of the foregoing including joint-ventures with foreign firms.

With the broadly *laissez-faire* approach to inward direct investment adopted by the UK (subject to the comments in Chapter 6), it might be considered that there has been relatively little attention given to the alternatives by government. In fact, there are specific instances where one of these alternatives has been chosen: support for British Leyland (now the Rover Group) to maintain an

65

indigenous presence in the motor industry; support for Inmos with the aim of giving the country a domestic chip-making capacity; the formation of the British National Oil Corporation and Britoil as indigenous vehicles for exploiting North Sea oil resources; and even the limitations placed on foreign shareholdings in the Thatcher privatisation programmes are all cases in point. In some cases the option might be to discourage any investment, foreign or domestic, if the latter was seen as contributing to excess capacity and instances exist of financial assistance being withheld on such grounds. The importance of the 'alternatives' is not merely of short-term concern. The long-term aim of policy must be to develop a healthy, competitive indigenous industry, irrespective of whether the initial impetus is provided by foreign direct investment or any of the alternatives noted above; the ability to use the foreign sector as a launching pad for establishing an indigenous industry should be incorporated into any cost-benefit assessment.

ECONOMIC IMPACT OF INWARD DIRECT INVESTMENT

The remainder of this chapter examines the impact of inward direct investment on the UK from a micro perspective, focusing on a number of broad issues — technology transfer and innovation; market structure; trade and the balance of payments; employment and productivity; and linkage and spillover effects. The general paucity of data and research evidence is a problem which must be admitted immediately; and, furthermore, much recent work has had a regional emphasis and is included in Chapter 4. The starting point for this section is, therefore, to go back to the work of Steuer and his colleagues which was sponsored by the Board of Trade/Department of Trade and Industry and published in 1973 as *The impact of foreign direct investment on the United Kingdom*.[5] There have been other government-sponsored studies before and since then. For example, Dunning's 1958 work on American investment in British manufacturing was financed by the Board of Trade and his 1986 book on Japanese participation in British industry came out of a report for the Department of Industry; while Hood and Young's 1983 study of MNE subsidiaries in the UK assisted areas was sponsored by the Department of Industry and various regional arms of government.[6] These and other studies have been more partial in scope than Steuer, and so a discussion of the latter is used to set the scene for the following issue-by-issue review and evaluation.

The Steuer Report focused on essentially the same questions as are discussed here. As regards the *technology* impact of multinationals in the United Kingdom, the authors took a 'debunking' approach, suggesting that the arguments both for gain and for loss were not very persuasive. The allegedly negative considerations were summarised as: (i) if foreign investment involved the acquisition of British firms, the research achievements of these companies might be lost to the British economy either because foreign interests acquire the property rights or research organisations are disbanded; (ii) foreign MNEs may not undertake R & D in Britain; and (iii) the country might in a general sense become technologically dependent. On the positive side: (i) affiliates may draw on the research efforts of the parent company at low or zero costs; (ii) new products are made available at lower costs and marketed more effectively; and (iii) linkage effects diffuse the benefits of new products and processes throughout the economy. If there was a general conclusion it was that independent technology was not necessary for British prosperity.

The *balance of payments* findings of Steuer *et al.* were less ambiguous. On the assumption that the government did not change its macro-economic policy in response to the foreign investment, the authors' modelling work indicated that the net balance of payments effect would be favourable, the order of magnitude being about ten per cent of the output of foreign-owned firms. The model was fairly robust with regard to changes in assumptions about the proportion of output exported and the greater efficiency of foreign subsidiaries; but negative effects would arise with particular government expenditure or taxation policies. Of course much inward investment during this period was of an import substituting kind, making for reasonably straightforward analysis. The same is not true of the 1980s, as has been shown.

On the subject of *monopoly and competitive structure*, Steuer *et al.* argued that there was no evidence that the activities of MNEs had led to more industrial concentration in the UK than would otherwise have occurred. While foreign investment was recognised as being an activity of oligopolistic firms, the data showed that MNEs tended to enter industries which were more concentrated in any event. The higher rates of return earned by US affiliates, furthermore, seemed to be due to a more productive use of labour and capital rather than to exploitation of a monopolistic or oligopolistic position.

Other topics covered included the regional impact: industrial relations, labour disputes and labour utilisation; and national sovereignty. Leaving aside the first of these, on *labour issues* the conclusion was that 'the foreign subsidiary is an innovator here in industrial relations in ways that can lead to greater flexibility and higher productivity'; although 'casual evidence would suggest that the general extent of such an impact through spill-over has not been large' (p. 86). It was recognised that some foreign subsidiaries displayed a markedly anti-union policy, and given the bargaining power these firms possessed when backed by their parents, legislation could be necessary to facilitate workers' rights. Finally, while the research produced few examples of loss of *national autonomy* through inward investment, it was recognised that multinational organisations were less amenable to government directive than domestic companies, joint ventures, etc. and reference was made to the inadequacy of existing institutional arrangements in the United Kingdom for properly monitoring the activities of foreign subsidiaries.

In aggregate the conclusion was, 'That concerns over the multinational firm and inward investment on the grounds of monopoly power, technology and the balance of payments are not well founded. At the same time, some drawbacks have been indicated, as well as a substantial amount of uncertainty with respect to . . . (the) findings' (p. 12). And it was the latter provisos which led the authors to reiterate their call for closer monitoring by governments. Circumstances have changed considerably since this report, widening even further the possible range of outcomes and the uncertainties over gains and losses from inward investment. Moreover, the criteria for evaluation are somewhat different given global competition, the speed of technological change and so on. Before launching into the discussion of issues, therefore, Figure 3.1 is presented as a summary of some of the potential costs and benefits associated with inward direct investment in the UK.

TECHNOLOGY TRANSFER AND INNOVATION

It is a revealing and rather disturbing fact that despite the central role of technology in the development process and the key position occupied by multinationals as creators of that technology, the issue has aroused rather little passion in an inward direct investment context in the UK. The Steuer Report summarised above argued that the requirement for an independent technology was 'romantic nonsense' and that 'research comparative advantage should be

Figure 3.1: Some potential benefits and costs associated with inward direct investment in the UK

Impact issue	Potential benefits to the UK economy	Potential costs to the UK economy	Some criteria for evaluating impact
Technology transfer and innovation	Transfer of advanced product/process technology; local technology creation via subsidiary R & D; technology diffusion and indigenous 'spin-off'; improved competitiveness and quality of employment	Transfer of standardised technology in assembly operations and mature sectors; royalty and other technology payments; technology dependency	Sectoral distribution of inward direct investment; forms of technology transfers (packaged/unpackaged, embodied/disembodied); local R & D activity; terms of technology transfers; the extent of technology diffusion; technology concentration and dependence; corporate/ subsidiary strategies and coordination
Market structure	Reduction in entry barriers and concentration levels; improved efficiency directly and indirectly; reallocation of resources towards growth sectors	Increase in concentration levels through market power and defensive mergers; anti-competitive practices; vulnerability to changing comparative advantage through international linkages	Market shares of MNE subsidiaries; spillover effects; sectoral distribution of inward direct investment; changing corporate strategies
Trade and balance of payments	Direct investment inflows; increased exports and improved competitiveness; import substitution effects	Repatriation of profits, royalties, etc.; imports of parts and components; transfer pricing; limitations on local sourcing; restricted export franchises	Capital inflows and remittances to parent company; export/import propensity of MNE subsidiaries; changing MNE sourcing strategies
Employment and productivity	Direct employment created through plant openings; multiplier employment effect; improved quality of employment; advanced personnel practices	Job security effects; low skill content in assembly operations; impact on union bargaining power	Employment in foreign-owned sector; plant closures/rationalisations; management and labour practices; industrial relations performance; MNE subsidiary performance *vs* domestic firms, other MNE subsidiaries in UK and abroad

pursued like any other comparative advantage'.[7] In recent years the development of the microelectronics industry in the UK and elsewhere in Europe has attracted a good deal of policy attention, but underlying this is a realisation that Europe is an 'also ran'. In such circumstances there is a view, at least in the UK, that the attraction of a healthy flow of inward investment is crucial to establish a presence in certain key technologies and that by so doing the technology problem takes care of itself. It is certainly possible that a 'virtuous circle' could be created through inward investment, indigenous spin off and the subsequent development of indigenous leading edge capabilities; on the other hand, a 'vicious circle' of inward investment with low technology products and processes and few indigenous spin offs is perhaps equally possible.

While the concern here is with foreign investment and technology transfer, it should be made clear initially that transfers of know how may take a large number of forms. Amongst the major types of chnology transfer are:

Foreign technology → foreign-owned establishment (inward investment in new start or expansion; wholly-owned subsidiaries or joint ventures)

Foreign technology → indigenous establishment (whole range of non-equity agreements)

Research institution (+ university) → new start (resulting from research finding, a new product for existing enterprises or the transfer of university know how to industry through training provision; stimulus to research partly from industry, partly not)

Employees → new start (employee spin off from existing enterprises, indigenous or foreign-owned)

Technically advanced company → subcontractor (improvement in standards and techniques of subcontractors through own efforts or through assistance of contracting enterprise).

As to the nature of technology itself, it may be embodied in the form of capital goods, including machinery and equipment; or it may be disembodied in forms such as industrial property rights, unpatented know how, management and organisation, and design and operating instructions for production systems. Inward direct investment contains in a single package capital goods and a number of the forms of disembodied technology.

Technology effects of inward direct investment

While authors differ in degree, the technology impact of inward direct investment on the UK is generally thought to be positive, albeit of 'unquantifiable dimensions'.[8] Such benefits are deemed to derive from the concentration of foreign MNEs in the more technologically intensive sectors; the linkage of the subsidiary into the R & D and technology resources of the parent multinational, as well as the research and development undertaken by many MNE subsidiaries themselves; and technological diffusion into the indigenous sector. Enough has been said in this book already to show that these are rather broad generalisations. The slower pace of innovation in the United States economy and resultant loss of competitiveness, for example, has obvious consequences for technology transfer into UK subsidiaries. Simply taking the years up to 1975, there was evidence of a slowdown in the rate of new product innovation; although it was also true that the period of time between introduction in the United States and transfer abroad was shortening, countering to some extent the argument that subsidiaries produce outdated goods with mature technologies.[9]

There are a few indicators available on the subject of the technological intensity of foreign direct investment in the UK. The stock of inward investment remains heavily concentrated in technologically advanced sectors, and, while it is necessary to be cautious in inferring this, there is an implication of the utilisation of advanced product and process technologies. What is clear is that the composition of the direct capital inflow is changing — away from the more technology-intensive (MTI) sectors towards less technology-intensive sectors, as Table 3.1 indicates. Care is needed in concluding too much from the figures shown. The concept of MTI embraces a wide range of industries, companies, markets, products and technologies. The distinction between MTI and LTI is quite arbitrary and sectors such as mechanical engineering and vehicles might legitimately have been regarded as mature industries. And industries may be reclassified, witness the argument in Chapter 1 that the automobile sector was moving back towards the technological frontier in terms of rates of innovations. Nevertheless, there is additional evidence to indicate that the categorisation is of some value. One study showed that the UK subsidiaries of MTIs grew at a much slower rate than those in LTIs over the period 1977–81. Furthermore the more technology-intensive foreign-owned MNEs expanded abroad in sales terms at a much faster rate than in the UK

71

Table 3.1: Sectoral distribution of inward direct investment flows in manufacturing industry in the UK

	1972–6 Inward investment £m	%	1977–81 Inward investment £m	%	1981–3 Inward investment £m	%
Chemicals and allied	355.7	18.1	893.6	20.6	611.4	43.5
Mechanical and instrument engineering	668.4	33.9	1,016.9	23.5	527.1	37.5
Electrical engineering	176.7	9.0	507.2	11.7	235.2	16.7
Motor vehicles	86.7	4.4	262.9	6.1	−593.0	−42.2
Rubber	50.2	2.6	−10.4	−0.2	−81.5	−5.8
More technology-intensive sectors[a]	1,337.7	67.9	2,670.2	61.7	699.2	49.8
Food, drink, tobacco	355.7	18.1	727.5	16.8	561.0	40.0
Metal manufacturing	35.4	1.8	178.4	4.1	−99.9	−7.1
Textiles, leather, clothing and footwear	23.7	1.2	2.9	0.1	37.1	2.6
Paper, printing, publishing	119.8	6.1	287.3	6.6	18.0	1.3
Other manufacturing	205.0	19.4	461.1	10.6	188.8	13.4
Less technology-intensive sectors[a]	739.6	32.1	1,657.2	38.3	705.0	50.2
Total manufacturing	1,970.9	100.0	4,327.4	100.0	1,404.2	100.0

Note: a MTI industries spent at least two per cent of their net output on R & D in 1974; LTI industries spent less than this percentage.
Sources: Dunning, J.H. (1979), 'The UK's international investment position in the mid-1970s', *Lloyds Bank Review*, 132, Table 5; and *Business Monitor*, MA4, 1981 and 1983.

over the same period.[10] This tends to support the view that MNEs will locate new products and production methods in countries where income, demand and output are high or growing, rather in the relatively stagnant UK economy, the implication being that the UK could end up with a growing proportion of standardised products and processes.[11] This issue is touched on again later in the chapter when questions of productivity differences between UK affiliates and those in other countries such as Germany are studied.

Undoubtedly there exists a need for studies at the corporate-specific level to investigate these and other technology-related questions. At present the limited evidence is derived from technology rankings made by foreign subsidiary executives in the UK. The results of one sample survey which compared foreign affiliates' product and process technology with that of domestic UK firms in the same industry, sister affiliates and home country plants are presented in Table 3.2. Although it is not shown, quite a high proportion of executives were unable to make a judgement on their technology, particularly relative to other group affiliates in Europe. Such comparisons are dependent on the method of affiliate control adopted by the parent, some making inter-plant data freely available, others not. Product range differences also reduce the ability of a manager to make comparisons with other firms. Where comparisons were possible, the results for foreign MNEs in the UK suggest generally superior technology to UK domestic firms, similar technology to sister affiliates and similar to less advanced technology to that in home country plants. Care has to be taken in accepting managers' opinions on these issues, although the results are along the lines that might have been anticipated.

The cost of technology transfer is a further issue which is commonly considered, especially in a host developing country context. The only information on this concerns royalty payments to related concerns abroad for licences, patents, trademarks, etc. as shown in Table 2.1 and Figure 2.9 in the previous chapter. There is little to add to the comment made there, although when royalty payments are related to inward direct investment flows, the costs do seem high. Thus in the years 1972–7, royalty payments to related concerns abroad amounted to 38 per cent of inward direct investment (excluding unremitted profits); the equivalent figure for the period 1978–83 was 44 per cent.

Table 3.2: Ratings of UK affiliate product and process technology

	Level of technology in foreign affiliates in the UK[a] Compared to UK firms (%)	
	Product technology	Process technology
More advanced	57.0	49.1
Similar	39.5	37.7
Less advanced	3.5	13.2
Total	100.0	100.0
	Compared to sister affiliates (%)	
More advanced	6.8	6.8
Similar	83.8	78.4
Less advanced	9.5	14.9
Total	100.0	100.0
	Compared to home country plants (%)	
More advanced	5.2	8.5
Similar	70.7	61.5
Less advanced	24.1	30.0
Total	100.0	100.0

Note: a Based on a sample size of 140, but 'don't knows' have been excluded from the tabulations given.
Source: Hood, N. and Young, S. (1983), *Multinational investment strategies in the British Isles*, HMSO, London, Table 1.9.

Technology and R & D

There are a number of reasons for believing that the location of an R & D function at subsidiary level may produce significant benefits for the UK affiliate and the UK economy:

The R & D unit at subsidiary level can act as a conduit for technology transfer from the parent MNEs, and thereby speed up flows of new products and processes
The presence of an R & D unit, particularly if it is effective in new product development, may encourage MNEs to delegate wider responsibilities to the subsidiary. Aside from manufacturing responsibility for the product, these may include marketing, wider market area franchises and generally greater autonomy
The R & D units themselves may be a source of pressure for greater autonomy and responsibility
To manage the R & D unit and R & D professionals, higher grade plant management may be required

R & D engineers may prove the most likely source for spin off indigenous enterprises, given their awareness of new product opportunities
Studies have shown that there is a tendency for R & D units to evolve into higher level work over time, even if they are set up initially on a very small scale and with a limited role.

Of course, none of these benefits is certain. The arguments above to some extent run counter to earlier discussions on globalisation and with this centralisation and integration. Furthermore, there may be good reasons for MNEs centralising R & D, including the maintenance of effective communications with production and marketing, and economies of scale in research and development itself. Moreover, even with subsidiary R & D, the benefits are dependent upon what happens to the research results.

The aggregate statistics on R & D in foreign-owned firms in the UK for a series of years are presented in Table 3.3. In 1981 £582 million was spent on R & D by foreign affiliates, split between funds obtained within the UK (64 per cent), funds from overseas (29 per cent) and financial support from the UK government (seven per cent). The table indicates that R & D employment in foreign firms has been declining, slowly but steadily, as a proportion of the total. By comparison MNE affiliate R & D expenditures have just about been holding fairly steady in share terms. In terms of R & D intensity (as measured by R & D/sales ratios), there has not been much difference between foreign controlled and all manufacturing enterprises, where both are adjusted to include company-funded R & D only. Wages and salaries paid to R & D employees in foreign firms were about 20 per cent higher than those paid to research and development personnel in UK manufacturing industry as a whole in 1981 (this was slightly greater than the 15 per cent wages and salaries differential which existed between multinational and all employees in manufacturing in the same year).

Two sets of factors need to be considered in relation to these results. The first concerns the issue of parent versus subsidiary R & D, and the second relates to the attractiveness of the UK as an R & D location *vis-à-vis* other host countries. It is well known that multinational research and development spending is concentrated in home country locations, although a gradual expansion of offshore R & D in US MNEs occurred up to 1982 at least, particularly in the area of development work, designed to support the marketing efforts of foreign subsidiaries. Data from US Department of Commerce

Table 3.3: R & D expenditure and employment in foreign-owned firms

| | R & D expenditure and employment in foreign-owned firms (as % of total)[a] | | | | | | | |
| | Gross expenditure | | | | Employment | | | |
	1972	1975	1978	1981[b]	1972	1975	1978	1981
Chemicals and allied products	17	26	26	27	14	23	23	23
Mechanical engineering	11	24	25	28	11	19	19	27
Electrical engineering (including electronics)	18	19	16	17	16	17	13	12
Vehicles (including aerospace)	14	12	8	6	15	15	10	8
Other products	14	15	25	22	11	14	21	17
All products	15	18	18	18[c]	14	17	16	15[c]

Notes: *a* R & D of overseas-controlled enterprises as a percentage of all enterprises performing R & D.

b 1981 figures refer to 'intra-mural R & D expenditure' and may not be comparable with data for earlier years. If a consistent series was produced on the basis of intra-mural R & D only, the foreign-owned share also shows a slight decline in 1981 rather than stability, as above.

c Total numbers employed in R & D in MNE subsidiaries were 26,100 and intra-mural R & D expenditure totalled £582.4 million.
Source: *Business Monitor*, MO14, 1975, 1978 and 1981.

Benchmark Surveys indicate that the US affiliate share of total American MNE R & D spending rose from 6.6 per cent in 1966 to 8.6 per cent in 1977, with a further marginal rise to 8.8 per cent in 1982. Since then the trend is more uncertain. There has been a growing capital intensiveness in R & D which could be expected to reduce the attractions of lower labour cost locations outside the USA. More speculatively, there are suggestions of a revival in confidence in the United States concerning the country's own scientific and technological capabilities, so that US MNEs may not be looking abroad for intellectual power to the same extent as in the past. And specifically related to the UK, the brain drain issue may be operating against this country as a desirable R & D base, with scientists moving to the greener pastures of research centres in America itself.

There are specific industry factors at work too. In pharmaceuticals there are signs of pre-clinical development work being centralised to a greater degree than formerly, and while the clinical phase of development (adaptation to different regulatory systems, etc.) is still decentralised, the work is now commonly subcontracted

Table 3.4: R & D in US majority-owned affiliates abroad

	R & D expenditure as % of total sales		R & D employment as % of total employment	
	1977	1982	1977	1982
All countries	0.9	1.2	1.5	2.3
Developed countries	1.0	1.3	1.8	3.1
EEC[a]	1.3	1.6[a]	2.1	3.8
France	1.6	1.0	1.8	2.3
Germany	1.5	2.2	2.2	5.1
UK	1.3	1.8	2.4	3.8
Developing countries	0.4	0.5	0.6	0.5

Note: a Includes Greece.
Source: US Department of Commerce, *US direct investment abroad 1977*, Washington, D.C.; US Department of Commerce, *US direct investment abroad: 1982 benchmark survey data*, Washington, D.C.

overseas. The UK had been particularly successful in attracting research from the pharmaceutical MNEs, and Brech and Sharp estimated that at the end of the 1970s 11½ per cent of the industry's global research was undertaken in Britain, although only 3½ per cent of the world's drugs were consumed there.[12] It is difficult to know the up-to-date position and there have been suggestions of reductions in pharmaceutical R & D programmes because of low returns. A recent small scale study did not find evidence to support this; where R & D programmes in UK subsidiaries were phased out, they have tended to be replaced by other R & D projects because of the high success rate in R & D innovation and the contribution made by universities and other research centres in Britain.[13] Considering the country location of US subsidiary R & D more generally, Table 3.4 shows that the UK has not declined in popularity as a centre for research and development. However, as a continuation of a trend which was apparent between 1966 and 1977, in the five years up to 1982, R & D/sales and R & D/employment ratios grew much more rapidly in Germany than in Britain.

Turning to the company level, it becomes apparent that foreign subsidiary R & D spending and employment in Britain must be heavily concentrated, because a high proportion of firms undertake no R & D. In one sample of US and Continental European subsidiaries, 40 per cent undertook no research and development work. As will be discussed in the next chapter, the absence of R & D is one indicator of what is termed the 'branch plant syndrome'.[14] The R & D performing firms in the sample were seen to be much larger in employment terms, and where R & D was present in the smaller affiliates, these were, without exception, MNEs with no other manufacturing plants in Europe outside the home country. Supporting previous remarks, affiliate R & D was heavily oriented towards development work (75 per cent of spending) as opposed to research; in fact this breakdown is not too dissimilar to that for all UK private industry. Finally, average employment in R & D departments was around 14, 3.5 per cent of total employment in the companies concerned, with half of these R & D jobs being taken by graduate personnel.

What has been absent in research in the UK are attempts to relate the presence or absence of R & D to measures of plant performance and contribution to the economy. However, Haug *et al.*, comparing R & D-intensive and non-R & D-intensive US electronics affiliates, revealed that the former were more export oriented and had more extensive primary and secondary sourcing roles outside Europe (although they were also larger in employment terms and generally older); R & D units seemed to provide a mechanism for facilitating technology transfers from the parent MNEs and the proportion of commercial applications from the research results was high and tended to be based in the affiliates themselves.[15] While the sample size was rather small, the results of this study were encouraging, and provide some clear lessons for policy makers in the encouragement of research and development.

MARKET STRUCTURE

A whole range of impact issues relate to market structure considerations and multinationality. A number of these shade into topics discussed elsewhere in this chapter; while the nature of the effects themselves is commonly difficult to determine, being dependent very much on the characteristics of individual markets and on how existing firms within these markets respond to the multinational threat (or opportunity). For example, concentration levels may be reduced by MNE entry and an element of competition injected; and there were numerous examples of this occurring, certainly in the pre-World War Two years, such as the establishment of the Goodyear Tyre Company and the Firestone Tyre Company in a sector where Dunlop had a dominant position.[16] The entry of foreign banks into the cosy banking oligopoly which existed hitherto is a more recent illustration. Conversely, concentration may be increased as overseas companies enter fragmented markets, with rather profound effects on indigenous producers, as with Japanese presence in the colour television sector demonstrated. The economic impact will, in addition, depend upon entry methods used by foreign MNEs, particularly as between the formation of greenfield ventures and acquisitions. Both chauvinism and the classic anti-trust dilemmas reared their ugly heads on several occasions in the late 1980s in relation to actual takeover cases such as STC/ICL, threatened takeovers (Ford and Austin Rover) and, indeed, cases where only minority foreign holdings were involved (the Sikorsky-Fiat stake in Westland Helicopters). In all countries where market structures are affected by an initial entry or takeover from abroad, furthermore, there will be further rounds of effects as companies strive to compete and jockey for position. It has been suggested that the next wave of Japanese inward investment will have a major catalytic effect on European and US companies in Western Europe, as they step up defensive cross-frontier mergers to rationalise capacity.[17]

The 1958 work of Dunning on American investment in British manufacturing revealed that 87 per cent of US affiliate employees were in industries where the subsidiary was either the dominant (or sole) producer or among the largest producers within an oligopolistic market structure.[18] As in the results of the later Steuer Report, it was suggested that the effect of the US presence was a mixed one, with examples both of the break up of monopolies and of greater concentration. Overall there was little evidence that the competitive structure of UK industry had been adversely affected by American multinationals.

More recent studies at the aggregate level have largely supported earlier findings. The work of Fishwick (1982) on MNEs and economic concentration in particular European countries including the UK, focused in its conclusions on the viewpoint prevalent in certain circles in the 1960s and 1970s concerning the growth of multinational domination.[19] The allegation was that concentration and MNE operations would expand until the small number of multi-nationals possessed greater power than national governments. In questioning these predictions the author provided evidence that:

Concentration was not increasing significantly, at aggregate or sectoral level, in those countries for which data existed
MNE operations were no longer being extended within Europe — rather there was some evidence of withdrawal

79

Competition in oligopolistic industries, in the form of price cutting, increased advertising and product innovation, had occurred on a scale inconsistent with theoretical predictions of collusion.

The conclusions of the above were based on conventional measures and statistical approaches, but rather than summarise these, it is more useful to refer to work by Dunning published in 1985.[20] Using regression analysis on data for the period 1971–9, comparisons were made between the structural characteristics of three groups of manufacturing firms, namely foreign-owned MNEs in the UK, UK companies producing in the UK and the overseas production of UK MNEs. Referring to comparisons between the first two of these groups, the findings were as follows. Relative to UK-owned firms manufacturing in the UK, foreign affiliates in the UK:

— Produced in sectors with above average productivity or profitability; and in industries where the productivity of foreign affiliates was highest relative to that of domestic firms
— produced in sectors with above average net capital expenditure per employee
— Concentrated in sectors where competition was oligopolistic, as reflected in an above average concentration ratio. (These relationships are only partially apparent from tabular data at the industry level as Table 3.5, which shows foreign-owned shares of employment and concentration ratios, reveals)
— Concentrated in growth sectors, especially when growth was defined to include exports
— Concentrated in sectors in which the trade intensity of the UK was increasing. This was seen as a reflection of intra-plant product specialisation, and the internalisation of economic activity across national boundaries.

In addition, there was no evidence that the subsidiaries of foreign-based MNEs were more vertically integrated in their UK activities than were indigenous firms.

The results from the various pieces of research thus show a substantial degree of accord. Certainly MNEs have had an impact on the UK economic structure which is different from that of domestic firms, with the indication that the multinationals 'assisted the UK's economic restructuring in the 1970s towards higher allocative and technical efficiency'. It is useful, however, to pick up

Table 3.5: Foreign-owned shares of employment and five firm concentration ratios, by industry, 1983[a]

SIC class	Industry	Foreign-owned share of employment	Five firm concentration ratio (by employment)
35	Vehicles	62.8	63.1
33	Office machinery	39.0	48.0
25	Chemicals	32.9	41.7
37	Instrument engineering	23.1	27.1
48	Rubber and plastics	21.1	23.6
32	Mechanical engineering	19.3	22.7
34	Electrical and electronic engineering	16.2	34.7
49	Other manufacturing	14.9	22.6
47	Paper, printing and publishing	14.4	21.9
22	Metal manufacturing	13.3	60.8
41/42	Food, drink and tobacco	11.7	50.7
26	Man-made fibres	9.8	93.0
31	Metal goods n.e.s.	8.3	16.6
24	Non-metallic minerals	6.6	43.6
45	Footwear and clothing	3.5	19.2
43	Textiles	2.9	34.0
46	Timber and furniture	2.0	11.9
36	Other transportation	1.9	28.7
23	Other minerals n.e.s.	1.5	44.6

Note: a Ranked by foreign-owned share of employment.
Source: *Business Monitor*, PA1002, 1983.

on Dunning's next point which was that 'by promoting structural independence between national markets, MNEs have made the UK economy more vulnerable to international demand and supply conditions'.[21] It is necessary initially to question whether on the basis of multinational operations and international competition it is relevant to talk about concentration levels on a uni-national UK level; and even if competition is essentially UK-centred, a foreign affiliate in Britain possesses advantages from being part of a multinational group which can override simple associations between size and market power, etc. Leaving this aside, the issue once again turns to the Chapter 1 themes of global firms and global industries: the dilemmas that were posed concerned the requirement for interaction with the rest of the world for reasons of competitiveness, as against loss of structural autonomy and the greater volatility deriving from international demand and supply conditions, but also from more footloose investment. Policy issues which arise relate to incentive bidding for mobile international investment and the necessity to try to put a lid on this through supranational action; conversely, the need for greater adjustment assistance arises when MNEs adapt more quickly to demand fluctuations and technological change than domestic enterprises. There are, in addition, questions relating to subsidiary roles within multinational corporate systems.

Despite the indications of positive impacts on resource allocation, it is clear that some foreign MNEs have achieved a dominant market position in certain product areas in the UK which, in instances, has led to allegations of anti-competitive practices and subsequent investigation under UK or EEC legislation. Furthermore, takeover bids from abroad have proved contentious on occasions, with investigation by the Monopolies and Mergers Commission. Various acquisition issues and merger policies are discussed further in Chapters 5 and 6 respectively.

TRADE AND BALANCE OF PAYMENTS

The trade and balance of payments effect of foreign MNEs remains one of the most important impact issues associated with inward direct investment in the UK, given the long term deterioration in the country's international competitive position and the large and grow-ing trade deficit in most manufacturing industries (see Chapter 1). As in the other impact areas under discussion, the trade and balance of payments effects are wide ranging and include important first-order (direct) and second-order (indirect) effects (see Figure 3.1). First-order trade and balance of payments effects arise through the impact of direct investment inflows on the capital account; the impact of profit repatriation and other remittances to the parent company on invisible payments; the export and import propensities of foreign subsidiaries; and the import substitution effect. Second-order trade and payments effects arise from changing multinational sourcing policies which affect subsidiary exports and imports; the overall impact of foreign MNEs on industrial efficiency and competitiveness; and long term export prospects which may depend more on intra-firm rather than 'arm's length' trade.

As in the technology area discussed earlier, inward direct invest-ment is generally thought to have had positive effects on the UK's trade performance and balance of payments, although major concerns remain regarding the high import propensity of foreign-owned subsidiaries in sectors such as automobiles and electronics.

82

Dunning's 1958 study identified several major trade and balance of payments benefits associated with the early flow of US direct investment in the UK.[22] These included the higher export propensity of US-owned subsidiaries; their concentration in sectors for which international demand was growing at the time (e.g. agricultural machinery, earth-moving equipment, automobiles, office equipment, etc.); subsidiary access to the global marketing network of the parent company; the general competitive stimulus provided by inward direct investment; and the potential for UK component suppliers to export to other parts of the multinational network. Dunning's conclusions were supported by the Steuer Report which, as already seen, concluded that the overall balance of payments effect was favourable to the order of ten per cent of the output of the foreign-owned sector.[23] This conclusion was based on regression analysis which took into account five key balance of payments impacts, namely, the export effect; the import substitution effect; the import effect; the repatriation effect; and the overall balance of payments effect. Dunning's 1976 study reinforced these early conclusions regarding the favourable trade and balance of payments effects of inward (mainly US) direct investment in the UK.[24] In 1970, the value of US subsidiary exports, after correcting for industry differences between the US-owned and indigenous sectors, was approximately £500 million in excess of the value of profit, interest and dividend repayments to parent companies.

Table 3.6 presents data on various direct balance of payments effects of inward direct investment in the UK during the period 1972–81. It should be noted that the table does not measure the overall balance of payments impact since no account is taken of the indirect or second-order effects identified above. However, the table does indicate a large and favourable direct contribution to the UK's balance of payments. Between 1972 and 1981, inward direct investment contributed a total of £5 billion to the capital account after excluding the amount of such investment financed locally. The current account effects are more difficult to estimate due to the absence of data on the import propensity of the foreign-owned sector. Nevertheless, as in Dunning's 1976 study, total remittances to the parent company were well below the value of foreign subsidiary exports, with the magnitude of difference being approximately £72 billion over the period covered by the table, giving a net positive balance of payments effect (excluding imports) of approximately £77 billion.

As mentioned, the data shown in Table 3.6 exclude the negative

Table 3.6: Some balance of payments effects of inward direct investment in the UK, 1972–81[a]

	1972	1973	1974	1975	1976	1977	1978	1979	1980	1981[c]
					£m					
Current account										
Exports by foreign-owned enterprises	+2,758	+3,469	+4,684	+5,736	+7,417	+9,483	+10,460	+12,000	+13,525	+12,822
Payment of interest, profits and dividends	−253	−363	−371	−378	−499	−595	−806	−852	−1,151	−1,298
Payment of royalties, etc. to overseas parent companies, branches, subsidiaries and associates	−78	−94	−121	−151	−180	−214	−254	−288	−324	362
Services rendered by overseas parent companies, branches, subsidiaries and associates	−65	−78	−86	−114	−151	−210	−232	−281	−319	−344
Current account balance excluding imports of raw materials and intermediate products	+2,362	+2,934	+4,106	+5,093	+6,587	+8,464	+9,168	+10,579	+11,731	+10,818
Capital account										
Net overseas direct investment in the UK[b]	+104	+390	+603	+368	+258	+489	+541	+496	+1,735	+125
Net balance of payments effect (excluding imports of raw materials and intermediate products)	+2,466	+3,324	+4,709	+5,461	+6,845	+8,953	+9,709	+11,075	+13,466	+10,943

Notes: a All industries, excluding oil.
b Total direct investment minus unremitted profits of subsidiary and associated companies.
c An update of this table is not possible due to a change in reporting requirements regarding exports.
Sources: *Business Monitor*, MA4, various years; CSO, *UK Balance of Payments*, various years.

balance of payments effects resulting from the high import propensities of certain foreign-owned subsidiaries and, indeed, this has become a major source of concern in the UK in recent years, especially in sectors such as automobiles, information technology and chemicals. In automobiles, both Ford and General Motors, in addition to the well-publicised Nissan case, have come under strong government pressure to increase the local content of cars sold in the UK market (see below).[25] The negative trade balance in the information processing industry has similarly been attributed to the foreign sourcing policies of MNE subsidiaries, with companies such as Hewlett-Packard remaining net importers into the UK despite the high export propensity of their UK subsidiaries.[26] Similar criticisms have been made against Japanese MNEs in the UK (see Chapter 5), while in the chemical industry, a rapid increase in imports in 1983 (+20 per cent compared with the previous year) was attributed to a change in sourcing policies by foreign MNEs in the industry.[27]

Several studies have attempted to evaluate the balance of payments effects of such changing MNE sourcing policies. Panić and Joyce correlated the net trade performance of different UK manufacturing industries with the extent of foreign participation (measured in terms of the foreign subsidiary share of net output) over the period 1971–8.[28] The correlation coefficients showed that the net trade ratio was more favourable in manufacturing sectors with a high level of foreign participation, indicating a favourable trade and balance of payments effect associated with the presence of foreign-owned firms. Conversely, the biggest deterioration in net trade ratios over the period was also recorded in sectors with a high level of foreign participation. Thus, the net trade effect of foreign MNEs was still positive, but declining. This was explained in terms of the increasing import propensity of foreign MNEs operating in the UK. Hamill (1985) updated Panić's study to cover the period 1978–83, with similar conclusions, namely, that the trade performance of those UK industries with a high level of foreign ownership deteriorated more rapidly than other sectors over the period 1978–83, but especially after 1980.[29]

The motor vehicle industry experienced the largest deterioration in net trade performance of any British manufacturing sector over the period 1978–84 (see Table 1.1). Over this period, vehicle exports (in money value) increased by only 13 per cent, as compared with a 118 per cent increase in the money value of imports.[30] Although a significant proportion of this increase in imports was due to the pressures of foreign competition, recent evidence suggests that most of the deterioration in the sector's trade balance can be blamed on the sourcing strategies of MNE producers, including Ford, General Motors (Vauxhall) and Peugeot (Talbot), which have significantly reduced their exports from the UK while, at the same time, increasing their 'tied' imports from plants in Continental Europe.[31] The study by Jones provided a detailed analysis of the impact of changing MNE strategies on the trade performance of the British vehicle industry. The main conclusions of the study are summarised below, with Figure 3.2 presenting some of the results diagrammatically:

The market share of 'non-tied' vehicle imports into the UK has stabilised at around 35 per cent following a rapid increase during the 1970s

The main increase in import penetration since 1974 has been in 'tied' imports from the Continental European plants of Ford, General Motors and Peugeot (e.g. Ford Fiestas built in Spain; Vauxhall Cavaliers built in Belgium). Such 'tied' imports increased their·share of the UK market from one per cent in 1974 to 22 per cent in 1984

There has, in addition, been a rapid increase in the volume of imported components used by the multinational producers, especially over the perid 1979–84, equivalent in value to an additional 150,000 imported cars

The real level of import penetration of the UK car industry is 66 per cent, i.e. 35 per cent 'non-tied' imports and 31 per cent 'tied' imports of finished cars and components

The UK content of cars sold in the UK by the multinational producers fell significantly between 1973 and 1984 from 88 to 46 per cent in the case of Ford; 97 to 42 per cent for Talbot; and 89 to 22 per cent in the case of General Motors

The multinational producers have ceased exporting built-up cars from the UK

In 1984 the value of 'tied' imports of finished cars and components was approximately £1,900 million, which represented 71 per cent of the total trade deficit in the sector

Both Ford and General Motors were net importers into the UK (£500 million and £600 million in 1984 respectively), while Talbot had a positive trade balance

The increase in 'tied' imports of components has had a major adverse effect on the UK component supply industry.

Figure 3.2: UK car trade and the multinationals

A   Import penetration in the UK car market, 1969–84

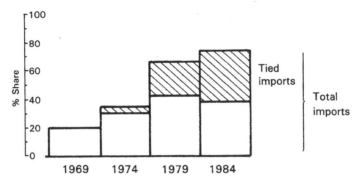

B   UK car sales and imports by manufacturer, 1984

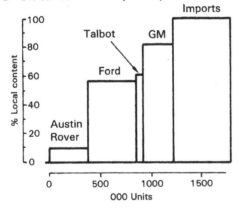

C   Car exports by manufacturer

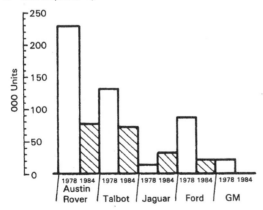

Source: Jones, D.T. (1985), *The import threat to the UK car industry*,
Science Policy Research Unit, University of Sussex.

The empirical evidence reviewed in this section suggests an overall positive trade and balance of payments effect associated with inward direct investment in the UK. This would be further increased if the second-order effects of MNEs on industrial efficiency and import substitution could be quantified. Very real sources of concern remain, however, with respect to the high import propensity of certain foreign-owned firms, as indicated above. It has to be said that in the vehicle industry there were some recent signs of an increase in local content due to the depreciation of sterling against Continental European currencies, especially the German Mark, which has increased the costs of imported components.

An additional source of concern regarding the trade and balance of payments effects of inward direct investment relates to the concentration of British exports within a small number of the largest industrial enterprises — many of which are foreign-owned. According to a Department of Trade inquiry, over half of all British exports are accounted for by just 87 enterprises, most of whom are multi-nationals.[32] Furthermore, a high proportion of both total exports (29 per cent) and imports (50 to 60 per cent) are with related parties abroad. The future trade performance of the British economy, therefore, may be dependent as much on the sourcing policies of MNEs (both foreign-owned and UK-owned) as on the question of international competitiveness.

EMPLOYMENT AND LABOUR EFFECTS

Despite the attention given spasmodically to the other impact items, there is little doubt that policy attitudes in the UK are still conditioned very strongly by the employment effects of inward direct investment, with the major issues being the direct and indirect (multiplier) effects of foreign MNEs on aggregate employment levels; the impact on the regional distribution of employment (which is examined in detail in Chapter 4); the nature and type of employment created (skill levels, sex composition, permanent vs temporary jobs, etc.); and the related issue of job security (see Figure 3.1).

While the focus on the job creating (or destroying) effects of inward direct investment is understandable given the high level of UK unemployment, there are other important employment and labour effects associated with foreign MNEs. In particular, the transfer of innovative foreign personnel and labour utilisation practices and the impact of such transfers on productivity and efficiency in both the foreign-owned and indigenous sectors (through the spillover of management practices) have been identified as some of the major benefits deriving from inward direct investment in the UK.[33] Although there have been many explanations offered for the deterioration in British competitiveness (see Chapter 1), one of the most frequently cited explanations was the adversarial nature of British labour/management relations. Aspects of the so called 'British disease' with possible detrimental effects on competitiveness included union militancy and restrictive practices; multi-unionism; informal bargaining and unofficial strikes; the role and influence of shop stewards; excessive wage demands; poor communications systems; and ineffective disputes procedures.[34]

While UK labour problems have been much exaggerated, the poor perception of British industrial relations had a major influence on the Conservative Governments in power since 1979, with the encouragement of a new realism in labour relations being a major element in the Conservative Party's 'supply side' strategy of regenerating the British economy.[35] To this end, legislation has been introduced covering the closed shop; secret ballots before strike action; the election of union officials; unlawful industrial action; picketing; and union immunity from legal action in industrial disputes. The government's aim of installing this new realism in British labour relations has met with a considerable degree of success, with many companies introducing radical new working practices.[36] The major trends in the emergence of a 'new industrial relations' have included a reduction in trade union bargaining power and in the role and influence of shop stewards; an increase in the number of non-union plants; longer term and more clearly defined collective agreements; flexible working practices; a shift by many employers towards the use of a 'core' and 'periphery' workforce; a greater emphasis on 'open door' communications; harmonisation; and more stringent recruitment procedures.[37] In addition to the encouragement provided by government policy, the introduction of these new practices has been stimulated by a number of other factors, including the transfer of foreign personnel practices by MNE subsidiaries in the UK (see Figure 3.3).

In terms of the direct employment impact of inward investment, Dunning's 1958 study identified three major benefits deriving from the early flow of US investment in the UK, including an enlarged volume of employment; the variety of employment created including female employment and an improvement in skill levels; and employment creation in depressed areas.[38] In addition, Dunning identified

Figure 3.3: Influences on the new industrial relations in the UK

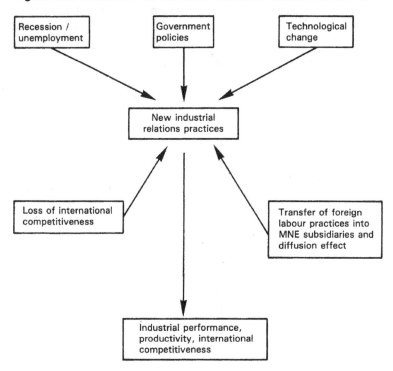

Source: Hamill, J. (1986), *Foreign multinationals: labour and industrial relations effects*, paper presented at an IRM/SIBU conference on 'Scotland and the multinationals', Glasgow, 18 September.

major employment and social benefits deriving to local communities from the concentration of US firms in particular areas including Dagenham, Luton, Dundee, Southampton, Slough, etc. Overall, it was concluded that the net employment effects of US investment were positive, despite the fact that the presence of American-owned firms had exacerbated labour shortages during the immediate post-war years leading to upward pressures on wage rates.[39]

The Steuer Report of 1973 did not examine in detail the aggregate employment effects of inward direct investment, although some evidence was presented regarding the composition of employment in the foreign-owned sector, based on a case study of the electrical engineering industry.[40] This highlighted little difference between foreign-owned and indigenous firms in the industry with respect to

Table 3.7: Employment in foreign-owned and all manufacturing enterprises, selected years 1963–8

Year	Foreign-owned employment (000s)	% change between years	All manufacturing (000s)	% change between years	Foreign-owned employment as proportion of total employment (%)
1963	539.0	—	7,695.0	—	7.0
1968	693.5	+28	7,249.0	−5	9.6
1971	742.7	+7	7,458.8	−2	9.9
1973	821.5	+10	7,268.3	−2	11.3
1975	925.7	+12	7,118.7	−2	13.0
1977	961.9	+3	7,090.4	−4	13.6
1979	974.2	+1	6,485.0	−8	15.0
1981	858.1	−12	5,777.9	−11	16.0
1983	736.0	−14	5,077.8	−12	14.0

Source: *Business Monitor*, PA 1002, various issues.

the education/skill composition of the workforce, but foreign-owned firms had a tendency to employ younger people and to provide more workforce training. Stopford's 1979 study on behalf of the ILO concluded that both inward and outward direct investment had positive impacts on UK employment levels.[41] On the inward side, there had been a more rapid increase in foreign-owned relative to indigenous employment in all sectors (except metals) over the period 1971–5.

Table 3.7 shows the broad trends in aggregate employment levels in the foreign-owned and indigenous sectors over the last two decades or so. During the 1960s and 1970s, employment within foreign-owned manufacturing firms increased at a faster rate than in manufacturing industry as a whole. Indeed, for most of the 1970s foreign-owned employment continued to expand even though manufacturing employment as a whole was in decline. This resulted in a consistent increase in the foreign-owned share of total manufacturing employment. Both the foreign-owned and indigenous sectors experienced a sharp reduction in employment levels during the most recent recessionary period 1979–83, with the rate of decline in the former being marginally higher than in the indigenous sector.

The foreign-owned employment data shown in Table 3.7 include the employment generated by new entrants. From a job security perspective, the most relevant measure is the employment trend in existing subsidiaries and this is shown in Table 3.8. Decision making regarding investment and divestment are amongst the most centralised decision-making areas within MNEs, and this will create obvious concerns regarding job security at subsidiary level. Similarly, it is possible to quote examples of significant job losses arising in the UK from the closure or rationalisation of MNE subsidiaries (see Chapter 5). However, the table indicates that in broad aggregate terms job security was not under greater threat in the foreign-owned sector, at least up to 1981.

Turning to the issue of the quality of employment, reference has already been made to the earlier Steuer Report, which identified little difference in the skill composition of employment between foreign-owned and indigenous firms in the electrical engineering industry. A recent study by two of the authors provided a detailed breakdown of the composition of employment within foreign-owned firms in the chemical, mechanical and electrical engineering industries.[42] When this was compared with Department of Employment data covering the composition of total employment in the three industries, it appeared that the skill content of employment in the

Table 3.8: Employment change in foreign-owned and UK-owned manufacturing enterprises, 1975–81[a]

	1975–8		1978–81	
	Foreign-owned %	UK-owned %	Foreign-owned %	UK-owned %
Employment change in survivors	+6	−1	−15	−16
Employment los in closures	−3	−3	−7	−6
Net change	+3	+4	−22	−22

Note: a Excluding the employment effects of new openings.
Source: T. Killick (1982), 'Employment in foreign-owned manufacturing plants', *British Business*, 26 November.

foreign-owned sector was lower than in the indigenous sector (Table 3.9). Both sectors employed approximately the same proportion of craft and similar employees, but the foreign sector apparently employed fewer managerial, professional, etc. workers and a higher proportion of semi- and un-skilled manual workers relative to indigenous firms.

In terms of personnel and labour practices, the preference of many foreign-owned subsidiaries to import parent company practices into the UK has been long recognised. Both the Dunning (1958) and Steuer (1973) studies provided a large number of examples of the transfer of foreign labour practices, with the aim of improving labour utilisation and productivity at subsidiary level.[43] Some of the innovative labour practices already introduced by the early 1970s included the preference for company as opposed to industry-wide bargaining to allow greater flexibility in wage determination; wage rates in excess of the industry average in order to attract skilled labour; an emphasis on individual performance-related payment schemes; profit-sharing; non-unionisation; more generous employee fringe benefits; factory design; improvement in communications procedures; and more professional recruitment and selection procedures. More recent studies have confirmed that significant differences still exist in the personnel and labour practices of foreign-owned and indigenous firms in the UK in relation to many of these areas; and that these are due mainly to the transfer of parent company practices.[44]

The transfer of foreign labour practices by MNEs in the UK has

Table 3.9: Workforce characteristics of foreign-owned and all manufacturing enterprises in the chemical, and mechanical and electrical engineering industries

| | % of total employment | |
	Foreign-owned	All firms
Managerial, professional, clerical, foremen and other non-manual	31	40
Craft and similar	18	19
Other manual	51	41
	100	100

Sources: Department of Employment Gazette; Hood, N. and Young, S. (1983), *Multinational investment strategies in the British Isles*, HMSO, London, Table 1.17.

recently attracted a considerable degree of public and media interest, especially in relation to foreign subsidiaries in the electronics industry and with respect to the distinctive personnel approach adopted by Japanese-owned subsidiaries. A House of Commons Employment Select Committee was established in 1986 to examine this area, especially in relation to the impact of such practices on productivity levels in foreign-owned companies, and whether such practices (e.g. non-unionisation) gave MNE subsidiaries a competitive advantage over indigenous firms.[45] Several studies have shown that MNE subsidiaries in the UK have higher levels of labour productivity compared with indigenous firms.[46] The Steuer Report attributed such differences to the larger capital inputs used by foreign-owned firms, whereas recent work by Sawers attributed labour productivity differences to various aspects of the labour utilisation practices adopted by UK subsidiaries, at least as far as German and Japanese MNEs were concerned (see Figure 3.4).[47] The transfer of innovative foreign labour practices could also be expected to reduce the incidence of labour disputes in foreign-owned subsidiaries, although the evidence regarding the relative strike-proneness of foreign as compared with indigenous firms is inconclusive.[48]

While it is clear that productivity in foreign-owned factories in the UK is significantly higher than in domestic firms, there is much more uncertainty about intra-MNE performance. Pratten's study of 1976 found that labour productivity in his sample of British plants was 27 per cent lower than in German plants, when comparisons

Figure 3.4: Factors making for high productivity

1. Products designed for ease of manufacture
2. Technically advanced and well-planned production equipment
3. Emphasis on continual improvements in production methods
4. Flexible labour force, with simple skill-related payments system
5. Tight manning levels
6. Good labour relations, with emphasis on provision of information to employees and mutual respect
7. Maintenance as prevention rather than cure; with operatives responsible for own machines
8. Clear responsibilities for performance at all levels
9. Careful recruitment and selection procedures

Source: Sawers, D. (1986), 'The experience of German and Japanese subsidiaries in Britain', *Journal of General Management*, 12(1), Table 1.

were made between MNEs with factories in both countries. The Sawers' work compared productivity in German and Japanese affiliates in the UK with that in their parents' factories; all the Japanese subsidiaries considered that their productivity was well below that in their parent operations and some of the German subsidiaries believed that productivity could be lower in certain areas in Britain than in Germany.

LINKAGE AND SPILLOVER EFFECTS

The evidence from this chapter has indicated that the multinational sector in Britain is highly dynamic (especially in comparison with indigenous firms — comparisons with MNE operations in other developed countries are not so favourable); and the economy has benefited structurally from this and from the attendant commitment to high productivity, and the growth and export orientation of the foreign-owned companies. The downside of this dynamism is the volatility of the sector, exacerbated by changes in international competitiveness which have adversely affected the dominant group of investors — American multinationals. In these circumstances the presumption of net benefit from the foreign presence in the future is dependent upon a continuing flow of new investment. Given such uncertainties, linkage with and diffusion into the indigenous sector is crucial for any lasting benefit from inward investment in Britain — for example, the formation of spin-off enterprises, backward linkages through locally-procured inputs leading to the emergence of an indigenous supply industry, forward linkages into product manufacture, relationships with the general scientific and business community and so on. The acid test is to question whether anything would remain if the multinationals departed. While information is limited, a number of these topics are touched on from the regional perspective in the next chapter. The discussion here is restricted to supply and subcontract linkages between the foreign and domestic sectors and other technological and managerial spillovers.

The local content issue was discussed in the previous section from the perspective of the balance of payments consequences of overseas sourcing. The focus here is rather in terms of the explanations for particular supply links and whether suppliers have been encouraged to improve their quality, price, delivery terms etc. because of the influence of MNE subsidiaries. In 1954 between one half and two thirds of the gross output of a sample of US manufacturing firms in Britain was outsourced, mainly from UK suppliers.[49] For 23 Japanese manufacturing subsidiaries in the UK, 1982 data showed the following:[50]

Sales	£235m
Purchases from other firms for further production	£161m
of which from:	
UK firms	£68m
Imports	£93m

So 68 per cent of sales value was outsourced, split 29 per cent/39 per cent between UK supplies and imports; or, expressed differently, 42 per cent of purchases were obtained from UK suppliers and 58 per cent were imported. While not directly comparable, another sample survey of US and European affiliates, which was concerned with input sources rather than purchases in relation to gross output or sales, indicated a figure of 57 per cent of 1980 inputs being obtained from UK as opposed to foreign sources; the figure for US subsidiaries alone was 55 per cent.[51]

The Japanese data, which indicate a greater reliance on imported supplies as compared with US affiliates at a roughly similar stage of development in the 1950s, are partly a reflection of exchange rate considerations in the two periods. In addition, however, the greater quality control exercised by Japanese firms over suppliers' goods and the more closely integrated procurement policies operated by Japanese MNEs represent other explanations. While it is necessary to be very cautious in deriving conclusions from the two US data

Table 3.10: Process plant contracting industry: proportion of UK contractors' plant procurement[a] from United Kingdom sources (%)

	UK-owned contractors	US-owned contractors
1977–8		
UK projects	81.5	75.7
Overseas projects	63.0	50.9
1978–9		
UK projects	91.5	62.4
Overseas projects	56.7	52.0
1979–80		
UK projects	92.0	58.1
Overseas projects	73.3	52.4

Note: *a* By value.
Source: Monopolies and Mergers Commission (1981), *Enserch Corporation and Davy Corporation Limited: a report on the proposed merger*, Cmnd. 8360, HMSO, London, September, Table 3.3.

sets, there is an indication of a substantial rise in the proportion of imported supplies. This, of course, is compatible with earlier comments regarding the growth of intra-firm product specialisation and trade intensities.

Before turning to a discussion of MNE/supplier relationships, it is interesting to refer to one further piece of evidence on the subject of the procurement behaviour of foreign firms, this time from an industry perspective. Table 3.10 compares UK- and US-owned process plant contractors in terms of procurement in the UK: for each of the three years studied and for both UK projects and overseas projects, British firms placed a higher proportion of orders with suppliers in the UK. Differences in procurement policy, differences in types of project and, for export markets, different requirements for credit or recourse to ECGD facilities were indicated as some of the reasons that might account for disparities in the behaviour of the two sets of contractors.

Corporate policy as regards subsidiary roles and decision-making authority delegated to subsidiaries clearly plays an important part in sourcing strategy. Large MNEs frequently have a central purchasing organisation to obtain economies of scale regarding prices and uniformity of quality. The group's central purchasing organisation will shop on a global basis to arrange acceptable terms with a suitable number of approved suppliers. Even if the possibility of 'local' sourcing exists, this is often more likely to be expressed in terms of Europe rather than simply the UK. Then the choice of actual suppliers will depend upon quality, price, delivery, technical standards, capacity and financial credibility. Interviews with foreign affiliate managers regarding UK suppliers have shown substantial unanimity in their results, with criticisms being levelled at vendors in terms of poor quality, high prices and unsatisfactory delivery dates (see also Table 4.9 and the accompanying discussion). Indeed, the poor quality of British supplies and associated high proportion of defective goods, together with the weaknesses of British management in tolerating this situation, were seen as some of the major explanations for lower productivity in UK subsidiaries as compared with parents' factories.[52]

For British suppliers which showed commitment and perseverance there is evidence of significant benefits from the interaction with foreign companies in terms of assistance with quality control, testing and inspection procedures; advice on product design and equipment and production methods and problems; and the provision of detailed information in the form of specification, drawings and designs. But in relation to the totality of British industry and the problems of British competitiveness, the benefits provided by the foreign presence can only be regarded as very marginal at best. And there have been partially offsetting criticism of foreign customers from the suppliers' perspective. These include allegations of the requirement for unreasonably rigorous quality standards even by parent MNE standards, and inconsistency in ordering policies.

The comments in the previous paragraph lead on logically to the more general question of whether foreign MNEs have produced much in the way of managerial and technological spillovers into British industry as a whole. Figure 1.2 in Chapter 1 showed that British competitive weaknesses lay in problems at the micro level and perhaps chiefly the software element of the latter, namely corporate management. Analysis of foreign firm activities can show how performance may be improved across these micro dimensions. On the other hand, the improvements are not easy to achieve, requiring, as they do, technical competence, application and the will to learn. As one author remarked, 'There seem to be no deep mysteries about successful industrial management; re-importing evidence that Victorian virtues of application and hard work still matter may be the most valuable management know-how that foreign subsidiaries can contribute to British industry.'[53] There must have been specific circumstances in which there have been significant management and technical spillovers, and the most obvious of these derives from the competition of foreign MNEs. But, much of the writing on this subject focuses on the Japanese multinationals in Britain, which are both very small in number and highly concentrated sectorally. Therefore, the possibility of widespread benefits is inconceivable. Indeed it could be argued that the major spillover benefit has accrued to American MNEs and their subsidiaries, many of which have assiduously attempted to learn from the Japanese!

CONCLUDING REMARKS

This chapter has looked at the broad economic impact of inward direct investment on the UK, including some debate on a number of fairly topical issues. Not surprisingly, given the difficulties in measuring impact identified in the introduction to the chapter and data deficiencies, no firm, let alone quantifiable conclusions can be established regarding the extent to which such investment has been good or bad for the UK. The weight of the evidence probably still points towards net benefit, but with much more variability than was the case when earlier studies were undertaken. And certainly there remains considerable scope for improving the contribution of foreign MNEs to the economy, not least in terms of establishing stronger linkages with the indigenous sector. To do this, however, requires a solution to the whole problem of British competitiveness; and if the latter were solved there would be little requirement for inward investment at all!

One topic which was not discussed in this chapter, but which is relevant to MNE impact across the range of issues reviewed is that of control and decision-making. It has been concluded that 'as regards the most crucial long-term and strategic decisions, control has been moving towards the centre'.[54] And even among the generally recently established Japanese affiliates, there is evidence of a fairly close influence on and control over management philosophy and style and decision making. These trends are hardly surprising in the light of the discussion in this chapter, and indeed of the strategic and environmental changes highlighted in earlier chapters. It then has to be asked whether this loss of autonomy at subsidiary level in the UK matters. As the authors have questioned elsewhere, 'Would the survival and growth of the subsidiary be more assured with greater autonomy? Would the subsidiary be better managed, more innovative and entrepreneurial, and so on?' It would be premature to volunteer an answer to these questions at this point in the book. Many of the results presented in this chapter can be more easily understood and interpreted within a corporate strategy framework, with the centralisation/autonomy debate being an important component of this. This is the focus of Chapter 5.

NOTES

1. On this subject it is interesting to cite a leader article in *The Sunday Times*, 23 February 1986 on the subject of 'Blimpish Britain': 'The Little Englanders are once more in full cry . . . they condemn efforts to buy bits of British industry as subverting our economy and turning us into an appendage of Wall Street, Tokyo or some other alien counterpart, ignoring the fact that many British household names have been foreign-owned for years. The Little England litany comes just as easily from the Tory old guard as it does from the militant left. Listen to Britain's dinosaur trade unions sniping at Japanese manufacturers who bring badly needed investment and jobs to South Wales and North East England but have the temerity to demand something as unBritish as a continuous production agreement. Then listen to those Tory MPs who wrap themselves in the Union Jack any time an American company offers to take British Leyland subsidiaries off the taxpayers drip feed and knit them into a world marketing team capable of taking on the Japanese.'

2. *Business Monitor*, MA4 supplement, 1981

3. Pelling, H. (1986), *America and the British left: from Bright to Bevan*, Adam and Charles Black, London, p. 99

4. See Bos, H.C., Sanders, M. and Secchi, C. (1974), *Private foreign investment in developing countries*, D. Reidel, Dordrecht; and Lall, S. and Streeten, P. (1977), *Foreign investment, transnationals and developing countries*, Macmillan, London

5. Steuer, M.D., Abell, P., Gennard, J., Perlman, M., Rees, R., Scott, B. and Wallis, K. (1973), *The impact of foreign direct investment on the United Kingdom*, HMSO, London

6. Dunning, J.H. (1958), *American investment in British manufacturing industry*, Allen and Unwin, London; and (1986), *Japanese participation in British industry*, Croom Helm, London; Hood, N. and Young, S. (1983), *Multinational investment strategies in the British Isles; a study of MNEs in the assisted areas and in the Republic of Ireland*, HMSO, London

7. Steuer, *Impact of foreign direct investment*, p. 46

8. Stopford, J.M. and Turner, L. (1985), *Britain and the multinationals*, John Wiley, Chichester, p. 188

9. Vernon, R. and Davidson, W.H. (1979), *Foreign production of technology-intensive products by US-based multinational enterprises*, a study funded by the National Science Foundation, Boston, Massachusetts, 15 January, mimeo

10. Hamill, J. (1985), *Multinational enterprises and the UK's trade performance: 1978–83*, Strathclyde International Business Unit working

paper 85/4, University of Strathclyde, pp. 11–12

11. Ibid.

12. Brech, M. and Sharp, M. (1984), *Inward investment: policy options for the United Kingdom*, Chatham House papers 21, Routledge and Kegan Paul, London

13. The work was undertaken by MBA students of one of the authors, completed in 1987

14. Hood, N. and Young, S. (1976), 'US investment in Scotland: aspects of the branch factory syndrome', *Scottish Journal of Political Economy*, 23 (3), pp. 279–94

15. Haug, P., Hood, N. and Young, S. (1983), 'R & D intensity in the affiliates of US-owned electronics companies manufacturing in Scotland', *Regional Studies*, 17(6), pp. 383–92

16. Dunning, *American investment in British manufacturing*, p. 159

17. Turner, L. (1987), *Industrial collaboration with Japan*, Chatham House papers 34, Routledge and Kegan Paul, London

18. Dunning (1958), *American investment in British manufacturing*, p. 157

19. Fishwick, F. (1982), *Multinational companies and economic concentration in Europe*, Gower, Aldershot

20. Dunning, J.H. (1985), *Multinational enterprises, economic structure and international competitiveness*, John Wiley, Chichester

21. Ibid., pp. 47–8

22. Dunning, *American investment in British manufacturing*, pp. 291–8

23. Steuer *et al.*, *Impact of foreign direct investment*, p. 8

24. Dunning, J.H. (1976), *US industry in Britain*, EAG business research study, Wilton House, London

25. *Financial Times* (1984), 15 February

26. *Financial Times* (1984), 21 February

27. *Financial Times* (1984), 14 February

28. Panić, M. and Joyce, P.L. (1980), 'UK manufacturing industry: international integration and trade performance', *Bank of England Quarterly Bulletin*, March

29. Hamill, *Multinational enterprises and the UK: 1978–83*

30. Ibid., p. 13

31. Jones, D.T. (1985), *The import threat to the UK car industry*, Science Policy Research Unit, University of Sussex; and House of Lords Select Committee on the European Communities (1984), *The distribution, servicing and pricing of motor vehicles*, HMSO, London, August

32. Department of Trade and Industry (1978), 'Direct exporters and credit terms of exports in 1976', *Trade and Industry*, 32(3), 31 July

33. National Economic Development Council (1983), *The Department of Industry's strategic aims*, NEDC, London, p. 13

34. Caves, R.E. and Krause, L.B. (1980), *Britain's economic performance*, Brookings Institute, Washington, D.C.

35. Tebbit, N. (1983), 'Industrial relations in the next two decades: government objectives', *Employee Relations*, 5(1), p. 3

36. Hamill, J. (1986), *Foreign multinationals: labour and industrial relations effects*, paper presented at an IRM/SIBU conference on 'Scotland and the multinationals', Glasgow, 18 September

37. Ibid.

38. Dunning, *American investment in British manufacturing*, pp. 298–303

39. Ibid., p. 299

40. Steuer *et al.* (1973), *Impact of foreign direct investment*, pp. 78–86

41. Stopford, J.M. (1979), *Employment effects of multinational enterprises in the United Kingdom*, working paper 5, International Labour Office, Geneva

42. Hood, N. and Young, S. (1983), *Multinational investment strategies in the British Isles*, HMSO, London, Table 1.17

43. Dunning, *American investment in British manufacturing*, pp. 298–303; Steuer, *Impact of foreign direct investment*, pp. 48–68

44. Hamill, J. (1983), 'The labour relations practices of foreign-owned firms in the UK', *Employee Relations*, 5(1); and (1984), 'Multinational corporations and industrial relations in the UK', *Employee Relations*, 6(5); Buckley, P.J. and Enderwick, P. (1985), *The industrial relations practices of foreign-owned firms in Britain*, Macmillan, London

45. The Select Committee was established in early 1986 to compare the industrial relations practices and policies of foreign-owned companies operating in the UK with their British counterparts, with specific reference to their relations with trade unions, their industrial relations performance, their management techniques, and the effect of such policies on productivity, profitability and job security. At the time of writing, the Committee's investigations were still in their early stages and no conclusions or policy recommendations had emerged.

46. See Stopford, *Employment effects*, pp. 34–36; Buckley and Enderwick, *Industrial relations practices*, pp. 24–25; Pratten, C.F. (1976), *Labour productivity differentials within international companies*, occasional paper 50, Department of Applied Economics, University of Cambridge

47. Steuer, *Impact of foreign direct investment*, pp. 78–86; Sawers, D. (1986), 'The experience of German and Japanese subsidiaries in Britain', *Journal of General Management*, 12(1), autumn, pp. 5–21

48. A good summary of the empirical evidence regarding the relative strike-proneness of foreign-owned firms in the UK is given in Buckley and Enderwick, *Industrial relations practices*, Ch. 6

49. Dunning, *American investment in British manufacturing*, p. 195

50. Dunning, *Japanese participation in British industry*, p. 103

51. Hood and Young, *Multinational investment strategies*, pp. 132–3

52. Sawers, 'Experience of German and Japanese subsidiaries', pp. 5–21

53. Ibid., p. 21; see also Trevor, M. (1983), 'Does Japanese management work in Britain?', *Journal of General Management*, 8(4), pp. 28–43

54. Young, S., Hood, N. and Hamill, J. (1985), *Decision-making in foreign-owned multinational subsidiaries in the United Kingdom*, working paper 35, International Labour Office, Geneva, p. 58

4

Foreign Multinationals in the UK
Assisted Areas

To this point in the book, the discussion on the effects of multi-national activity has related primarily to the UK economy as a whole. This approach fails to consider the differential spatial impact of MNEs within the country. A fundamental plank of British industrial/social policy has been the use of policy instruments to attract inward investment, from elsewhere in UK and especially from overseas, to the less favoured Northern and Western areas of the country, with the objective of alleviating regional economic disparities. These assisted areas have thus been the major target regions for foreign direct investment. This is likely to continue to be the case, and although the 'regional' emphasis in policy has diminished quite significantly in favour of more general and innovation-oriented industrial strategy measures, the promotion of inward direct investment continues to be geared towards regional attraction efforts. The assisted areas have had a long association with inward investors, many of whom would scarcely be recognised as 'foreign', and concentrations by nationality — the Japanese in Wales — and by sector — electronics in Scotland's 'Silicon Glen' — can be identified. This relationship has continued to the present time, with some of the highly significant investment announcements in the mid/late 1980s including Nissan in North East England, the Finnish paper company Kymmene-Stromberg in Scotland and Samsung Electronics, the first South Korean electronics company to manufacture in Britain, again in the North East.

This chapter on the foreign MNE position in the assisted areas is highly relevant at the present time, following the disappearance of a significant part of the country's manufacturing base over the past decade or so. But the frighteningly high levels of unemployment associated with this have not been experienced in London and the

South East of England. Indeed close to full employment, labour shortages and a booming housing market are characteristic of parts of the South. By contrast, pockets of industrial desolation have emerged in the North, Wales and Scotland, with a whole generation growing up not knowing what it is like to work. Viewed from the South, there are still, regrettably, many who would attribute these problems to bloody-minded unions, local politics and a reliance on government handouts at all levels. So the political and social divisions created may yet cause major upheavals within the 'United' Kingdom. Within this environment, multinationals are welcomed with open arms in the assisted areas and with no-holds-barred competition between and within the regions themselves to obtain inward investment. The beneficial job effects of MNEs are obvious, and the new products and technologies brought by inward investors have improved the industrial structures of the assisted areas. The more fundamental questions relate to long-term competitiveness and the impact of MNEs on the innovative and entrepreneurial potential of the regions.

Although the main policy discussions in this book are contained in Chapter 6, it should be apparent from the above that the impact of foreign MNEs in the UK assisted areas must be considered within the context of regional aid schemes. This chapter, therefore, begins with a scene-setting review of UK regional policy, before extending to an assessment of the contribution and problems associated with MNEs in the assisted areas at a fairly aggregate level. The later sections of the chapter focus more heavily on companies and sectors, the subject of high technology industry in the regions being given especial attention in the latter regard. There is a strong emphasis in parts of this chapter on Scotland: this is chiefly a reflection of information availability, but it is also, and unashamedly, related to the authors' own interests.

REGIONAL POLICY IN THE UK

Background of regional policy and regional policy instruments

Regional policy in the UK has a history dating back to the Special Areas Act of 1934, and has operated with the aim of attempting to alleviate 'imbalances between areas in employment opportunities'.[1] According to a 1983 White Paper, 'Regional industrial incentives also enable the United Kingdom to compete effectively for internationally mobile investment. Inward investment projects . . . can improve the national economy through their contribution to output and employment . . .'[2] While accepting that an economic case for regional industrial policy can be made on this and other grounds, one argument for continuing the policy at the present time is seen by Government to be social. The coverage of areas available for regional assistance has varied over time, but the northern areas of England, together with Wales, Scotland and Northern Ireland, contain most of the 'assisted areas', whether development or intermediate areas in current terminology. As at 1985, 35 per cent of the working population of Great Britain lived and worked in areas eligible for assistance.

The instruments of regional policy have varied over time. The regional employment premium (REP), which was a job-related subsidy, was in existence between 1967 and 1977. Again industrial development certificates (IDCs) were very important during the 1950s and 1960s, before being progressively eased in the following decade and removed in 1982; the aim of IDCs was to direct mobile industry to the assisted areas by limiting industrial development elsewhere.

Since 1972 the main instruments of regional industrial policy have been regional development grants (RDGs), regional selective assistance (RSA) and advance factory building. Historically, RDGs were payable almost automatically on both new and replacement investment in land, buildings and plant in manufacturing, mining and construction industry; 1983 rates of grant in Great Britain amounted to 22 per cent in special development areas and 15 per cent in development areas. Additionally, RSA (Section 7 of the Industrial Development Act 1982) was available for projects which met certain criteria, including good prospects of viability and the creation of new jobs or the safeguarding of existing ones in the assisted areas; such projects had to be shown to benefit both the regional and national economies and require assistance to make them happen. Grants which were negotiable but which might amount to 10 to 15 per cent of fixed capital costs, loans on favourable terms and help with removal and training costs for employees were all available under the terms of RSA.

A major review of regional policy by the Thatcher Administration led to changes in the system from 1984, designed to make regional policy more cost effective and to reduce what was seen as the public expenditure burden of the policy. Alongside changes in the map of assisted areas, RDG was reduced to a single rate of 15 per cent and was subject to a cost per job limit of £10,000 (alternatively a job grant of £3,000 was payable for each new job created, for labour intensive projects). Preferential treatment was accorded to the small firm sector by normally waiving the cost-per-job ceiling for companies with fewer than 200 employees. RDGs were no longer payable on replacement investment, but the sectors available for assistance were expanded from manufacturing to include a number of service industries (excluding retailing and tourism). Discretionary RSA remained available as a topping up element for new projects and expansions creating employment, and for modernisation or rationalisation projects which maintain or safeguard existing employment.[3]

These changes represented a fairly significant realignment of policy, especially when viewed from the perspective of regions competing for internationally mobile inward investment projects. In fact, the Conservative Government might have liked to have abolished regional assistance altogether, but refrained from doing so for a variety of reasons, including the weak state of the party outside the South of England, and the fact that EEC countries need to identify assisted areas in order to be eligible for aid from the European Regional Development Fund.[4] There were, of course, major criticisms of the previous regional policy structure. These related to the payment of grants on occasions to large, highly capital-intensive, sometimes locationally immobile projects — into this category might perhaps come RDG payments of £92 million in 1982–3 to BP for the oil terminal at Sullom Voe and £19 million to Occidental for oil-related developments in the Orkneys — and, while not locationally tied, it was alleged that Hoffman-La Roche received £350,000 of public money for every permanent job created at its Vitamin C plant in Ayrshire, Scotland; the focus on manufacturing despite the growth potential in service industry; and the designation of assisted areas at a time when high unemployment had spread to formerly prosperous areas such as the West Midlands. Moreover, some of the payments made under the regional policy banner were highly controversial, as with the De Lorean and Lear Fan projects in Northern Ireland; and others, including aid payments to Timex and Hyster, were investigated by the EEC Commission to establish whether Community rules on incentive levels were being contravened.[5]

The net effect of the various changes is still difficult to ascertain, depending on the balance between capital intensive projects which may perhaps no longer go ahead and the improved viability of some labour intensive investments, the stimulus to service industries, etc. There is a strong view in the assisted areas that their competitive position has been impaired when bidding for new inward investment projects against countries such as the Republic of Ireland. It has been suggested, for example, that some of the major electronics projects of recent years would not have come to Scotland under the new grant regime, where the assistance per job created would be at least 50 per cent less than that allowed previously. The removal of assistance for replacement investment could also be damaging if companies are becoming more footloose as was suggested in Chapter 1. The shortening of product life cycles, meaning more rapid replacement, is an issue too. What is equally significant is that the regional dimension of policy is becoming less important within the total expenditure package on industrial and social strategy measures. If it is accepted that regional policy has been effective in the past in creating and safeguarding manufacturing jobs in the assisted areas, then valid concerns may be expressed about the future. And since jobs associated with foreign investment projects have been a significant component of this, then equal concerns exist for prospects in the overseas-owned sector.

Employment creation and regional policy

Inevitably, the impact of regional policy has been subject to continuing scrutiny in both academic and government circles. A recent estimate of gross employment creation by domestic and foreign firms was 500,000 manufacturing jobs in the assisted areas of the UK over the period 1961–81.[6] It was accepted, however, that a substantial difference was discernible between the late 1960s and the later 1970s, the job creation effect of regional policy being nearly 2½ times greater in the former than in the latter period. Most of the difference could be accounted for by relative demand pressures in the national economy in the two periods, and by the operation of IDC policy which was active during the 1960s but largely abandoned by the late 1970s.

Virtually no work has been undertaken on the impact of regional policy on jobs created by foreign firms specifically, although the comparative responsiveness of indigenous and foreign firms to regional aid and their subsequent performance in assisted areas has been the subject of some debate.[7] Using data on firm moves during the period 1960–71, Ashcroft and Ingham indicated that foreign

Table 4.1: Ratio of the share of total employment in manufacturing due to first-time inward investors to the share of total manufacturing employment

	1971–5	1976–80
Mainly non-assisted regions	0.5	0.3
Mainly intermediate area regions	0.2	0.2
Mainly developed area regions	3.3	4.0

Source: Department of Trade and Industry (1983), *Regional industrial policy: some economic issues*, DTI, London, Table 28.

mobile companies were more responsive than indigenous companies to the financial incentives available in the development areas, and overseas companies did not appear to be influenced by the intensity of IDC controls.[8] A DTI study, based on more recent data, has indicated that foreign manufacturing companies establishing their first presence in the UK found the development areas more attractive than other areas, and concluded that this was *prima facie* evidence of the positive impact of regional industrial policy (see Table 4.1). As a broad estimate, an employment creation figure of 10–15,000 jobs per annum in the overseas-owned sector has been quoted for the UK as a whole in recent years, although only a part of this could be attributed to regional policy.[9]

The significance of regional policy in these job creation figures quoted is dependent upon the importance which MNEs place upon financial assistance as opposed to other factors in their locational decision-making. In this regard, 1983 survey evidence relating to US and Continental European companies has shown market access to be the major factor behind the choice of the UK as a location, though regional incentives were considered important by a significant minority of companies.[10] In terms of choice of location within the UK, the role played by regional incentives was rather greater, being considered of some importance by around two thirds of the sample making greenfield investments in the assisted areas. As regards type of policy instrument, the predictable RDGs were claimed to be more important than RSA (which supports other work which has shown that regional development grants are more commonly incorporated into investment appraisal calculations).[11] What emerged from this 1983 study was that companies locating in Northern Ireland typically attached more importance to government financial assistance. Given the higher level of incentives and more broadly based incentive system operating there, this does at least suggest some rationality in locational decision making.[12]

Apart from the effect on the initial locational decision, some attempt was made to identify the significance of regional incentives in expansionary decisions and in influencing project characteristics. In regard to the former, only companies which had undertaken capital investments leading to increased plant output were included in the analysis; the conclusion was that the impact of regional incentives was just as great in expansionary decisions as in the initial investment decision. This is quite an important result in view of the removal of RDGs from replacement investment in 1984. The survey results indicated that the impact of regional assistance affected mainly the scale and capital intensity of expansionary projects; additional equipment for the manufacture of existing or new products; and (for a smaller proportion of firms) the timing of technology introduction.

Dunning's 1986 work on Japanese investment in the UK confirmed that the initial *raison d'être* for investing was primarily to supply the UK or EEC markets; with tariff and non-tariff barriers and the appreciation of the yen in relation to the £ being specific reasons for switching from exporting from Japan to manufacture in Europe.[13] On regional incentives, the view was that grants did not affect these locational fundamentals, although the amount and timing of the investment and location within the UK was considered to be, at least marginally, affected by grants. Dunning continues, 'One engineering affiliate also mentioned that the level of grants . . . affected the rate at which it replaced machinery and equipment, and therefore its ability to keep up with its competitors. This is clearly likely to be most relevant in the rapidly innovating sectors and those in which additional assurance of the good faith of the UK economy is needed.'[14]

In another (1984) study of Japanese involvement in the consumer electronics industry in the UK, it was indicated that 36 of the sample 100 companies operating in the assisted areas considered that incentives were 'of significance' in influencing decisions on planned investment projects over the following three year period.[15] This supports the conclusions noted above for American and Continental European investors and puts question marks over the government decision to withdraw RDG support for such projects.

Costs of employment creation. The difficulty with such survey work is that it does not permit a quantitative assessment of the impact of

Table 4.2: Regional selective assistance (Section 7) to foreign-owned companies

Year	Number of offers	Total assistance offered (£m)	Assistance offered as % of total Section 7 assistance	Total value of projects assisted (£m)	Number of jobs	
					Created (000)	Safeguarded (000)
1978–9	128	29.5	25	295	9.7	4.8
1979–80	126	29	23	340	10.1	6.8
1980–1	88	46	39	495	13.3	2.9
1981–2	83	50	47	531	10.2	8.8
1982–3	115	47	32	448	10.9	6.3
1983–4	152	65.6	37	176	11.9	9.8
1984–5	154	121.3	51	1,339	17.1	4.0
1985–6	124	107	52	1,369	12.8	8.7
Total — (8 years)	970	495.4	40	4,993	96.0	52.1
Average per year	121	61.9	—	624	12.0	6.5

Sources: *Industry Act 1972: annual report; Industrial Development Act 1982: annual report* — various issues.

regional policy to be made, and, therefore, rather little can be sensibly said on the costs of job creation in the assisted areas. Data are available on one component of expenditure, namely regional selective assistance (RSA) offers to overseas firms, and these are shown in Table 4.2. In the eight years to end March 1986, nearly £500 million in discretionary assistance was offered to MNEs, representing 40 per cent of all Section 7 assistance and over half in the two most recent years. In terms of number of offers, the share of foreign companies in the total is much smaller. The difference reflects the larger average size of overseas-owned firms and related projects, but also the higher grant levels offered (in percentage terms) for projects which are or may be claimed to be internationally mobile.

Taking the figure cited in the table on RSA offers and jobs created or safeguarded gives a discretionary assistance cost per job of £3,346 over the whole period rising to £5,749 in 1984–5. If an estimate for regional development grants (RDGs) was included, then direct assistance per job has been about £10,500. Estimates by Brech and Sharp and Dunning relating to Japanese investment suggest direct assistance per head of £4,730 and around £3,000 respectively.

These various estimates exclude other items of assistance which were payable, including land and factory building, and it is arguable that some of the assistance available under Section 8 'Support for Major Projects' of the 1982 Industrial Development Act should be incorporated. Section 8 assistance is available nationally for major projects which are in the country's interest, but has been used chiefly for projects which were internationally mobile. Thus, in 1978–9, £18 million was offered under the terms of Section 8 to Hoffman-La Roche for its Vitamin C plant at Dalry in Scotland (an assisted area). By end March 1986, it was claimed that this support measure had attracted to the UK 42 internationally mobile projects involving capital expenditure of £184 million.

More important than the financial omissions is the job creation actually attributable to regional policy instruments: the sensitivity of this is illustrated by the fact that suppose between one quarter and one third of the job figures (a reasonable guesstimate perhaps) quoted in Table 4.2 could be attributed to financial incentives, this would raise the employment cost to between £31,500 and £42,000 per employee.[16] Undoubtedly, the inward investment attraction agencies in the UK would argue for a much higher proportion of job creation to be linked to regional aid (and their own efforts), on the grounds of the intense competition within Europe for mobile international projects.

The rest of this chapter is concerned with the operation of foreign-owned companies once they have set up in the assisted areas — and not only their employment behaviour. Despite the focus on jobs at the regional level, it is more important to ascertain whether the influx of MNEs has stimulated competitiveness, productivity and growth in these areas (questions which are generally ignored in debates concerning the effectiveness of regional policy).

GROWTH AND PERFORMANCE OF FOREIGN-OWNED MANUFACTURING INDUSTRY IN THE ASSISTED AREAS

Employment trends and plant movement

The previous chapter has already revealed the steadily expanding employment penetration of MNE subsidiaries within the UK as a whole until recently. In the years immediately after World War Two, American companies particularly, seeking access to the dollar-deficient European market, saw Britain as a welcoming port of entry, and were often willing to be steered into government-built factories away from the south of England. And a good number of the famous names which make up the 'Fortune 500' invested in the peripheral areas during this time. In the early and mid-1950s, regional policy was applied fairly weakly and it was the 'active' policy period of the following 15 years, when IDC controls were strengthened, the regional employment premium introduced, etc. that coincided with a strong movement of foreign-owned industry into the assisted areas. This is best illustrated by the motor industry. Ford and General Motors had had operations in the South and Midlands of England since the 1920s and 30s, and until the 1950s additional investments mostly took place in existing locations. In the major phase of expansion coming in 1960, on the other hand, the use of stick (the refusal of industrial development certificates) and carrot (loans and grants available under the 1960 Local Employment Act) steered Ford to Halewood and Vauxhall to Ellesmere Port, both on Merseyside, and Rootes (later Chrysler and then Peugeot) to Linwood in Scotland — all in development areas; while BMC also set up tractor, truck and car assembly operations in the assisted regions. This was the largest piece of industrial dispersal that has ever been attempted in the United Kingdom, with 41,000 jobs being made available in the development areas between 1960 and 1965 as a result of the movement of vehicle firms.[17]

The assisted areas benefited more generally from the flood of American capital into Europe during this time, including, for example, the first phase of electronics investments through companies such as Motorola, National Semiconductor, General Instrument Microelectronics and W.L. Gore. The upheavals of the 1970s saw not only a slowdown in the growth of foreign investment and in Britain's share of US investment in Europe (see Chapter 2); but also the weakening of IDC controls as an instrument of regional policy for new and expansionary investments and the emergence of divestment and rationalisation as an issue among the established MNEs, many of which were by then very large in employment terms. The number of offers of RSA to foreign firms (Table 4.2) confirms, nevertheless, the continuing attractiveness of the assisted areas in the 1980s, as Japanese and Continental European MNEs began to invest in increasing numbers.

Employment trends

Within this broad framework, Figures 4.1 and 4.2 record the trends in employment in foreign-owned and all manufacturing companies in the assisted areas from 1963, with the South East of England being included as a comparator. It is suggested that in employment terms the assisted areas benefited substantially up to 1973: of the 280,000 job growth in the foreign-owned sector in the UK as a whole between 1963 and 1973, nearly 52 per cent took place in the assisted regions. From 1973 to 1977, 192,000 further jobs were added by MNEs, with the assisted areas taking 35 per cent of these. Since that time, substantial retrenchment has occurred, with the assisted areas faring marginally worse than the country as a whole in the period when world and UK economic problems were biting hard. Figure 4.3 records similar trends in multinational-related employment for the individual assisted areas: what is shown is a significant reduction in regional disparities between 1963 and 1973, but then great fluctuations in employment levels because of the size and timing of divestments and contractions in MNE activity; the sharp fall in employment in Scotland is, however, especially noteworthy.

It can be concluded, therefore, that during the 1960s, foreign direct investment made a substantial contribution towards a reduction in regional employment inequalities, but this trend stopped during the 1970s. Important questions are inevitably raised by the

113

Figure 4.1: Employment in foreign-owned manufacturing companies in the assisted areas and the South East

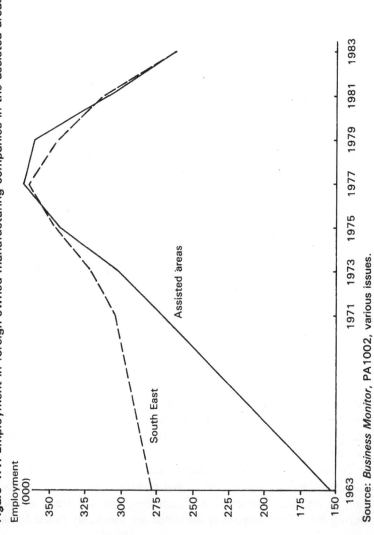

Source: *Business Monitor*, PA1002, various issues.

Figure 4.2: Employment in all manufacturing companies in the assisted areas and the South East

Employment
(000)

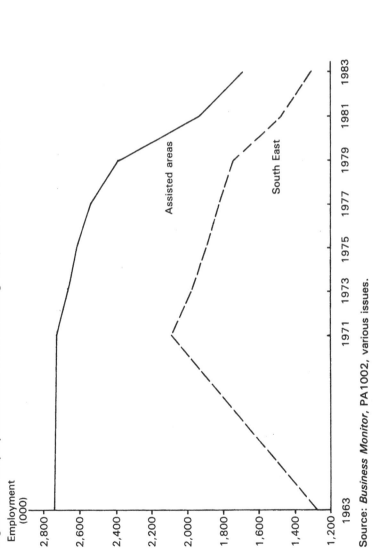

Source: *Business Monitor*, PA1002, various issues.

Figure 4.3: Employment in foreign-owned manufacturing companies in the assisted areas

Employment
(000)

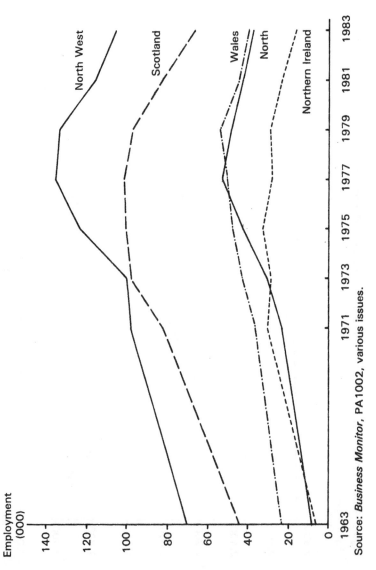

Source: *Business Monitor*, PA1002, various issues.

patterns observed. Is there an indication in the figures that active regional and/or expansionary economic conditions are necessary to improve the foreign employment position in the assisted areas? Does the recent employment decline say anything about the stability or otherwise of peripherally-located MNE branch plants, in relation both to indigenous companies and to more centrally-sited MNE headquarters' operations? To begin to examine these and related questions it is necessary to disentangle the various components of change in the foreign sector, as between new openings and expansions, divestments and contractions, and acquisitions. Thus the patterns shown in the figures above represent the net effect of a series of influences at work during the period considered.

Manufacturing plant openings

Over the last decade, there has been a marked reduction in the inter-regional movement of manufacturing industry, but within this overall trend foreign moves into the assisted areas held up very well.[18] Indeed, the assisted regions' position improved in the five years up to 1980:

Assisted areas share of openings of
manufacturing units of first-time inward investors[19]

	Units	Employment
	%	%
1972–7	48.3	61.9
1976–80	75.5	85.9

Looking at all openings of foreign-owned plants, whether first-time inward investors (as above) or expansions/relocations of established MNEs in the UK, Table 4.3 shows a less bullish but still very healthy position for the assisted areas. Over one half of all foreign plant openings took place in the assisted areas during the years 1966–82. The data in Table 4.3 cannot be directly compared with the figures quoted in the previous paragraph, but the interpretation of the difference is that first-time investors continued to be strongly attracted to the assisted areas, whereas MNEs expanding or relocating within the UK have become more involved in short distance moves. Inter-regional moves over longer distances, even within a country as small as the UK, may be perceived as being more risky in a recession-hit environment.

Even with a weakened IDC policy, therefore, the assisted areas continued to be attractive locations, especially for first-time

117

Table 4.3: Openings of foreign-owned plants, by region

Years	UK	English non-assisted areas	English assisted areas	Wales	Scotland	Northern Ireland	Total assisted areas
				Numbers of openings			
1966–72	480	224	116	30	94	26	256
1973–7	345	189	59	27	50	20	156
1978–82	236	97	48	47	24	20	139
1983	8	n.a.	n.a.	1	6	1	8
Total	1,069	510	223	105	164	67	559
Closures since 1973	316	156[a]	32[a]	41	49	38[b]	160
				Per cent of total UK openings in period			
1966–72	100.0	46.7	24.2	6.2	17.5	5.4	53.3
1973–77	100.0	54.8	17.1	7.8	14.5	5.8	45.2
1978–82	100.0	41.1	20.3	19.9	10.2	8.5	58.9
1983	100.0	n.a.	n.a.	12.5	75.0	12.5	100.0
Total	100.0	47.7	20.9	9.8	15.3	6.3	52.3

Notes: a Closures of those setting up since 1966; excludes any closures in 1983.
b Openings since 1954 which closed in 1973 or later.
Source: *Hansard* (1984), 29 February–7 March.

investors. The role of other regional policy instruments has been shown to be important, and various new factors have entered the equation. The promotional activities of the regional agencies, Locate in Scotland (LIS), Wales Investment Location (WINVEST) and the Industrial Development Board for Northern Ireland (IDB) have become more intensive and professional. At the same time the stock of investors of particular nationalities or in particular industries has become large enough to produce some agglomeration economies which will affect the attraction of industry.

To end on a more cautionary note, the success of the assisted areas must, of course, be judged not only in a British context but also in relation to the performance of neighbouring competitive locations, particularly in this context the Republic of Ireland. Over the period 1975–82, Ireland attracted 582 new overseas projects excluding projects originating in Great Britain. Comparative figures for the UK would relate to RSA offers for new (excluding expansionary) projects; these are not available for the assisted areas as a whole, but the comparative figure for Scotland was 85 projects. The Irish performance is a reflection both of the resources committed to promotional activity and the incentive package offered to inward investors. What is particularly disturbing is that these comparisons relate to a period prior to the cuts in British regional incentives from 1984.

Manufacturing plant closures

Despite the healthy position on openings, a general allegation concerning branch plant activity in the assisted areas (whether multi-plant indigenous companies or multinationals), is that the operations lack roots and because of this are the first candidates for closure when times get hard. For one four-year period (1978–81) Department of Trade and Industry work showed little difference between foreign-owned and all firms in Great Britain in terms of jobs lost in closures and contractions, and the same conclusion applied to employment performance in the assisted areas specifically.[20]

Despite this, there could still be cause for concern if, for example, closures or contractions of MNE subsidiaries were concentrated among large firms in dependent communities. There is no doubt that in their build up phase a number of multinational subsidiaries in sectors such as vehicles and vehicle components, office equipment and consumer durables did become very large employers of labour, and in general, plant size in foreign-owned industry has been much larger than in the indigenous sector. As

119

Table 4.4: Large plant closures in the UK, 1978–82

Closures of plants employing more than 500 people in 1978	UK	England	Wales	Scotland	Northern Ireland
Total manufacturing (no. of plants)	286	243	10	24	9
Foreign-owned manufacturing (no. of plants)	48	32	3	8	5
Foreign-owned (as % of total)	16.8	13.2	30.0	33.3	55.5

Source: *Hansard* (1984), 28 February–7 March.

Table 4.4 reveals, a number of these large MNE operations closed during the 1978–82 period, with the assisted areas appearing to be hardest hit (although data are not available for the English assisted areas). The most spectacular of these were in Scotland, including Monsanto Textiles, Goodyear Tyres, Massey-Ferguson, Singer Company, Talbot Scotland and SCM Typewriters. Northern Ireland was, however, most adversely affected in relative terms, with the factories of British Enkalon and Michelin being two of the largest closures.

Judgement on such closures has to be kept in perspective. It would be churlish to condemn multinational divestments out of hand, when no thought was given at a policy level to the consequences of large size and employment concentration while these companies were in their expansionary phase. There is, even so, cause for reflection concerning the timespan over which the benefits from MNE operations may be assumed to apply, especially in current circumstances with shortening product and technology life cycles. The globalisation and technology imperatives would indicate more rapid restructuring of enterprises, although smaller plant sizes will mean reduced dislocation problems for communities if divestment does take place.

Before leaving this issue, it is worth focusing briefly not on the comparison between the assisted areas and the country as a whole, but rather the assisted areas and the core region of the South East. It is common to hear the comment that job losses in South East operations will be less marked during recession periods because of the status of the ventures in terms of decision-making responsibility. For the limited 1978–81 period there is no evidence to support this contention from the data above. Arguably, a more valid way of testing such a hypothesis is to compare peak employment in plants with employment in a more recent year. This procedure was followed in a recent Hood and Young study for the DTI.[21] For the sample of MNE subsidiaries in the assisted areas, 1980 employment was one third below peak compared with a reduction of under 17 per cent in the South East enterprises in the same industry sectors. To reinforce the point, the decline in jobs in the South East sample of MNEs was smaller than in any of the assisted areas taken separately.

The acquisition issue in a regional context

The patterns of plant openings and expansions, closures and contractions do not explain the employment trends shown in Figure 4.1. In fact by these measures, the peripheral areas of the UK were benefiting in net terms in comparison with other regions from MNE activity, at least during the time periods studied. The explanation for the apparently contradictory findings lies in the relative location of acquisition investment within the UK. Takeovers involving foreign companies are not subject to any formal monitoring, which *inter alia* would enable a statistical picture to be built up; and may be referred to the Monopolies and Mergers Commission or not on exactly the same criteria as apply to any other acquisition. There is some evidence that in contrast to new investment from overseas, the extension of foreign interests through acquisition was focused mainly on the more prosperous and faster growing regions of the UK, particularly the South East.[22] Since the latter is the core region with all its attractions, and the location with the largest stock of firms, this is hardly surprising. As to the explanations for the acquisition activity, takeovers may be a risk-reducing strategy in a period of environmental turbulence. With the large numbers of liquidations within the UK, MNEs should be able to pick up assets fairly cheaply. And, in addition, awareness of takeover possibilities must have increased as the MNE presence has grown and become an established part of the industrial scene.[23] The conclusion from the present perspective is that the apparent shift in MNE-related jobs in favour of the South East is somewhat illusory; in terms of new inward investments these are continuing to favour the assisted areas.

Inter-regional foreign-owned manufacturing position

The discussion to this point has mostly related to the assisted areas as a whole, whereas in fact the most detailed work relating to the implications of foreign direct investment has been undertaken at the level of the individual region. Summarising the position in terms of employment contribution, MNEs are most important to the economy of Wales and least important to the North. Thus in 1983 the foreign-owned share of all manufacturing employment ranged from nearly 19½ per cent in Wales to under 13 per cent in the North, compared with the assisted area average of 15.5 per cent (see also Figure 4.3 for trends).

The North is the only region which is truly under-represented in terms of foreign employment contribution. Going back to the early 1960s the region accounted for just over 1½ per cent of foreign employment in the UK. The number of foreign jobs tripled between 1963 and 1971 and continued to grow sharply up to 1977. Any problems are thus of more recent origin; and have been due to a higher closure rate than the assisted area average in recent years. This in turn may be bound up with the industry mix in the Northern region in which labour-intensive sectors such as textiles, clothing and leather goods and glass, as well as instruments, are strongly represented. To an even greater extent than elsewhere, therefore, the 'branch plant syndrome' has been very apparent. For the future, the position may be more encouraging, given the decision by Nissan to establish their factory at Washington in North East England; and particularly if the planned Nissan expansions go ahead and auto industry suppliers and perhaps other Japanese firms move into the area. Interestingly, in December 1985, Komatsu of Japan announced that it was investing over £12 million in the former Newcastle upon Tyne premises of Caterpillar Tractor to produce hydraulic excavators and wheeled loaders.

The issue of the behaviour of multinationals during the recession-hit years from the mid-1970s onwards is of especial importance in the light of preconceived notions. Studies by a variety of authors in different regions have tended to reach similar conclusions, namely that multinationals have shed employment at a slower or similar rate to that of indigenous enterprises. In Northern Ireland, Harrison noted that employment in foreign-owned projects did not fall as rapidly as overall manufacturing employment in the 1974–9 period.[24] In Scotland, analysis by the Industry Department for Scotland established that both in terms of closure rates and overall employment performance, branch plants performed better than all other units opened during the same period.[25] For the North West of England, Lloyd and Shutt found that although locally-controlled firms contracted employment more slowly, there was little difference between the rate of contraction in foreign and UK externally-controlled MNEs; both of the latter groups reduced their blue collar employment by over a quarter in the 1975–80 period.[26] It is interesting that the villains of the piece have begun to be seen as British-owned multinationals![27] Undoubtedly, the most optimistic findings refer to Wales where 1976–80 data showed surviving foreign-owned plants declining much less than average, although the employment performance in the indigenous sector was adversely influenced by steel and related closures. These studies are now rather out of date but there is no reason to expect significant differences in the results for the 1980s.

Negative findings have been restricted to the Northern region (as suggested above), where 1979 work established that externally-controlled plants were much more vulnerable to closure than those controlled within the region. The high closure rate of (previously independent) plants acquired by companies with their headquarters outside the region was especially important in this pattern. The Scottish results are of interest too, since the concentration of closures in a small number of very large enterprises does mean that the conclusions reached are heavily dependent on the period selected for analysis. The depressing consequences of partial or total multi-national divestment on dependent communities were brought out clearly in the present authors' work.[28] Particularly important was Talbot at Linwood, where the car plant closed in May 1981 with the direct loss of 4,800 jobs, making it the largest single mass redundancy in Scotland; follow up research by the Manpower Services Commission revealed 57 per cent of the former workforce continuously unemployed in the twelve months after closure.[29] Critics of regional policy and growth-pole theory can find ample material to support their case in these examples, but the critics of multinationals less so. Looking around Scotland, closure of the Invergordon aluminium smelter, the pulp mill at Fort William and the BL truck plant at Bathgate have caused or will cause as much devastation as the 'multinationals in retreat'.

The inter-regional investment and divestment patterns are tied in with the industry mix in foreign direct investment. Since MNEs are concentrated in high technology and growing sectors, their performance during recession should be more robust. In the North, suggestions of a more labour-intensive bias in the MNE-owned industrial structure may be important insofar as greater vulnerability to international competition is implied. The emphasis on engineering in Scotland is much higher than elsewhere, an industry in which increasing worldwide competition and technological change have been important themes.

Output and productivity in foreign-owned companies in the assisted areas

The discussion to this point has been almost exclusively concerned with employment questions, a consequence of the employment emphasis in regional policy, but also data availability. From the viewpoint of competitiveness and long-run prosperity, the performance of MNEs in terms of capital investment, output and productivity is, however, crucial. For the UK as a whole it was indicated in Chapter 3 that by these measures, MNE subsidiaries were making a substantial contribution to improved efficiency in the economy, although differences in industrial structure, size of plant, etc. explain part of the performance differential. Considering the assisted areas in total, a similar conclusion is warranted in regard to productivity: Table 4.5 reveals that net output per employee in foreign companies was one quarter higher than in all manufacturing industry in 1981. This was, nevertheless, a smaller differential than had existed in earlier years, for Census of Production figures for 1971 showed a gap of 40 per cent in comparative net output per employee and this widened to close on 50 per cent by the middle 1970s. The partial change since that time would seem to support more general evidence of the beneficial shake-out effects of recession on the indigenous sector.

It is also interesting to look at the productivity performance of MNEs in the assisted areas in comparison with all MNE subsidiaries in the United Kingdom. During the years from 1971 to 1983, there was generally a small but consistent balance in favour of assisted area MNE subsidiaries: the differential in terms of net output per head was as high as 12 per cent in 1973 but had slipped to a marginal one per cent by 1983 (net output of £21,138 per employee in the assisted areas compared with £20,833 in the UK overall, as Table 4.5 shows).

Among the assisted areas themselves, there were quite wide differences both in terms of net output per employee in the MNE

Table 4.5: Net output per employee in foreign-owned and all manufacturing enterprises, 1983

	UK	South East	North West	North	Wales	Scotland	Northern Ireland	Total assisted areas
Foreign-owned (£)	20,833	22,724	21,337	20,078	22,531	22,070	15,390	21,138
All manufacturing (£)	15,910	17,697	16,063	16,610	16,658	16,523	12,874	16,144
Ratio	1.31	1.28	1.33	1.21	1.35	1.34	1.20	1.31

Source: *Business Monitor*, PA1002, 1983.

sector and in comparisons of foreign-owned and all manufacturing performance. At the beginning of the 70s, the North West, Wales and, most strikingly, Northern Ireland stood out from other regions with very high net output figures in the foreign sector. The Northern Ireland productivity levels may have been distorted at that time by a small number of large capital-intensive operations and at the end of the 70s decade it was Wales which was way ahead of the remaining areas. By 1983, the most marked improvement was in Scotland, a result presumably related to the closures of large, low productivity MNE plants and growth in the high productivity electronics sector. As Table 4.5 reveals, net output per head in Scotland and Wales was similar to that in the South East, and these three areas were well above the UK average for multinational firms.

Despite the fact that the productivity differential between foreign-owned and all manufacturing firms narrowed in the years up to 1983, the multinational sector continued to invest at a higher rate and accounted for a growing share of net capital expenditure (Table 4.6). This bears out the trend in RSA offers to foreign and all companies, and supports previous evidence that the MNEs have been less adversely affected by recession conditions than their British counterparts. It also suggests that the overseas-owned sector will be in a better position coming out of the recession. To that extent the apparently improved productivity performance in indigenous companies is rather illusory, being produced by labour-shedding but not backed up by new investment.

Nature of multinational activity in the assisted areas

Characteristics of the assisted areas

It is probably apparent from the foregoing that at the regional level in the UK there has been a much more continuing interest in the multinational phenomenon than in the country as a whole. In part this is a function of the regional aid focus of policy, but the other issue which has dominated discussion concerns the nature and characteristics of branch plants in regional economies. And it is the evidence relating to the latter which has tempered the optimistic findings relating to investment, jobs and productivity. Considering the differences in structural characteristics between depressed and more prosperous parts of the country, academic work has suggested that:

Table 4.6: Net capital expenditure[a] of foreign-owned and all manufacturing enterprises in the UK assisted areas

Net capital expenditure	1971	1973	1975	1977	1979	1981	1983
Foreign-owned (£m)	169.1	157.8	267.7	402.5	664.6	707.7	618.7
All manufacturing (£m)	996.2	978.9	1,639.9	2,041.7	2,889.6	2,245.9	2,220.6
Foreign-owned as % of all manufacturing	17.0	16.1	16.3	19.7	23.0	31.5	27.9

Notes: a Net capital expenditure includes new building work plus acquisitions less disposals of land and existing buildings, vehicles and plant and machinery; latest data refer to a revised definition of 'manufacturing'.

Source: *Business Monitor*, PA1002, various issues.

Many of the assisted areas, especially in relation to the South East, have an industrial milieu less favourable to successful entrepreneurship: a somewhat unfavourable rate of product innovation; a relatively low level of employment in the business services sector; an occupational structure characterised by a low proportion of managerial and professional jobs; and a high level of dependence for manufacturing employment on branch plants owned by national or international companies whose UK head offices and research and development facilities are concentrated in the South East. Clearly these characteristics are inter-related.[30]

Before developing this theme, it should be pointed out that these weaknesses did not always exist, nor, therefore, are they inevitable. As Firn and Roberts note, 'The Clyde Valley in the last quarter of the nineteenth century had almost the same aura and image amongst the industrial nations of the world as Silicon Valley has at present.'[31]

Returning to the present, the evidence reveals that the inter-related set of regional problems do not derive from or refer exclusively to multinational branch plants. With the growing interdependence of the United Kingdom, it has not been possible to speak of separate regional economies for many decades. The widening of share ownership, acquisitions of locally-headquartered companies by large national or international UK enterprises, the widening of markets through internally-generated growth, are all processes which have encouraged the centralisation of headquarters and other decision-making activities in the South East of England and reinforced the concentration of business service employment in that area. It is recognised that:

The acquisition of companies indigenous to a region and the establishment of branch plants can clearly bring local advantages. A new branch plant can bring jobs to an area and diversify its industrial structure, whilst a takeover may result in the introduction of new management practices and a widening of the market opportunities for the local company. In addition, the presence in the region of national and international companies may result in a more rapid spread of new technologies and working practices. Similarly, the fact that a company is owned and controlled within a region does not guarantee its success.[32]

Notwithstanding these points, it is argued that increasing external control will weaken the economies of the assisted areas: higher order control fuctions together with R & D will be located outside the region; and externally-controlled plants may be less integrated into the regional economy in terms of their purchasing of materials and business service inputs. The low proportions of managerial occupations, low levels of R & D and the poor range of sophisticated services available locally in turn may mean that the rate of new firm formation (particularly technologically innovative firms) will be reduced.

Multinationality and branch activity

The question which needs to be answered in the present context is whether multinationality adds another dimension to this branch plant syndrome. There has, in fact, been rather little work on comparing locational patterns and characteristics of the various groups of externally-owned enterprises, as between foreign MNEs, British multinationals and multi-plant national enterprises. Considering the foreign sector only, it might be anticipated that American MNEs new to Europe would see advantages in keeping plant and head-quarters functions closely aligned and regional economies would therefore benefit. There is some evidence to support this view in Chapter 5 which discusses multinational strategies. Subsequent expansion on a multi-plant and multinational (within Europe) basis would eliminate the rationale for a headquarters operation in the UK assisted areas; and a desire to reduce information and contact costs would suggest a capital city or adjacent location somewhere in Europe. For Continental European MNEs an HQ in the UK assisted areas is most improbable. To date at least Japanese companies in Europe have tended to stick to a single site, and a separation of manufacturing from other functions is usual. Indeed Dunning in his work on Japanese investment in Britain noted that in some cases the sales office might not even be in the same country as, for example, Mitsubishi's output from its Scottish factory was exported to its warehousing and sales operation in Düsseldorf. Crum and Gudgin's work would seem to lend support to some of these views:[33] it was found that 97 per cent of the detached head offices of foreign manufacturing companies in the *Times* 1000 list of 1974–5 were located in the South East; in the case of overseas head offices attached to production sites, however, a much more dispersed pattern was in evidence.

Overall, it was found that only 6½ per cent of the headquarters of the leading thousand foreign companies were located in the development areas in 1974, a lower share than was discernible for the largest indigenous companies.[34] Moreover there seemed to have been a slight decline in the position of the development regions between 1974 and 1977.

Extending from this, attempts have been made to identify the exact characteristics of multinational activity in the assisted areas in comparison with the South East, and also in comparing the position between the assisted regions themselves. There is no question that the South East does stand out from the regions in terms of levels of managerial and professional jobs, the existence of R & D, etc. in the multinational sector. As noted above, part of the explanation lies in the concentration of detached head offices in the South. Comparisons between plants in the South East and the assisted areas also reveal higher proportions of UK headquarters/administrative offices, sales offices and R & D departments in the former region.[35] In addition, the proportion of managerial and professional employees in MNE plants in the South East is a good deal higher than in the assisted areas. This Hood and Young work indicated that the differences were most marked for the location of main sales offices, where the results showed that nearly all South East plants acted in this capacity compared with just over 40 per cent of MNE operations in the assisted regions. This finding was linked in with the high level of warehousing activity found in the South East, indicating that the subsidiaries had a strong selling and distribution as well as manufacturing role, as befits their location relative to major markets.

It should be added that it is not simply the presence or otherwise of particular types of activity at plant level that is important, but also the nature of that activity. There have been suggestions that even where assisted area plants appear to have certain functional responsibilities, as in research and development, decision-making activity may still relate chiefly to routine problem solving rather than innovation.

The other issue which has been discussed at some length concerns the purchasing policies of multinational plants in the regions. Low supply linkages with the local economy are regarded as characterising these investments, and when taken together with the maintenance of other backward linkages outside the region in administration and finance, could raise fears of the emergence of a dual economy as between indigenous and foreign industry. This dual economy argument has been supported by the work of Hoare

130

in Northern Ireland, and has been both supported and partially rejected in studies of the Republic of Ireland.[36] There are clear assisted area dimensions to this issue, since the overall degree of industrialisation, the availability of local suppliers and sub-contractors, etc. will vary regionally. On the other hand, multi-national strategy dimensions relating to production and marketing integration internationally and the role of centralised purchasing will be important too.

Multinational acquisitions and implications for the assisted areas

Despite the fact that merger activity has been concentrated in central regions of the UK, there has been growing concern since the late 1970s over the effects of inward acquisitions in the peripheral areas. In Scotland, for example, the catalyst was the contested acquisition of major Scottish companies Highland Distillers, Royal Bank of Scotland and Anderson Strathclyde; all three had bids for them by externally-controlled enterprises turned down by the Monopolies and Mergers Commission (MMC) either wholly or partly on regional grounds (although the Secretary of State subsequently permitted the acquisition of Anderson Strathclyde by London-registered Charter Consolidated).

Until recently there has been little evidence on the impact of inward acquisitions on regional development and, moreover, the conclusions have been rather impressionistic. Leigh and North, in work relating to takeovers in 1973 and 1974, indicated that acquisition resulted in the removal of high level functions but the retention of relatively routine middle-management functions; while Smith has suggested that 'technological asset stripping' may have been associated with takeovers in the Northern region.[37] These and other studies have suggested real costs and benefits associated with inward acquisitions, whether from elsewhere in the UK or from abroad, but provide little quantification. A major piece of research on inward takeovers in Scotland covering the period 1965–80 went much further in terms of systematic analysis, indicating that:

Returns on capital and sales in acquired companies tended to fall as a result of the acquisition; sales improved significantly, with employment not being affected overall

Acquisition was shown to be associated with a marked reduction in autonomy, with managerial functions being lost

Associated with the above, local linkages were adversely affected, especially professional service linkages, such as accountancy.

It was concluded overall that while judgement on the net benefits and costs of inward acquisition could not be made, 'there must be an expectation of detriment to the Scottish economy'.[38] It should be noted, however, that foreign-owned acquirers accounted for only 17 per cent of the acquisitions, so the results relate mainly to other UK-owned acquiring firms. Even so, the weight of evidence from this and other work does suggest that takeovers may be reinforcing some of the long standing weaknesses of the assisted areas, and further damaging their self-generating growth possibilities. The acquisition question is taken up again in the next chapter, and the topic of merger policy is discussed in Chapter 6.

Policy questions and the future

Accepting the weaknesses of the assisted areas, which derive in large part from factors associated with external control, the real problem comes in devising policy measures which might counteract the situation. Chapter 6 of this book looks at policy in some detail, but at this point it is worth making a few preliminary observations, particularly since these relate to the use of regional policy instruments. Since RSA has always been 'selective' and the trend is towards greater selectivity, it could conceivably be possible to use the 'additionality' concept in regional assistance offers to try to up-grade MNE affiliates (in terms of headquarters activity, R & D, local purchasing, etc.). Whether this offers real possibilities is dubious in the light of the poor supply of sophisticated business services at local level, and limited demand as the headquarters functions of indigenous companies move closer to the market centre. The danger of making the South East less attractive in the process and thereby encouraging more MNEs to think in terms of Brussels, Paris and other Continental locations is also present.

As to the future, the question is whether the globalisation and technology imperatives require a reconsideration of the branch plant phenomenon. Given the view of a 'branch plant' as a production only facility, there are still big differences between branch plants according to the technology incorporated into the manufacturing process. Thus hi-tech branch factories will be operating some or all of the components of computer-integrated manufacturing, whereas manual assembly may still be in evidence in the low-tech facilities.

Even this classification would need to be considered with care, however, since low volume or specialised manufacturing will still not be amenable to automation. More work is clearly required in this area. On the theme of globalisation and branch plants, it has to be asked whether the encouragement of greater autonomy at subsidiary level, with associated R & D functions, etc. is desirable in a situation where international competitiveness seems to require more centralisation and integration. The danger in such a situation is that the subsidiary may be left out on a limb. This topic is taken up in more detail in the next chapter, when some models of foreign subsidiaries in the UK are developed and their relative performance assessed. For the moment it is worth illustrating some of the dilemmas, drawing on the example of IBM in Scotland. 'Big Blue's' subsidiary at Greenock would seem to fit almost exactly into the mould of a classic branch plant, as an assembly facility with no marketing or R & D, and little likelihood of these functions being allocated to plant level given global corporate policy. Yet the assembly operation is highly automated, plant 'status' by the measure of graduate employment is high and the Greenock productivity record undoubtedly had a bearing on the decision to locate IBM PC assembly at the plant in 1983. The long-term employment, trade and technology contributions to the Scottish economy cannot be denied.

Foreign-owned service industry in the assisted areas

The weaknesses of the service sector in general in the assisted areas have been alluded to in the previous discussion, but little can be said in detail about this or about the foreign-owned component. Major interest here relates to the business service sector, comprising management consultancy and executive search, advertising, accountancy, insurance, banking, engineering design and legal practices. These are heavily market-oriented activities with the growth of service MNEs being linked to the prior expansion of manufacturing multinationals. So the majority of such offices began their lives in Europe supplying clients already supplied in other countries. Typically thereafter the branch offices develop in the local markets and eventually find the bulk of their business coming from indigenous clients in the host country. Considering the distribution of business service activities in US companies within Europe (strictly only Belgium, France and the UK were considered) Dunning and

Norman estimated that the United Kingdom accounted for nearly half of the total in the mid-1970s, with an especially strong representation in the banking sector.[39] It was suggested that 25,000 people or more were employed in the UK in these business service MNEs, but the overwhelming proportion of employment was in Central London or areas close by, attracted by information requirements, access to markets and the general advantages of agglomeration. It was only in the case of engineering consultancy firms that the general advantages of a central location were less apparent.

The important question in the present context is whether or not there is any potential for mobility among these business service MNEs. Location of Offices Bureau data indicate about 160,000 job moves (indigenous and foreign firms) from Central London between 1963–4 and 1979–80.[40] Most of these were short distance moves, nevertheless, and a mere five per cent of the job moves were to the assisted areas. As noted previously the government has encouraged moves of service industries to the assisted areas by means of the Office and Service Industries Scheme (OSIS). It has been estimated that moves from London and the South East accounted for about half of all jobs associated with projects receiving offers up to the end of September 1983, that is about 17,800 jobs.[41] For a variety of reasons including those given above it is doubtful if many of the companies involved were foreign MNEs. Thus, for example, only the largest of the management consultants in the Dunning and Norman sample could see any scope for decentralisation and even then any hive-off would involve only routine operations. Clearly the low level of demand for business services by manufacturing MNEs in the assisted areas is a major factor.

Several points can be made. Firstly, responsibility for the purchase of services may not reside at branch plant level in the regions. Figure 4.4 shows the patterns of responsibility for business service purchases in a small sample of MNE subsidiaries in West Central Scotland, indicating that accounting, computing and engineering services were generally under the control of local management, whereas advertising and promotions, market and economic research, and general management and marketing services were usually centralised at UK or European headquarters' levels.[42] Secondly, even if authority notionally resides at plant level, corporate purchasing policies formulated at head office may specify particular outside suppliers to be used. Thirdly, subsidiary managers may be forced to purchase outside the local area particularly for specialised services because of inadequate local provision. In this instance a

Figure 4.4: Responsibility for purchase of services in
Strathclyde-located manufacturing MNE subsidiaries[a]

Case 1	Insurance handled at UK HQ; advertising and promotions, market and economic research, general management and marketing partly handled at UK sales HQ
Case 2	Insurance, advertising and promotions, market and economic research, general management and marketing handled at UK HQ
Case 3	Advertising and promotions, public relations, market and economic research handled at European HQ in Brussels
Case 4	Advertising and promotions, general management and marketing handled by corporate international organisation
Case 5	Advertising and promotions, public relations, market and economic research, general management and marketing handled by UK HQ

Note: a Services covered — 1 Accounting, 2 Other finance, 3 Insurance,
4 Advertising and promotions, 5 PR, 6 Market and economic research,
7 General management and marketing, 8 Computing, 9 Engineering
services, 10 Other services.
Source: Authors' survey data.

'Catch 22' situation exists, with low demand and poor supply reinforcing each other. The low demand from the multinational sector, moreover, has to be considered together with centralisation pressures among indigenous manufacturing firms and the probable decline in business service demand at regional level associated with this trend.

The position is not totally negative. The major cities in the United Kingdom will often have branch offices of major service MNEs such as McKinsey, Price Waterhouse, Arthur Anderson, Coopers and Lybrand, PA Management Consultants, etc. The accounting firms, in particular, may be significant employers; although, conversely, in some other cases the branch office may be little more than a 'post box', designed to capitalise on the 'buy local' policies of local authorities and government agencies.

Of more importance is the fact that in particular regional economies the level of demand for certain business services may be such as to encourage multinational service activity: this is especially true for the banking industry in Scotland in the light of North Sea oil. Prior to the discovery of oil, there was only one foreign bank which had established itself in Scotland. This was the Bank of Nova Scotia, which opened a branch in Glasgow in 1964. Thereafter, between 1970 and 1981, about 17 foreign banks providing full banking services opened branches in Scotland.[43] In addition there was a large influx of foreign banks with representative offices, merchant

135

banks and finance houses. A number of these have developed considerable expertise in specialist fields and trade on this. For instance, Manufacturers Hanover Trust Co has a large and active investment trust business; the Bank of America is strong in documentary credits and collection, etc. For the American banks particularly, North Sea oil has been the major stimulus to activity and can be traceable back to their oil connections in the United States. Similarly the foreign-owned merchant banks located in Scotland are heavily involved in North Sea activity, for example, in the setting up of exploration consortia. As of 1986, with the slump in oil prices and sharply reduced levels of activity in the North Sea, there were signs of some retrenchment in foreign banking activity.[44]

The development of North Sea oil and gas reserves proved an irresistible attraction for many other groups of firms. In 1985, it was estimated that there were at least 700 offshore supply companies in Scotland, which sold over 80 per cent of their output to the offshore market.[45] There is relatively little information either on the service industry component of this or of foreign MNE involvement. Services include the provision of catering, medical and diving equipment and services; the operation of supply/tug vessels to transport materials and equipment from shore to rig, helicopter operations, design and project management, computer services, welding and inspection services, etc. It has been estimated that about half of the offshore supply companies are controlled either from other parts of the UK or from abroad: but in the service sectors, especially low-tech services, MNE involvement would not be expected to be high.

The importance of foreign MNEs derives from the central role of the oil companies, which are at the core of a huge subcontracting network. The oil majors rely on the services of specialist engineering contracting firms, which in turn take responsibility for supervising oil field design and specifications, and the tendering of contracts to engineering and service firms. In the higher technology activities, MNE activity is extensive, and as will be shown in the policy sector of this book, inward investment has been stimulated by the discriminatory policies of the Offshore Supplies Office. Some British firms have broken into these higher technology operations, including the John Wood Group of Aberdeen, which grew in little over a decade from being a medium sized firm involved in traditional local industries to one of the major petrochemical engineering concerns in the UK. The company's strategy has involved buying oil expertise through the recruitment of experienced offshore oil managers; joint ventures with foreign partners; and the acquisition of smaller specialist companies. It is interesting to relate the company's view concerning its joint venture experience: 'Such joint ventures have less than a 50/50 chance of long term success mainly because in a situation where the local company has no technology, any joint venture with an experienced partner appears to be a relatively cheap and safe way of getting into the specialist market. In the long term, however, it can be very expensive and an ongoing contribution from both participants is an essential ingredient of success. Problems have also arisen where the level of investment and rate of return aspirations have been incompatible.'[46]

In a situation where the major problem is one of increasing the level of service activity in the assisted areas (whether undertaken by foreign or indigenous enterprises), there has been little debate about the wider impact of MNEs in the service sector. To a greater extent than in manufacturing, foreign service firms will be competing in sectors where there is already an indigenous presence: questions of additional *vs* displacement investment, and of beneficial competition *vs* undesirable market power, therefore loom large. In the banking sector, there is little doubt that the new foreign entrants have had a stimulating effect on the Scottish banks, encouraging diversification domestically and internationally, greater efficiency and aggressiveness and (along with the challenges posed by North Sea oil) increased flexibility and innovativeness in bank lending policies. In the advertising industry, by contrast, it would be unsurprising to see adverse impacts on small, entrepreneurial indigenous enterprises. Yet a different case is the engineering consulting industry, where even large indigenous enterprises are managerially weak, and struggling to secure overseas markets to offset the decline in public sector business in the UK. New foreign entrants are setting up in the assisted areas, as, for instance, the US-owned Holmes and Narver which announced the establishment in 1984 of a major engineering consulting company with plans to employ 160 people, including architects, design engineers and draughtsmen; depressingly, the company withdrew only two years later.

THE ELECTRONICS INDUSTRY IN THE ASSISTED AREAS[47]

Most of this chapter has been concerned with the broad picture of foreign ownership in manufacturing and non-manufacturing industry in the assisted areas of the United Kingdom. When consideration is given to recent trends in inward direct investment, however, and these trends are projected into the future, it becomes very apparent that the electronics industry will be the key sector at least for the remaining years of this century. The importance for the assisted areas of a strong representation in this industry cannot be over estimated, given its position as the principal user and supplier of core technology for economic development. The aim of this section of the chapter is thus to outline and evaluate the position of the electronics industry in these regions, against the backcloth of the specific targeting of this sector for industrial development by agencies such as LIS and WINVEST.

Background of the electronics industry in the UK

There is no question that the overall position of the electronics industry in the UK is very weak. This is reflected in a whole variety of indicators: import penetration for the industry as a whole stood at 54 per cent in value terms in 1982, with a trading surplus in 1975 having deteriorated into a £1.5 billion deficit seven years later; by 1984 the deficit in office machinery and data processing, and electrical and electronic engineering (Classes 33 and 34) had reached £2.4 billion (Chapter 1, Table 1.1). Domestic production in several of the largest or fastest growing sub-sectors, moreover, is dominated by the presence of foreign-owned manufacturers. The indigenous industry is relatively strongest in the capital equipment sub-sectors of defence and telecommunications, but in the former case there are limited civil/commercial spin offs and the latter has suffered from the vagaries of public procurement policies. The indigenous sector lacks the benefits of the technological complementarities, between components, consumer and computer industries, enjoyed by Japan and the United States. The British companies are further criticised for not concentrating on leading-edge businesses, so their share of world markets has declined and output growth has suffered. Finally, Britain's record in generating major innovations in microelectronics has been very poor.

Despite or perhaps because of the above the United Kingdom is still the most favoured location in the world for electronics MNEs, especially American multinationals.

Location of the electronics industry in the UK

In investment terms the South East of England dominates the UK electronics industry, with one half of manufacturing employment in this region; and an even greater concentration of service employment given that, for example, around 70 per cent of computer service companies are based in the South East. Locationally, the Thames Valley and the M4 corridor in particular dominate the industry, with strong growth also taking place along the M11 from Epping Forest to Cambridge ('Silicon Fen'). The advantages of the area include a critical mass of highly skilled personnel; access to good communications, with Heathrow Airport a major plus point; a core of government research establishments, important for defence contractors; a marked absence of trade union traditions and a semi-rural work environment. Government innovation assistance to industry, designed to help firms adopt new technologies and products, has also been strongly skewed towards this area. And of even more significance is public investment in defence procurement: the equipment budget of the Ministry of Defence was six times as large as regional policy spending in 1983, with the non-assisted areas being the major beneficiaries of defence contracts. A number of these points emerged in the earlier discussion on the characteristics of assisted *vs* non-assisted manufacturing industry, whether foreign or indigenous. The apparently even greater centralisation pressures in the electronics sector, are reinforced by the favourable innovation environment, necessary for high technology industry, which exists in the South East.

Despite this south eastern concentration of the electronics industry, movement into the assisted areas can be inferred from the statistics on regional policy spending. Over the period 1972–83, regional selective assistance offers to the electronics industry have represented between one fifth and one quarter of all RSA offers, and this proportion has increased, as would be expected, in recent years. The vast majority of this electronics industry expenditure has, moreover, gone to foreign companies.

What is especially important in the regional growth of the electronics sector is its concentration in particular assisted areas, notably Central Scotland. As the data in Table 4.7 reveal, for the years 1979–83 Scotland accounted for 55 per cent of RSA offers by value in Great Britain and 45 per cent of the associated jobs, figures which were nowhere near matched by any other regions. The regional policy influence on the growth of the industry in Scotland cannot be

Table 4.7: Offers of regional selective assistance to the electronics industry, Scotland and Great Britain

	Great Britain	Scotland[a]	Scotland's share of Great Britain (%)
1972–83			
Number of offers	615	174	28.3
Offer value (£m)	179	89	49.7
New jobs	74,000	31,000	41.9
Safeguarded jobs	39,500	12,500	31.6
1979–83			
Number of offers	345	104	30.1
Offer value (£m)	127	69	54.3
New jobs	39,000	17,500	44.9
Safeguarded jobs	17,000	4,500	26.5

Note: *a* Data relate to indigenous and foreign firms, but in the 1980–3 period, overseas firms accounted for 83 per cent of the assistance offered to the electronics industry in Scotland by value and for 70 per cent of jobs created or safeguarded. In the year 1984–5 specifically, offers to overseas-owned electronics firms in Scotland accounted for 86 per cent of assistance to the industry and 87 per cent of jobs.
Sources: Industry Department for Scotland; IDS (1986), 'The electronics industry in Scotland', *Statistical Bulletin*, No. C1.1, January, contains information on 1984–5 RSA offers.

denied, but the focus of assisted area expansion in this region does indicate that other factors must also be considered.

One of the other variables is undoubtedly the electronics industry development strategy pursued by the Scottish Development Agency, through its Electronics Division and its associate organisation, Locate in Scotland. Part of this strategy has involved intensive and targeted promotional activity, particularly in the United States but latterly also in Japan. To a greater extent than in the other assisted areas Scotland does possess attributes around which the promotional campaigns can be built: these include a long tradition of engineering excellence; a base of electronic skills, fostered by government purchasing for the UK defence sector, with Ferranti playing a central role in the industry's development since the end of World War Two; an independent research capability and capacity within Strathclyde and Glasgow Universities and the Wolfson Microelectronics Institute at Edinburgh University in such fields as VLSI, artificial intelligence and opto-electronics; and the ability to recruit (and equally importantly in this sector, retain) scientists, technologists and technicians.

On the basis of such factors, the industry in Scotland grew to employ 45,800 people in 1984, before falling back slightly in 1985. At its 1984 level, the industry accounted for 10½ per cent of total manufacturing employment in Scotland, in the form of 210 companies.[48] Sixty one of these enterprises were foreign-owned, and they made up 49 per cent of electronics employment; the American component of foreign ownership is very high and in 1984 the 46 US plants employed 19,700 people out of the total in the overseas-owned sector of 22,600. Foreign ownership is especially high in the important electronics components sector, which contains within it the major US and Japanese semiconductor fabrication plants: these firms were responsible for an estimated one fifth and four fifths respectively of Western European and UK integrated circuit production in 1983.

Excluding Central Scotland, the only other assisted area with any significant representation of the electronics industry is South Wales, in which 14,000 people were employed in 1981 (foreign and indigenous companies). Observers have suggested that, unlike the position in Scotland, South Wales has few advantages beyond regional assistance and accessibility ('the subsidised end of the M4 corridor').[49] Thus it lacks the research and development platform and the small indigenous sector evident in Central Scotland and, moreover, has an occupational structure with relatively low numbers of technically skilled and managerial employees.

The foreign-owned electronics industry in Wales is dominated by Japanese multinationals.[50] Thus there were four Japanese consumer electronics companies which had a combined employment of 3,082 at the end of 1982. Following investment in sales and service facilities in the late 60s and early 1970s, the first manufacturing plant was set up in 1974, by Sony — a greenfield factory at Bridgend costing £6 million and employing 1,000 people. Matsushita followed two years later with a £3 million facility employing 400 people, and in 1980 Aiwa set up a plant specialising in the production of miniature hi-fi. The group is completed by the most problematic operation, namely the Hitachi investment which started out as a joint venture with GEC in 1979. In March 1984, Hitachi acquired GEC's 50 per cent stake in the joint venture, following a brief history which was fraught with management problems and poor industrial relations and a halving of the workforce. Hitachi was able to extract substantial concessions as a price for keeping the television plant open including a no-strike, single union agreement with the EEPTU (electricians' union), further redundancies and a general shift towards the Japanese operating style (and Japanese productivity levels). Following this group of investments, in 1985 two further Japanese electronics companies opted for Wales (Wrexham in North Wales), namely Brother Industries making electronic typewriters and Sharp Corporation producing video tape recorders.

Impact of foreign ownership in the assisted areas

It must be clear from preceding paragraphs that there are some very healthy signs in the electronics industry in Scotland, primarily due to the inflow of inward investment. Employment in the indigenous and foreign sectors together in Scotland has grown from around 7,400 in 1959 to the 1985 figure of 43,800. There are difficulties in estimating employment trends because of definitional problems and reclassifications, and such factors largely explain the intermittent employment growth recorded in recent years, despite the impressive stream of new or expansionary projects which has been announced. Nevertheless, employment in the industry grew from 39,400 in 1978 to 43,800 in 1985. This compares with the 'jobless growth' phenomenon which has been alleged for the UK as a whole.[51] Output has grown rapidly as Figure 4.5 shows: the rise in the six years to 1984 was 120 per cent in real terms, much of this being due to the data processing equipment industry which quadrupled its output over the period.

Productivity in the industry is well above the UK norm: in 1979 the ratio of net output per head in Scotland to that in the UK was 114.9. The American companies, although not the European-owned enterprises, have an impressive export record (Table 4.8), reflecting their role as suppliers of a Europe-wide market and beyond. And the proportion of R & D employees in the industry has been rising, at the expense of technical staff in design engineering — often adaptation of US models to European standards and requirements. Perhaps confirming the latter point, it has to be said that R & D in Scotland is a long way from the rarefied research battleground for fifth generation computers and the like. Nevertheless, there have been some meaningful recent developments such as the Engineering Centre at Honeywell opened in October 1986, which employs 130 research staff (including 80 graduates) in projects ranging from software development and design equipment to computer-integrated manufacturing.[52]

Figure 4.5: Output of electronics and all manufacturing industry in Scotland, 1978–84

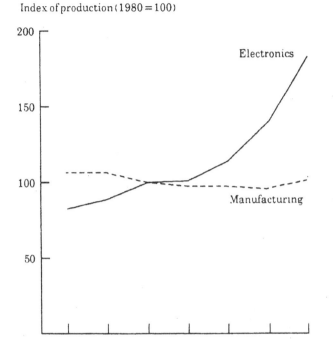

Index of production (1980 = 100)

Source: Industry Department for Scotland (1986), 'The electronics industry in Scotland', *Statistical Bulletin*, No. C1.1, January

Table 4.8: Market destination for Scottish electronics industry production, 1978[a]

Destination	US-owned firms	% of production European-owned firms	All firms
Scotland	7	7	7
Rest of UK	31	86	55
Europe	46	7	26
USA	7	—	5
Rest of world	9	—	7
Total	100	100	100

Note: *a* 1979 data are available from the Scottish Input-Output tables, and these indicate an export proportion of 52 per cent, substantially higher than the survey figures shown in the table.
Source: Booz, Allen and Hamilton (1979), *The electronics industry in Scotland: a proposed strategy*, Scottish Development Agency, Glasgow.

143

The optimism has to be qualified in any event when consideration is given to the linkages of the multinational industry with the local economy. The overseas sector is poorly integrated, with little secondary employment creation. This is evident from Table 4.9 which indicates only one fifth of purchases of components and subcontract services from Scottish suppliers in 1979. A more recent survey of 30 electronics MNEs in Scotland suggested that even this modest figure had been reduced, with 15 per cent of production input purchases being made in Scotland in 1984; the major source was England, which accounted for 38 per cent of inputs by value.[53] There are some explanations for this pattern which have nothing to do with the competitiveness or otherwise of Scottish suppliers. For example, central sourcing of components with global searches to achieve the best price, quality and delivery terms are normal. Nevertheless, managers in MNE subsidiaries in Scotland were pessimistic about Scottish suppliers because:

Few indigenous firms had the required technical knowledge in specific areas
There were few Scottish firms with sufficient capacity to be able to handle demand from foreign-owned enterprises
There seemed to be an unwillingness on the part of Scottish firms to become heavily committed to supplying MNE affiliates.

Reflecting the very complex and intractable nature of industrial problems in Britain as a whole, reasons for lack of success by Scottish electronics companies ranged from 'cultural attitudes through management weaknesses of assorted kinds to very specific technical problems'. As this SDA Newsletter went on to observe, 'The indigenous electronics community in Scotland does not exhibit the cohesion shown by dynamic economic groupings elsewhere and the consequent isolation can be a cause of opportunities passing unnoticed or threats emerging unexpectedly.'[54]

Securing and deepening the base of the industry in Scotland depends crucially too on the emergence of a strong domestically-owned industry. There was an indigenous sector of some 154 plants in 1985, a good number of which were Scottish- as opposed to other UK-owned. The Scottish-owned firms have emerged from a variety of backgrounds.[55] There have been a number of spin offs from large electronics corporations, including Fortronic formed by an executive from Hewlett-Packard; Findlay Irvine in industrial electronics and instrumentation set up by ex-Ferranti employees;

Table 4.9: Purchases of components and subcontract services by Scottish electronics OEMs, 1979

Origin of supplier	Electronics components (%)	Subcontract work (%)	Total purchases (%)
Scotland	12	30	19
Rest of UK	46	54	49
Europe	22	3	15
USA	13	8	11
Other	6	5	6
Total	100	100	100

Source: Scottish Development Agency (1982), *The Scottish electronics subcontracting and components supply industries*, SDA, Glasgow, May.

Rodime established by employees from Burroughs; and Office Workstations out of ICL. In addition there was an indigenous printed circuit board industry, comprising 16 companies in 1985. The first company in this sector was Exacta, later acquired by STC, from which a number of other firms have spun off; but the biggest pcb manufacturer in Scotland is now Prestwick Holdings. Another group of Scottish firms has emerged from the universities, including Lattice-Logic, producing silicon computers, VLSI courses and gate arrays, Seel Electronics, Intellimetrics and the Wolfson Microelectronics Institute; the science park phenomenon, associated with the universities, is important in Scotland as elsewhere in the UK. In other cases the companies, such as Kineticon and Future Technology Systems have emerged from the usual route of a business idea followed by the packaging of people and finance. The Scottish Development Agency has been heavily involved in the financing and refinancing of many of these ventures and, arguably, has done a great deal to offset weaknesses in venture capital availabilities in Scotland.

As to the nature of technological advance in the Scottish sector, some of the companies mentioned above have developed and deployed advanced technologies. Work by Oakey, furthermore, reached some favourable conclusions on small high technology firms in Scotland in relation to similar companies in the South East of England and the Bay Area of southern California.[56] The majority of Scottish firms are, however, low technology enterprises operating in the hi-tech electronics sector, and growth rates give no indication that a genuine 'high-flyer' will emerge on the National Semiconductor or Texas Instruments

Table 4.10: Selected performance indicators for Japanese and all manufacturing plants in Wales, 1981

	All manufacturing plants	Japanese-owned plants
Gross value added, as % of gross output	27	18
Wages[a], as % of gross output	12	6
Salaries[b] as % of gross output	6	4
Average wages[a] (£ per annum)	5,719	4,194
Average salaries[b] (£ per annum)	7,372	5,251

Notes: a Wages relate to operatives excluding jobbers.
　　　b Administrative, technical and clerical salaries excluding working proprietors.
Source: *Hansard*, written answer to Mr Austin Mitchell by the Secretary of State for Wales, 1 March 1984.

models. In addition, as with the case of Rodime, a manufacturer of Winchester disk drives which went public on the over-the-counter market in the USA in 1982, indigenous firms may feel it necessary to expand outside the UK in order to keep abreast of leading-edge technology. Reflecting such points, the Scottish Development Agency sees further targeted inward investment as one way to improve linkages within the industry. While being realistic, this further increases foreign dominance which was already as high as 94 per cent in employment terms in MLH (Minimum List Heading) 366, computers, in 1981 and at a level of 78 per cent in electronic components (MLH 364).

In evaluating hierarchies of regional development in the electronics industry in the UK, Central Scotland has been suggested as being in an intermediate position. The core functions in the industry are primarily located in the South East, admittedly, but to characterise Scotland as a branch plant location for electronics would be incorrect too. The industry in Wales seems in reality much closer to the branch-economy stereotype. The Japanese presence in Wales extends beyond electronics, but certainly the latter is the major sector, and, therefore, it is worth observing the performance data for Japanese MNEs shown in Table 4.10.

In part these results reflect the position of the electronic consumer goods sub-sector, which largely entails assembly operations, this has the highest proportion of low skilled employment of all sub-sectors and involves products of a low value-added kind. Moreover, it seems that some of the Japanese companies have not introduced their new generation, mass-market products into Wales.[57]

The survey work of Sayer and Morgan has identified other features of the electronics industry in Wales. Firstly, South Wales MNE plants were often the last to benefit from technology transfer within the multinational system, but this transfer still represented the major source of innovation in the region. Secondly, the personnel in the electronics plants were primarily engaged in 'routine occupations'. Thirdly, the purchasing policies of the multinational plants and the relative absence of an indigenous small-to-medium firm sector meant low regional multiplier effects. Fourthly, except for new entrants still in the process of building up employment, output growth was linked to stable or declining levels of employment.

It does seem apparent, therefore, that from an assisted area perspective the growth of the electronics industry is bound to widen regional differentials, while maintaining the centrist/periphery relationship between the South East and the assisted areas as a whole. Scotland is not too far from being able to break out from the latter relationship in manufacturing, given the growing university–industry coordination, the important role of the finance and banking community and the aggressive efforts of the Scottish Development Agency. Progress is not inevitable and the industry is very volatile, with a rate of closures (as well as openings) well above the average for manufacturing as a whole; and what must be feared is that Scotland becomes the victim of its (limited) success, so that the policy stance is changed before the policies have fully had time to work.[58] What can probably never be reproduced in a Scottish context or in any other assisted area is the wide and concentrated array of activities as exists in the M4/M11 areas, particularly in electronics-related business services, which in turn seems to be associated with a more entrepreneurial culture and a high rate of new firm formation.

CONCLUDING REMARKS

When the assisted areas of the UK are considered as a group, there is little question that beneficial impacts have been associated with the multinational presence. Being an advanced and dynamic group of firms, MNEs have had a positive effect on the industrial structures of regional economies, previously dominated by declining heavy industries. As the chapter has shown, moreover, the MNEs are more productive than indigenous industry and have continued to account for a disproportionate share of capital spending on buildings, plant and machinery. And with regional policy as an important attraction instrument, the proportion of incoming multinationals setting up in the assisted areas has been encouragingly high.

The impact of MNEs needs, however, to be judged against additional criteria to those above. Whether the regions have become more competitive, faster growing, more innovative and closer to self-sustaining growth, are all factors which need to be considered. When such issues are brought into the equation, judgement has to be much more qualified. The fact that headquarters functions of MNEs are commonly located outside the assisted areas, that local linkages are weak, and that there have been only fairly isolated examples of spin-off enterprises emerging from the multinational sector are telling findings, with no indication that there have been any improvements over time. It is true that the branch factories of the present day may be hi-tech production units, performing a crucial role within the European or global multinational system and .providing training and employment for skilled technicians and graduate staff. Yet by the crucial innovative and competitive criteria, multinationals have not had a favourable impact on the peripheral regions of the UK. In many ways the regional economies are classic dual economies, with the hi-tech MNE subsidiaries somehow cocooned, like the antiseptic work environs of their electronics factories, from the real problems of the regions. Apart from the points mentioned above, the lack of involvement of the companies in industrial affairs and in the wider industrial community is relevant too. For example, it is difficult to envisage a multinational company having the influence on industry which Ferranti undoubtedly has had on the electronics sector in Scotland: Ferranti had a lead role in the Scottish Development Group of electronics companies from 1945; senior Ferranti executives serve on nearly all the main industrial bodies, institutions, organisations and societies in Scotland; numerous multinational electronics firms in Scotland have recruited their core engineering and management staff in Ferranti, and the company has produced several entrepreneurial figures who have gone on to play key roles in the establishment and growth of indigenous electronics enterprises.[59] It should be noted that similar doubts about the wider role multinationals can play emerged in the report of the Alvey Committee relating to future British technology policy.

The problems noted above cannot necessarily be placed uniquely at the door of the MNEs themselves. For example, on issues relating to location of headquarters' functions, the pattern is evident with multi-plant indigenous enterprises also, as the latter become increasingly international and transnational. The American MNEs and especially their subsidiary managers in Europe are undoubtedly aware of some of the concerns expressed, especially as regards local sourcing, and are making efforts to remedy trade imbalances by increasing European-level purchases. There are self-interest motives, of course, such as reducing exchange risk and trying to increase European-level autonomy. The companies may move towards country-level trade balances, but it would be foolish to expect assisted area trade balances. The same set of arguments might be applied to research and development: within American companies, the European general managers will see R & D as a means of increasing autonomy and perhaps improving the security of European operations *vis-à-vis* sister operations in the Far East. But R & D could not be justified at every plant in Europe (although value engineering and some development work is feasible). More generally the companies could rightly argue that their role is not that of regional development agencies, and that the problems lie as much in the weaknesses of British industry and indigenous British companies as anything else.

The debate then turns to government policy and addressing the fundamental question of indigenous competitiveness. The conclusion of this chapter is that regional policy is necessary but not sufficient. It is necessary because without regional aid a significant proportion of new inward investment projects could go elsewhere — perhaps the South of England, but more likely the Republic of Ireland or Continental Europe. To abolish regional assistance altogether, moreover, and 'let workers move to the work' would not be successful for reasons which were all too apparent at the time this book was being written. These related to the North/South divide, vastly different levels of economic activity and from the huge house price disparities and the adverse effects of the latter on labour mobility. Finally, it is difficult to see what could replace inward investment and thus make regional policy redundant. The first chapter of this book showed that international business was taking many different forms including joint ventures, licensing agreements, etc. But all these alternatives involve local firms to a greater or lesser degree and the performance of the indigenous sector would hardly give grounds for confidence.

Still, regional policy as previously operated is decidedly not sufficient to regenerate the assisted areas. The question is whether regional aid could be operated in an even more selective way so as to increase linkages and more general multinational involvement in the economy; and/or if other policy measures could have a role. In essence the discussion is brought back to the comments in Chapter 1 on the competitiveness problem of the British economy; and final conclusions are ducked until the policy evaluation of Chapters 6 and 7. What can be concluded unequivocally is that MNEs have not and will not cure these deficiencies in the competitiveness of the United Kingdom assisted areas.

NOTES

1. Secretary of State for Trade and Industry (1983), *Regional industrial development*, Cmnd 9111, HMSO, London, December, p. 3
2. Ibid., p. 4
3. For details, see *Industrial Development Act 1982: annual report*, 1985 and 1986 issues
4. Jones, J. (1986), 'An examination of the thinking behind government regional policy in the UK since 1945', *Regional Studies*, 20(3), pp. 261–6
5. Young, S. (1984), 'The foreign-owned manufacturing sector', in Hood, N. and Young, S., *Industry, policy and the Scottish economy*, Edinburgh University Press; the Timex and Hyster cases cited in the next paragraph are also discussed in this source
6. Department of Trade and Industry (1983), *Regional industrial policy: some economic issues*, DTI, London, pp. 92–110
7. For example, Holland, S. (1976), *Capital versus the regions*, Macmillan, London; Yannopoulos, G.N. and Dunning, J.H. (1976), 'Multinational enterprises and regional development: an exploratory paper', *Regional studies*, 10, pp. 389–99; Blackburn, A. (1978), 'Multinational enterprises and regional development: a comment', *Regional Studies*, 12, pp. 125–7
8. Ashcroft, B.K. and Ingham, K.P.D. (1982), 'The comparative impact of regional policy on foreign and indigenous firm movement', *Regional studies*, 16, pp. 81–100
9. Quoted in National Economic Development Council (1982), 'Direct inward investment', *Memorandum by the Secretary of State for Industry to the NEDC*, NEDC (82) 7, January
10. Hood, N. and Young, S. (1983), *Multinational investment strategies in the British Isles: a study of MNEs in the assisted areas and in the Republic of Ireland*, HMSO, London, especially Part 4, Chapter 2
11. See the work of Allen, Begg, McDowall and Walker (1983), cited in DTI, *Regional industrial policy*, pp. 119–21
12. From the early work of Aharoni, subjective and irrational factors have been shown to play a part in locational decision-making by MNEs: Aharoni, Y. (1966), *The foreign investment decision process*, Harvard

Business School Division of Research, Cambridge, Massachusetts

13. Dunning, J.H. (1986), *Japanese participation in British industry*, Croom Helm, London

14. Ibid., p. 55

15. Brech, M. and Sharp, M. (1984), *Inward investment: policy options for the United Kingdom*, Chatham House papers 21, Routledge and Kegan Paul, London

16. The guesstimate is derived from the rankings of locational determinants in Hood and Young, *Multinational investment strategies*, pp. 168–171; for a review of studies on the subject (not specifically relating to inward investment), see McGreevy, T.E. and Thomson, A.W.J. (1983), 'Regional policy and company investment behaviour', *Regional Studies*, 17(5), pp. 347–58

17. Young, S. and Hood, N. (1977), *Chrysler UK: a corporation in transition*, Praeger, New York, pp. 256–60

18. DTI, *Regional industrial policy*, pp. 78–81

19. The source for the 1972–7 figures is *Regional Trends* (1981), HMSO, London, Table 10.5; and for the 1976–80 data Killick, T. (1983), 'Manufacturing plant openings, 1976–80 analysis of transfer and branches', *British Business*, 17 June, Table 3

20. Killick, T. (1982), 'Employment in foreign-owned manufacturing plants', *British Business*, 26 November

21. Hood and Young, *Multinational investment strategies*, p. 243

22. Smith, I.J. (1980), *Some aspects of direct inward investment in the United Kingdom, with particular reference to the northern region*, discussion paper 31, Centre for Urban and Regional Development Studies, University of Newcastle upon Tyne, March

23. Hood and Young, *Multinational investment strategies*, pp. 100–2 and 179–93

24. Harrison, R.T. (1982), 'Assisted industry, employment stability and industrial decline: some evidence from Northern Ireland', *Regional Studies*, 16(4), pp. 267–85

25. Industry Department for Scotland (1983), 'Employment performance of overseas-owned manufacturing units opening in Scotland, 1954–77', *Statistical Bulletin*, No. A1.1, May

26. Lloyd, P.E. and Shutt, J. (1983), *Recession and restructuring in the North West region: the policy implications of recent events*, discussion paper 13, North West Industry Research Unit, University of Manchester

27. Ibid., see also Gaffikin, F. and Nickson, A. (1983), *Job crisis and the multinationals: deindustrialisation in the West Midlands*, Russell Press, Nottingham

28. Hood, N. and Young, S. (1982), *Multinationals in retreat: the Scottish experience*, Edinburgh University Press

29. Manpower Services Commission (1984), *Closure at Linwood: a follow-up survey of redundant workers*, MSC, Edinburgh, April

30. DTI, *Regional industrial policy*, p. 5

31. Firn, J.R. and Roberts, D. (1984), 'High technology industries' in Hood and Young, *Industry, policy and the Scottish economy*

32. DTI, *Regional industrial policy*, p. 5

33. Crum, R.E. and Gudgin, G. (1977), *Non-production activities in UK*

manufacturing industry, Commission of the European Communities, Brussels

34. A point developed by Smith, *Aspects of direct inward investment*, Table 1.5

35. Hood and Young, *Multinational investment strategies*, Part 4, Chapter 4; the data have been analysed statistically in Young, S. and Stewart, D. (1986), 'The regional implications of inward direct investment', in Amin, A. and Goddard, J.B., *Technological change, industrial restructuring and regional development*, Allen and Unwin, London

36. Hoare, A.G. (1978), 'Industrial linkages and the dual economy: the case of Northern Ireland', *Regional Studies*, 12(2), pp. 167–80; Stewart, J.C. (1976), 'Linkages and foreign direct investment', *Regional Studies*, 10(2), pp. 245–58; and O'Loughlin, B. and O'Farrell, P.N. (1980), 'Foreign direct investment in Ireland: empirical evidence and theoretical implications', *Economic and Social Review*, 11, pp. 155–85

37. Leigh, R. and North, D.J. (1978), 'Regional aspects of acquisition activity in British manufacturing industry', *Regional Studies*, 12(2), pp. 227–45; Smith, I.J. (1979), 'The effect of external takeovers on employment change in the northern region between 1963 and 1973', *Regional Studies*, 13(5), pp. 421–37; ——— (1982), 'Some implications of inward investment through takeover activity', *Northern Economic Review*, February, pp. 1–5; and ——— (1985–6), 'Takeovers, rationalisation and the northern region economy', *Northern Economic Review*, winter, pp. 30–8

38. Bain, A.D., Ashcroft, B.K., Love, J.H. and Scouller, J. (1987), *The economic effects of the inward acquisition of Scottish manufacturing companies, 1965 to 1980*, HMSO, Edinburgh

39. Dunning, J.H. and Norman, G. (1979), *Factors influencing the location of offices of multinational enterprises*, LOB research paper 8, Economists Advisory Group Ltd, London, October

40. DTI, *Regional Industrial Policy*, pp. 78–85

41. Ibid., p. 84

42. This survey of the business services sector in the Glasgow area was undertaken by the authors as part of a wider SDA-commissioned study

43. Elder, D.W. (1981), *Scottish banking in the light of oil*, MBA dissertation, University of Strathclyde

44. Draper, P., Hood, N., Smith, J. and Stewart, W.S. (1987), *Scottish financial sector*, Edinburgh University Press

45. Scottish Development Agency (1980), *The international offshore oil and gas market*, Aberdeen; and Jenkins, M. (1981), *British industry and the North Sea*, Macmillan, London

46. Quoted in Mackay, T. (1984), 'The oil and oil-related sector', in Hood and Young, *Industry, policy and the Scottish economy*

47. Aside from other references quoted specifically, this section draws on Morgan, K. and Sayer, A. (1983), *The international electronics industry and regional development in Britain*, working paper 34, Urban and Regional Studies, University of Sussex, September; Sayer, A. and Morgan, K. (1984), *The electronics industry and regional development in Britain*, paper presented at an ESRC/CURDS workshop, University of Newcastle upon Tyne, March; and Firn, J.R. and Roberts, D. (1984), 'High

technology industries', in Hood and Young, *Industry, policy and the Scottish economy*

48. The data quoted here are derived from Industry Department for Scotland (1986), 'The electronics industry in Scotland', *Statistical Bulletin*, No. C1.1, January; Industry Department for Scotland (1986), 'Employment in the electronics industry 1975–85', *Statistical Bulletin*, No. C2.1, September

49. Sayer and Morgan, *Electronics industry and regional development*, p. 9

50. See Dunning, *Japanese participation*; and Brech and Sharp, *Inward investment: policy options*, pp. 69–70

51. Sayer and Morgan, *Electronics industry and regional development*, p. 4 and p. 20

52. *Glasgow Herald* (1986), 20 October, p. 15

53. McCalman, J. (1986), *What's wrong with Scottish electronics firms? Local sourcing by foreign electronic companies in Scotland*, working paper 2, Department of Management Studies, University of Glasgow, June

54. Scottish Development Agency (1986), *Electronics Scotland*, Newsletter of the Electronics Division of the SDA, Glasgow

55. The discussion draws *inter alia* on *Investors Chronicle* (1985), 24 May

56. Oakey, R.P. (1983), *Research and development cycles, investment cycles and regional development*, CURDS discussion paper 48, Centre for Urban and Regional Development Studies, University of Newcastle; and
——— (1984), *High technology small firms: regional development in Britain and the USA*, F. Pinter, London

57. On this topic of screwdriver plants, Turner argues that Japanese MNEs 'acknowledge that screwdriver operations are only acceptable as a provisional first step in the process of becoming a fully fledged multinational': Turner, L. (1987), *Industrial collaboration with Japan*, Chatham House papers 34, Routledge and Kegan Paul, London

58. One recent report argues that employment in Scottish electronics is very unstable; its ability to create jobs seriously over estimated; and that in the long term Silicon Glen will suffer job losses. See McInnes, J. and Sproul, A. (1987), 'Electronics employment in Scotland', *Fraser of Allander Quarterly Economic Commentary*, 12(3), pp. 77–82

59. Firn and Roberts, 'High technology industries' in Hood and Young, *Industry, policy and the Scottish economy*

5

Multinational Strategies and Operating Characteristics

Chapters 3 and 4 provided a review of the inward investment position in Britain, nationally and regionally, drawing on official statistics and the various studies which have been undertaken in this area. Inevitably, the focus was on MNE activities in the UK in isolation and there was only limited discussion of foreign subsidiary operations within the wider framework of multinational behaviour and performance. Consistent with the viewpoint of Chapter 1, the argument to be presented here is that a full understanding of the impact of MNEs can only be gained by looking at multinational strategies and operations at least European-wide, perhaps world-wide. Evolution and revolution in subsidiary relationships within the corporate whole, as reactions to constantly changing firm, industry and country factors and now to the all-embracing globalisation and technology imperatives, provides the background against which this chapter is written.

In the first half of the present chapter, a linkage is attempted between international strategies, foreign subsidiary roles in the UK and thence UK impact, thereby bringing together the broader material of Chapters 1 and 2 and the UK specific dimensions of Chapters 3 and 4. The second half of the chapter, providing a wide range of individual company case material, discusses a number of specific issues which relate to strategy, namely, the effects of industry variations, nationality of ownership, entry methods and ownership relationships. Separation of these items is important since government policy will tend to operate at this level.

SOME IDEAS ON INTERNATIONAL AND SUBSIDIARY STRATEGIES

Chapter 1 highlighted an international strategy model for large multinational companies which had been developed around the theme of globalisation and global competitiveness; this model essentially distinguished different combinations of production logistics and marketing policies, and degrees of integration within these and is reproduced in the upper half of Figure 5.1. The country-centred strategy entails MNEs treating markets on an individual basis with manufacturing operations in those countries where local demand will justify this: some industries are intrinsically country-centred as, for example, where high transport costs, legislative differences or other government policies act as a barrier to cross-border product and component flows. Otherwise the suggestion in the figure is that all the other strategies represent forms of global policies. While there is some evidence that global approaches are on the increase, it is still more common for MNE strategies to be *regional* in character focusing on, for example, the Americas; Europe, Middle East and Africa; the Far East; or some similar combination. Final goods and intermediate product flows might be substantial within the region, but regions themselves are essentially self-contained. The stage thereafter might be towards *hemispheric* strategies where, for instance, Europe and the Americas are treated as a single bloc. Possible variety in strategies becomes even more pronounced when small and non-dominant firms and industry variations are taken into consideration.

Will the technology imperative be likely to alter either the types of strategies or the incidence of particular strategies? Choice of strategy is deemed to be related to economic factors (economies of scale and scope, product differentiation, relative production costs at home and abroad, etc.) and political factors (the influence of host governments in regulating trade and investment, and as customers, suppliers and competitors). Any individual company's responses to these signals may vary according to how it believes it can best compete internationally but, broadly, Japanese success was historically based on export strategies, with an accelerating movement of manufacturing and assembly operations to major developed countries at present in the face of protectionist pressures and the appreciation of the yen. Conversely, high levels of foreign investment in manufacturing have been characteristic of major American MNEs, emanating from quite different economic signals. The discussion in Chapter 1 showed a

variety of international business consequences from the new technologies: perhaps the principal one from the present perspective relates
to the alleged replacement of economies of scale by economies of
scope, in which smaller factories and shorter production runs of any
given design, along with rapid shifts of design, are feasible. This
would seem to reinforce other arguments in favour of a high foreign
investment strategy at least in developed host country markets, with
local subsidiaries' manufacturing operations (and associated flexibility in product design and product mix) as well as decentralised
marketing being used as necessary to leverage competitive advantage.

From the present perspective the interest is in the outcome of
MNE strategies at subsidiary level in the UK. A good deal of
conceptual and empirical study has been undertaken on the subject
of subsidiary level strategies in Canada. One such piece of work has
suggested a distinction between the following groups of affiliates:[1]

Marketing satellite. Marketing subsidiaries which sell into the
local trading area products which are manufactured centrally
Miniature replica. A subsidiary which produces and markets
some of the parent's product lines or related product lines in the
local country; depending on the degree of product and marketing
modification undertaken by the subsidiary, there are three sub-
strategies: *viz* adopter, adaptor and innovator
Rationalised manufacturer. Where the subsidiary produces a
particular set of component parts or products for a multi-country
or global market
Product specialist. Where the subsidiary develops, produces and
markets a limited product line for global markets .
Strategic independent. Where the subsidiary is permitted
independence to develop lines of business for either a local,
multi-country or global market.

Some of the effects of these different types of subsidiary operations on the Canadian economy have been evaluated, with the
Miniature Replica group being the subject of a great deal of
criticism. To quote the Science Council of Canada: 'The subsidiaries
are truncated manufacturing operations that do no R & D, export
only to the United States and import components on a scale that
contributes to a huge balance of payments deficit.[2] The truncation
of product lines means that foreign firms manufacture most of the
parent product line but at high unit cost due to the smaller scale of

Figure 5.1: International and subsidiary strategies

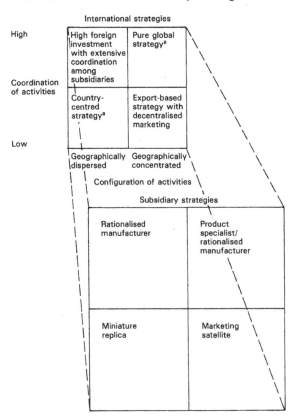

International strategies

	High foreign investment with extensive coordination among subsidiaries	Pure global strategy[a]
High		
Coordination of activities	Country-centred strategy[a]	Export-based strategy with decentralised marketing
Low		

Geographically dispersed   Geographically concentrated

Configuration of activities

Subsidiary strategies

| Rationalised manufacturer | Product specialist/ rationalised manufacturer |
| Miniature replica | Marketing satellite |

Note: *a* Strategic independent subsidiaries could emerge from either of these two international strategies.
Sources: Porter, M.E. (1986), 'Changing patterns of international competition', *California Management Review*, 28(2), winter; White, R.E. and Poynter, T.A. (1984), 'Strategies for foreign-owned subsidiaries in Canada', *Business Quarterly*, summer.

operations and using a high proportion of imported components. The product mixes allocated, associated short product runs and mature product ranges in a number of industries are widely regarded as having contributed to the relatively lower productivity in Canadian plants. By comparison, the Product Specialist and Strategic Independent subsidiaries were viewed as being beneficial from a host country perspective. In a Canadian context, most attention has been paid to the former, especially in connection with the concept of world

157

product mandates (WPMs), where the subsidiary is given total responsibility for all aspects of R & D, manufacturing and international marketing. Despite the assumption of substantial net benefit, this is a much debated subject. Will MNEs be willing to grant WPMs to subsidiaries when the outcome is likely to be loss of control of the subsidiary; a reduction in the parent's bargaining power due to its reliance on the mandate holder for supplies of the new product; less efficient global R & D; and possibly even the emergence of a rival producer?[3]

An attempt is made to link the models of international and subsidiary strategies in Figure 5.1 so, for example, an export-based strategy with decentralised marketing is likely to see Marketing Satellite businesses operating at subsidiary level. Similarly, a strategy involving extensive coordination among manufacturing operations globally (or regionally) would tend to produce a Rationalised Manufacturer at subsidiary level. Where there is less certainty concerning the outcome relates to the two extremes of the country-centred strategy by multinationals or the global strategy. In regard to the former, a Miniature Replica subsidiary could well be the outcome of a country-centred strategy, but it is also possible that such a subsidiary, perhaps due to successful performance, may be granted certain autonomy to develop its own lines of business; this would then fit the Strategic Independent category. In the same way, the Product Specialist or Strategic Independent could be the outcome of a global multinational strategy.

Whether or not the subsidiary groupings suggested are applicable in a British/European context is a matter of conjecture at this stage. Certainly the British market is not so insular as that of Canada, and the American MNEs, in particular, have tended to treat Europe as a single market area (and in the process have probably done more for European integration than all the politicians combined). Therefore, the 'local market' may not be the British market alone. Aside from this, there would seem to be sufficient commonality with the Canadian situation to use this subsidiary strategies model as at least a basis for discussion.

SUBSIDIARY STRATEGIES AT THE BRITISH AND CONTINENTAL EUROPEAN LEVEL

American MNEs in the immediate post-war period

When turning to discuss the topic of strategy in European specifically, it is necessary to take a time perspective. Thus the role of foreign manufacture is quite different, for example, when a single, newly-formed subsidiary is being considered as compared with a large and long-established affiliate or a multi-plant network. To illustrate the development of strategy, it is useful to consider the sequence commonly followed by an American multinational which established its first European manufacturing plant in the 1950s and 1960s. During this period of most rapid expansion of American multinational activity in Europe, a typical entry strategy would take the form of an initial greenfield manufacturing base in the UK. This was usually a follow up to an earlier export relationship with Britain and perhaps other European countries. The reasons for this huge wave of investment activity were discussed in Chapter 2 — essentially a response to firm-specific and environmental characteristics of the period — with the large market in Britain and cultural similarities favouring the UK as a manufacturing site.

Although most firms began manufacture in the UK, very few remained exclusively in the same site or in the same country. Most expanded their operations into Continental Europe, with Germany, France and Belgium being the most common locations. One sample study indicated that among a group of 1950s and 60s US entrants to Britain, the firms had a further one or two affiliates on the Continent by 1973.[4] In many cases, the location pattern which emerged was a consequence of a market-by-market approach to Europe. So the companies built manufacturing plants to serve their dominant markets or to ensure market access where public sector bodies or governments were important buyers. Inevitably the fact that the EEC and EFTA did not come into being until the late 1950s had a major influence on this entry strategy. And even thereafter the fact that these two economic blocs were separate meant that UK and Continental European subsidiaries supplied different markets. Many of these facilities were set up to parallel existing US operations, gradually transferring technology and products and adopting the US product range — classic *Miniature Replicas*, except insofar as the subsidiaries normally had a market franchise extending beyond the

Figure 5.2: Schematic representation of US multinational activity in Britain — example based on 1950s/60s entrants[a]

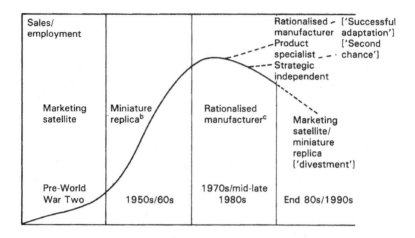

Notes: *a* Excludes companies pursuing exclusively country-centred strategies to supply the UK market alone, because of economic or political factors.

b Manufacture based on products transferred from the USA, but substantial exports, e.g. to EFTA, Commonwealth markets.

c By this time many US MNEs had several manufacturing operations in Europe, all of which had been going through an approximately parallel cycle to that illustrated for the British subsidiary.

UK to include the rest of EFTA and perhaps the Commonwealth.

This phase did not last long, as the schematic representation of strategy shown in Figure 5.2 suggests. The early 1970s saw the enlargement of the European Community, the first oil price shock, growing competition from Japan and indigenous producers in Europe, and the beginnings of the electronics revolution. Any one of these would have been sufficient to produce severe shock waves at both corporate and subsidiary levels: for example, NCR missed the move into electronics in their traditional products of mechanical cash registers and the numbers the company employed in the European region alone fell by almost half between 1970 and 1977.[5]

When the various industrial and environmental characteristics of the 1970s were brought together, the outcome in terms of strategy for many US multinationals entailed greater European integration in

160

manufacturing and marketing systems — the *Rationalised Manufacturer* stage. In the build up stage of foreign direct investment in Europe, a series of Miniature Replica subsidiaries emerged, with the product line manufactured in the various locations being generally similar. 1970s strategic reorganisation involved decisions being taken at corporate level to reallocate products and/or components between plants so as to integrate manufacturing operations horizontally or vertically. One study of 30 American MNEs which broadly fit the classification of 1950s/60s entrants to Europe showed that two thirds had gone at least part of the way in the direction of product or component specialisation by the end of the 1970s decade; in the main such specialisation was related to European rather than to worldwide operations.[6] Associated with these changes in product responsibilities were generally wider market franchises — instead of UK and EFTA, the market area served would encompass the whole of Europe and perhaps other areas such as the Middle East and Africa.

To illustrate the changes in strategy taking place, it is useful to take the case of Hewlett-Packard. Three stages of development could be identified in Europe up to the late 1970s:

Establishment of assembly plants, gradually moving into manufacture, first in Germany and then in the UK (Bedford 1961, before subsequently settling in South Queensferry, Scotland in 1966). The German factory supplied the EEC market and the British factory EFTA and Canada. Basically the same goods were manufactured in the two facilities, being products transferred from the US under licence.

With the entry of Britain into the EEC, a study group was set up to investigate the rationalisation of activities, since for some products the two plants were manufacturing in small, uneconomic volumes. The outcome was a product reallocation programme, with the UK and German plants each having responsibility for the entire European market with a range of non-competitive licensed products. A new factory at Grenoble in France was also included in this reorganisation. Product allocations were based on products closest to the independently developed lines of the plants: in the UK's case the latter was communications test equipment, and the licensed product allocation instruments.

The third stage saw European plants being encouraged to build up their own product lines with local R & D and worldwide marketing responsibilities, in parallel with products designed in

the USA and manufactured in Europe under licence. This stage
of development will be discussed at greater length later.

The other feature of many US multinational operations in Europe
during the 1970s was divestment, consequent on depressed market
conditions and Japanese competition, as well as technological
change which in some sectors sharply reduced factory space
requirements. About two fifths of the sample of 30 firms reported
earlier were involved in plant closures, with in total 20 divestments
being undertaken.

As Figure 5.2 shows, strategic change in the fourth phase of
corporate development has been a good deal less predictable. In
part, strategy has depended upon the success or otherwise of the
changes introduced during the 1970s: where American companies
have still been unable to match the competition from Japan, then
further divestment has resulted. Effective response to product life
cycle maturity has been an associated variable. At the extreme, UK
manufacturing would cease and the market would be supplied from
abroad with only a sales presence remaining (*Marketing Satellite*
business). In part also, divergent US corporate views about the most
efficient role for European subsidiaries have been important: in a
few cases, European subsidiaries have developed from Rationalised
Manufacturers to *Product Specialists* or *Strategic Independents*, as
in the Hewlett-Packard example, where the concept has been one of
fully integrated divisions both in the USA and abroad. Thus the
charter of the Telecommunications Division in the UK is to be 'the
world's leading supplier of dedicated measurement capability
needed to design, manufacture, install, performance-monitor,
troubleshoot and repair telecom equipment and networks'.[7] So the
operation is responsible for design, manufacture and worldwide
marketing of test and measurement products.

In other instances a *Rationalised Manufacturer* role has been
retained for European plants, even if the focus has been away from
regional integration to hemispheric or global integration. In fact it
is not yet clear how the globalisation imperative and global strategies
will be implemented at the level of European subsidiaries. The
concept of manufacturing in Europe for European markets, with
perhaps back up development work, and coordination via a European office or European headquarters is still paramount. Similarly
the impact of technology on strategy is uncertain: although based on
limited evidence, work of the authors suggests that rapid product
change and short production runs means that investment in

computer-integrated manufacturing will not be economic for many companies.

This discussion of 1950s/60s entrants has concentrated on the group of American MNEs where volume, scale and locational economies have favoured integration. Other entrants to Britain have continued with a market-by-market approach (Miniature Replica), and not simply in obvious sectors such as food and drink. For example, Ethicon, the manufacturer of sutures and related products has followed a similar strategy, driven by the labour intensive nature of manufacture and perhaps the demands of the National Health Service, etc.

Newer multinational entrants to Europe

As has been noted at various points, recent inward investment has been rather more varied in terms of home country and method of entry, although the United States is still the major source for new investments. Even among United States investors, however, the UK has not been an obvious first choice as a location in recent years, with export profits tax relief (now withdrawn) in the Republic of Ireland enticing MNEs like bees to a honeypot. Illustrative of companies drawn by Ireland's tax haven attractions was Digital Equipment Corporation, which set up its first European facility in Galway in the early 1970s. Factories followed in Ayr, Scotland (1976), Munich, Germany (1977), Clonmel, Republic of Ireland (1979) and Valbonne, France (1986); these, together with the repair facility in the Netherlands and an R & D Centre in Reading, bear witness to the extraordinarily rapid growth of this electronics producer. Moreover, the small scale VLSI assembly operation at Ayr (a recent addition to this plant's main role as a producer of small and personal computers) is being replaced by a totally new facility being built at South Queensferry on the opposite side of Scotland. The philosophy is one of European manufacture for European markets to ensure customer satisfaction, providing that this is cost competitive. The strategy is thus directed towards European integration, with the two systems plants in Scotland and Ireland being supplied by components manufacturers elsewhere in Europe. Even so, there are elements of a global approach in the statement by the vice president (European manufacturing) that 'We will not duplicate all of the worldwide manufacturing investments. Other Digital manufacturing facilities will continue to supply us with products and materials'.[8] And it is believed that the forthcoming VLSI plant in the UK is to have a worldwide charter. In general, of course, the newer entrants are at an earlier stage in their 'European life cycle' than DEC.

Aside from differences in locational patterns, a second factor which has been considered in European strategy to a greater extent than formerly is that of local sourcing and the balance of payments consequences of investing or not investing. Among the 1950s/60s US entrants, overconcentration of investment in one location (usually the UK) became a millstone which recent investors have sought to avoid. Few companies are perhaps able to emulate IBM which tries to maintain balance of payments equilibrium in its various European operations, but certainly in the electronics industry at least this is seen as a desirable goal.

Generally, the European strategies of US multinationals seem to be following a similar path to previously. As regards another group of recent entrants — the Japanese — inward investment was concentrated in consumer electronics, but is now more widely spread sectorally. Much has been made of the global marketing strategies of the Japanese, with investment in developed countries as a further stage along the road to global manufacturing also. To date in Europe, however, the suggestion is that European facilities will mostly serve European markets. Furthermore, recency of establishment means that networks of manufacturing plants have not emerged within the European continent; among the industrial electronics companies, e.g. NEC Semiconductors and Shin-Etsu such networks may never develop for, as Dunning points out, 'Micro electronic components are high value-added products, incur low transport costs and engage in automated methods of production; and . . . all these factors favour the centralisation of production.'[9] In general the Japanese MNEs are at the Miniature Replica stage in Britain, albeit with market franchises encompassing Europe as a whole.

Generalisations concerning Continental European MNE strategies overall and in Britain are difficult because of the variety — time and method of entry, sector, size and so on. There are cases of investors such as Philips, which in its electronic components' business had built up in Europe a rambling manufacturing network which was largely self-sufficient on a country basis. Strategic development proceeded exactly along the lines of the American model described earlier: in the face of rapid technological change and Japanese penetration of the market, European integration and divestment became the watchwords of the late 1970s and early

164

1980s; the UK subsidiary lost 50 per cent of its jobs, while gaining a European market franchise.[10] In other instances investment has been *ad hoc*, designed to serve the British market, with acquisition entry as a means of easing start up problems and accelerating market penetration. Work by Buckley and others on direct investment in the UK by smaller European firms identified eight takeovers in the 35 production subsidiaries studied, with the size of the UK market and the desire to service customers directly as major investment motivations.[11] Country-centred strategies were thus strongly in evidence, exports representing on average only 10–20 per cent of sales.

PROFILE OF MNE STRATEGIES IN THE 1980s AND IMPLICATIONS FOR THE UK

As at the mid-1980s, therefore, a cross-sectional view of the population of MNE subsidiaries in Britain would reveal a variety of strategy types, relating to period of entry, life cycle phase, sector, nationality and so forth. By no means all of the variation was identified in the previous discussion since, for instance, the chemical and petro-chemical MNEs were not considered. Manufacture and marketing for Europe in Europe is a fairly robust broad generalisation from the evidence available, although companies are at very different stages of implementing this. And there are substantial differences in approach between the integrated manufacturing and marketing MNEs and the country-by-country producers, or, again, the single location manufacturers. Nevertheless, a European focus is generally being maintained, even within a corporate strategy framework which for many MNEs is becoming increasingly global in nature.

Figure 5.3 attempts to identify some of the strategy profiles evident among foreign MNEs in Britain in the mid/late 1980s, including some comments on likely implications for the UK economy. As was indicated previously, Miniature Replica subsidiaries have been subject to a great deal of criticism in Canada but in Britain this category is subject to much more diversity. For one group, Miniature Replica status is simply an early life cycle stage for the firm; and for the other Miniature Replica groups, strategy is likely to be less country-centred than in Canada because of the adjacency of the Continental market.

Different types of Rationalised Manufacturer are in evidence depending on the focus of integration (European, hemispheric, global), market growth and corporate success. Even among the

Figure 5.3: Some examples of corporate strategies in the 1980s and implications for the UK

Type of multinational	Environment and broad strategy thrust	UK subsidiary strategy and characteristics
1. New/recent entrant to Europe, e.g. Japanese companies	Corporate comparative advantage based on technology, marketing skills, etc. Foreign direct investment to gain market access	*Miniature replica* Pilot plant — assembly plant — local manufacture. Increasing number and skill levels of employment; reductions in expatriate staffing Gradual widening of product range based on technology transfers from parent; possibility of low level R & D to facilitate transfers Increasing local content as manufacture commences. Moves into exporting. Limited HQ activity but based at plant
2a. Multi-site manufacturer in Europe (expansion, e.g. DEC, IBM, semiconductor firms)	Integrated operations, at European or global levels European or global production system, possibly utilising developing country locations for assembly Rapid but intermittent growth Expansion, including new sites, in Europe Automation of assembly and reduced activity in the Far East (semiconductor MNEs)	*Rationalised manufacturer* Significant job-expansion potential (constrained by views on optimum plant size) Substantial graduate employment, high proportion of females Little local R & D, but global competition ensures up-to-date technology at plant Substantial exports, imports and intra-firm trade

	European or global marketing and purchasing policies Standardised products	Small number of major manufacturerers, meaning reliance on maintenance of competitive position	Some moves to increase local sourcing (assisted by foreign direct investment by MNEs' suppliers) Sales and other HQ functions close to market centre
2b. Multi-site manufacturer in Europe (autonomy, e.g. Hewlett-Packard, NCR)	Growth environment Innovation environment	Autonomous developments at subsidiary level Export orientation	*Product specialist/strategic independent* Growth dependent upon subsidiary efficiency and success in market place R & D and marketing functions at subsidiary level
2c. Multi-site manufacturer in Europe (rationalisation, e.g. Caterpillar, US auto MNEs)	Increased competition Recession Technological innovation	Manufacturing improvement programmes Integration specialisation	*Rationalised manufacturer* Job effects dependent on subsidiary reorganisation/closure Reduced capacity requirements, rationalisation Changing skill mix of employment New technology based on parent R & D Degree of in-house manufacture reduced Plant specialisation, market area widening Increased intra-firm trade Centralised control systems Subsidiaries as branch plants ('cost centres') Decision-making activity at UK or European HQ level

Figure 5.3: *Contd.*

Type of multinational	Environment and broad strategy thrust		UK subsidiary strategy and characteristics
3a. Host-market oriented manufacturer (food to telecommunications)	Strategy influenced by nature of product (low economies of scale, high transport costs) or type of customer, e.g. host governments	Growth dependent on host economy Decentralised marketing and product development Parent support in innovation and drive to standardise where possible	*Miniature replica* Substantially integrated local manufacture Limited growth and employment decline with technological change Local R & D to meet customer requirements Possibility of changing ownership relationship with parent
3b. Host-market oriented manufacturer (European company, acquisition entrant)	Entry to gain market share and preempt competition		*Miniature replica* Integrated into local market, but low export orientation. Behaviour patterns similar to indigenous enterprises

Source: For examples of types of work on which the above is based, see references in text and especially Dox (1986), Hood and Young (1980, 1982).

expansionist firms (Group 2a), beneficial impact on the British economy, when measured across a range of variables, is by no means certain. Thus trade imbalances may persist unless there is a conscious effort by the companies or pressures from government to source locally. And the same point is true of the Product Specialist/ Strategic Independent subsidiaries. Hewlett-Packard, mentioned on several occasions in this chapter, can be used to illustrate the problem. In evidence to the Select Committee on Overseas Trade, the company stated that they would not balance imports against exports until the early 1990s, adding, however, that, 'Although we recognise that at present we contribute to the United Kingdom balance of payments difficulties, we are perhaps to a greater extent part of the long-term cure of those difficulties'. And, significantly, the company statement went on, 'We recommend that non-United Kingdom owned multinationals be encouraged to invest in the United Kingdom and, further, that a measure of the contribution of a multinational to the national economy be devised to foster a balance between manufacturing, sales and R & D as is practised in other countries such as West Germany'.[12] The problem curiously enough is a function of growth, for with a continuing transfer of licensed products from the United States, it takes time to find local suppliers of components, whereas domestic and export sales may build up quite quickly.

Some qualitative conclusions on UK impact in the areas of employment, balance of trade, technology transfer and entrepreneurial capacity are summarised for the six groups of subsidiaries in Figure 5.4. Several points should be noted on the areas of impact covered. First, the comments relate to the balance of trade rather than the balance of payments; capital inflows to set up the new entrant may be substantial, whereas for the established subsidiaries questions of management and licence fees, intra-group funds transfers and dividend remittances are important. Secondly, technology refers to transfers to the UK rather than diffusion within the UK: it has been suggested previously that the latter is generally quite limited, in part, of course, because of weaknesses in indigenous enterprises in the UK. Third, entrepreneurial capacity is a catch-all to encompass local autonomy, the existence of local R & D, international marketing responsibilities and so on.

This statement of the types of subsidiaries which exist in the UK does not take any position on what would be desirable. Indeed the figure shows the difficulty of judging 'desirability'. But the wide differences in contribution between subsidiary types does show the

Figure 5.4: Subsidiary strategies and UK impact

Type of multinational	Employment	Impact area Balance of trade	Technology transfer	Entrepreneurial capacity
1. Miniature replica — new/ recent entrant to Europe	Growing rapidly	Substantially negative — will be exacerbated if subsidiary acts as marketing agent for parent corporation	Substantial	Very limited
2a Rationalised manufacturer — multi-site manufacturer (expansion)	Growng — albeit in discrete steps dependent upon new product introduction, facility extension etc. High quality employment	Negative or positive	Substantial	Limited
2b. Product specialist/strategic independent — multi-site manufacturer (autonomy)	Growing. High quality employment	Negative or positive	Limited — depending on balance between own and parent induced developments	Significant — local R & D, international marketing responsibilities, etc.

2c. Rationalised manufacturer — multi-site manufacturer (rationalisation)	Declining or stabilised at much lower level than peak	Possibly positive	Mainly process	Limited — but successful rationalisation will mean efficiency of existing operations
3a. Miniature replica — host-market oriented	Stable or declining with technological innovation	Limited exports and imports — possibly positive in net terms	Limited	Some possibility of developments for UK market
3b. Miniature replica — host-market oriented	Stable or declining with technological innovation	Possibly negative — limited exports; imports from parent	Limited	Limited

merit of the strategic analysis approach, particularly when going on to consider the possibilities for policy intervention as in Chapter 6.

CASE EXAMPLES

The qualitative conclusions presented above regarding the link between corporate strategy and MNE impact are examined in more detail in the remaining sections of this chapter, using a wide range of individual company case examples.[13] In addition to the broad corporate strategy dimension, the selection of cases has been designed to illustrate the variation in MNE impact by industry, nationality of ownership, entry methods, and ownership relationships.

Industry variations

The costs and benefits associated with inward direct investment in the UK vary considerably on a sectoral basis, with MNE impact in, say, the textile industry being markedly different from impact in the information processing and microelectronics industries. In assessing such variations, some classification of industries is necessary, with several alternatives being available — more-technology versus less-technology intensive sectors; 'sunrise' versus 'sunset' industries, etc. Alternatively, industries may be classified to illustrate the variation in MNE impact over time in response to changing corporate policies, and it is this classification which is adopted in this section.

Three main industry groupings are examined. First, industries with a long history of inward direct investment but where many of the benefits traditionally associated with such investment have been substantially reduced in recent years as a result of corporate rationalisation and restructuring — mechanical and electrical engineering; vehicles; tyre and rubber products. Second, industries such as information processing and electronics which are continuing to attract a growing volume of inward investment, but where long-run impact depends on future strategy at both corporate and subsidiary levels. These two industry groupings correspond broadly to strategies 2c and 2a/2b respectively in Figure 5.3. Third, a heterogeneous group of industries selected to highlight the sectoral variation in multinational impact — chemicals; metals; food, drink and tobacco; textiles, etc.

Engineering, vehicles, tyres

Inward direct investment in these industries has a long history, dating back in many cases to the pre-World War Two era; and a high proportion of each sector's output and employment is still accounted for by some of the best known foreign-owned companies in the UK (e.g. Caterpillar; Massey-Ferguson; Hoover; Electrolux; Ford; Vauxhall, etc.). Over the last decade or so, most US MNEs in the three industries have substantially rationalised and restructured their global operations in response to the recession, technological change and stronger foreign competition, especially from Japan. The impact of such restructuring at UK subsidiary level has been largely as predicted in Figure 5.3 — large scale job losses, plant closures, and in most cases increased imports of parts and components. The nature and extent of such changes varies considerably by company, with some MNEs completely withdrawing manufacturing from the UK; while in others, rationalisation has been accompanied by significant new investment to improve the efficiency of existing operations.

The effects of corporate rationalisation on UK subsidiaries is illustrated clearly in the agricultural and construction equipment sector where inward direct investment by companies such as Caterpillar, Massey-Ferguson and International Harvester undoubtedly resulted in major benefits to the UK economy in the past. At their peak during the mid-to-late 1970s, these three companies employed more than 30,000 people in the UK with many more indirect jobs being created by the strong local sourcing policies of the companies. The UK's balance of payments benefited greatly from the export propensity of such companies. In 1981, exports from the UK accounted for 86 per cent of Caterpillar's UK production, 77 per cent in the case of Massey-Ferguson, and 74 per cent in the case of International Harvester. Markets supplied from the UK included Europe, Africa, Latin America, the Middle East and North America. The strong local sourcing policies of such companies also contributed positively to the UK's balance of payments. In Massey-Ferguson, for instance, the company's main UK manufacturing plant at Coventry produced axles and gearboxes in addition to the final assembly of agricultural and industrial tractors. Tractor components were manufactured at the Manchester and Baginton locations, while diesel engine supplies were located in the UK through the company's acquisition of Perkins engines and Rolls-Royce engines. At Caterpillar, parts and components for the company's main manufacturing plant at Uddingston, near Glasgow were supplied by its Newcastle plant.

Severe overcapacity in the industry, together with the emergence of companies such as Komatsu, pursuing unashamedly global strategies, has forced each of the three North American MNEs to embark on a belated cost reduction programme simply to ensure survival. Such programmes have involved substantial rationalisation and restructuring of their worldwide operations. Caterpillar, for example, launched a five-year rationalisation programme aimed at reducing 1986 costs to below 20 per cent of their 1981 level in constant dollar terms. Rationalisation involved the standardisation of parts and components, the search for lower cost sourcing locations, and plant closures. Five plants in the USA alone were closed between 1983 and 1984, with worldwide employment in the group falling from 89,266 to 1979 to 55,815 in 1985. The changes at Massey-Ferguson and International Harvester have been even more severe. Total employment at Massey-Ferguson fell from 68,200 in 1977 to less than 25,000 in 1985. Tractor production has ceased in the USA, while the company has been saved from complete bankruptcy on several occasions only by a refinancing package agreed between its major creditors and various host country governments, including the UK. At International Harvester, worldwide employment fell by more than 30,000 people in the two years 1981 to 1983, while in 1985 the company's agricultural equipment business was acquired by Tenneco Inc. The impact of such corporate restructuring on the UK subsidiaries of two of these companies is summarised in Figure 5.5.

Rationalisations and restructuring measures within the mechanical engineering industry have not been confined to the companies discussed above but would include Singer, Cummins Engines, Clark Equipment, Terex, etc., while in electrical/instrument engineering, corporations such as Timex and Hoover have introduced similar rationalisation measures.

The recent experiences of foreign-owned firms operating in the UK vehicle and tyre industries parallels that of the farm and construction equipment manufacturers. As in the previous example, direct investment in these two industries has a long history, with the growth of the vehicle industry encouraging inward investment by component manufacturers including the four large multinational tyre manufacturers, Uniroyal, Goodyear, Firestone and Michelin. The impact of recent corporate rationalisation on the UK subsidiaries of such companies is again summarised in Figure 5.5. Future prospects for the UK subsidiaries of these companies remains highly uncertain, with the possible exception of Ford, as the more extended discussion in Chapter 3 revealed.

Figure 5.5: Restructuring and rationalisation within selected MNE subsidiaries in the UK engineering and vehicle industries

Company	Impact of rationalisation on UK operations
Caterpillar	Closure of Newcastle plant in 1983 with loss of 2,000 jobs; significant job losses at Glasgow plant, with employment falling from 2,300 in 1981 to 1,200 by 1986. £62m investment in Glasgow plant announced in 1986 with new products and component manufacturing to be introduced; but no new investment transpired, and complete closure of Glasgow plant announced in early 1987
Massey-Ferguson	Substantial reduction in UK employment from 21,000 (1978) to 11,867 (1985) following reorganisation of UK operations. New refinancing package negotiated in May 1986 at both corporate and UK subsidiary levels. Future remains uncertain
Vauxhall (GM)	UK subsidiary has become an assembly operation only, with no design or product development, limited export propensity and high volume of imports following centralisation of European operations at Opel (W. Germany). Employment losses in excess of 12,000 since the early 1970s. Additional job losses (1,700) announced at Bedford Commercial Vehicle division in 1986
Ford	Cost cutting measures introduced at all UK plants; closure of foundry works at Dagenham announced in 1984. UK employment fallen by approximately 20,000 since 1979. Turnover, profits and exports, however, remain buoyant and the company has announced several large scale investments in recent years, including £65m at Halewood, £25m at Basildon, and £45m at three UK component plants
Chrysler/Peugeot	Significant rationalisation measures introduced following takeover by Peugeot of France, including closure of Linwood plant. Job losses approaching 20,000 since 1979, while turnover and exports have fallen rapidly. Exports totally dependent on supply of kits to Iran
Firestone	Company has ceased manufacturing in the UK following substantial rationalisation since 1978
Uniroyal	Tyre production has ceased in the UK, although a limited range of rubber and plastic products is still produced
Goodyear	Company continues to manufacture tyres in the UK, although on a much reduced scale following closure of Clydebank plant in 1981. Total UK employment fallen from 11,000 (1977) to less than 3,000
Michelin	Tyre production remains in UK but on a slightly reduced scale; 4,000 redundancies announced in 1982, including closure of Belfast plant. Additional 2,600 redundancies announced in 1985, mainly at Stoke

Source: Derived from company accounts and press reports.

Information processing and electronics

In comparison to the industries discussed previously, the recent behaviour and performance of some multinational firms in the information processing and electronics industry is more encouraging from an impact perspective. The industry has continued to attract a growing volume of inward direct investment, both through the expansion of existing facilities and through new greenfield plants. The propensity of many of these foreign-owned firms in the sector to establish manufacturing plants in the assisted areas was discussed in Chapter 4. In addition to the job-creating effects of such investment, benefits to the economy derive from the high export propensity of most foreign enterprises, high levels of productivity and efficiency, and local R & D and technology transfer (in a few cases); while further benefits may derive from the 'innovative' personnel and industrial relations practices adopted.

The case of IBM illustrates clearly the potential benefits to the economy from inward direct investment in the industry. The company currently employs almost 20,000 people at 40 different UK locations, including two manufacturing plants at Greenock, Scotland and Havant, Southampton. As Table 5.1 shows, the UK subsidiary of IBM expanded rapidly during most of the 1970s and early 1980s. The company is one of the UK's leading exporters and employment in the company has increased by approximately 7,000 since 1973. But even 'Big Blue' is not immune from competition and strategic miscalculations, and pre-tax profits fell by 19 per cent in the year 1986 as the company lost market share to low cost clones like Amstrad's PC 1512. The success of the IBM manufacturing operation in the UK was, however, reflected in the announcement in April 1987 that the IBM System 2 personal computer, the company's response to the clones, was to be assembled at Greenock for European, Middle East and African markets.[14]

Where IBM is rather unusual is in the fact that the UK subsidiary has a major role in innovation, with the Hursley development laboratory being responsible for the research and development of display equipment, software and low cost disk storage equipment. The Hursley facility is the largest IBM development laboratory outside the USA. There is in addition a scientific centre located at Peterlee which undertakes research into computer software and applications, especially for medical and social uses. The location of a substantial volume of R & D activity in the UK has resulted in the creation of additional job opportunities for highly skilled personnel.

Table 5.1: Sales, profits, exports and employment at IBM UK 1973–86

	Turnover (£m)	Pre-tax profits (£m)	Exports from UK (£m)	Employment in UK
1973	278	54	130	12,428
1974	345	60	161	13,206
1975	396	72	178	13.440
1976	494	87	239	13,391
1977	579	110	264	13,814
1978	759	147	334	14,905
1979	880	162	431	15,498
1980	954	152	452	15,590
1981	1,002	161	420	15,362
1982	1,240	225	523	15,916
1983	1,677	255	745	16,511
1984	2,349	325	1,175	17,672
1985	3,043	521	1,582	19,256
1986	3,080	421	1,430	n.a.

Source: Extel Statistical Service and company accounts.

Whether or not there is much technological benefit for the UK economy is more debatable, since the R & D lab is mainly operating in support of the parent rather than specifically IBM UK — a 'corporate technology unit' in the terminology of Ronstadt.[15] Approximately one third of the company's UK employees are university graduates or equivalent. IBM has pioneered a number of novel personnel and industrial relations practices in the UK, including a single-status workforce; an 'open door' policy which encourages the maximum communication between all employees regardless of status; and the provision of wage levels and employee fringe benefits which are thought to be considerably in excess of the industry average. The non-recognition of trade unions is another part of this human resource management package.[16]

Other existing foreign-owned computer companies in the UK have been growing rapidly, with expansionary investments being announced by firms such as Digital Equipment (DEC); and new entrants are continuing, one of the most recent being the high flying Compaq corporation. In some cases plans have been postponed because of the world recession in the industry, the semiconductor sector being particularly affected, and several manufacturers have introduced short-time working, with two plants (General Instruments and Burroughs) being closed in 1986 and 1987. Such

177

cutbacks, however, appear to be a short term response to demand pressure, with the overall foreign capital stake in the industry continuing to expand. Nevertheless, instability is likely to be a feature of the industry for the future because of intense competition, demand volatility, and the fairly short life cycle of products, more of which are becoming of a fashion nature.

Several additional sources of concern remain regarding the activities of firms in the information processing and semiconductor industries. The high export propensity of the foreign-owned sector is partly counterbalanced by the high import propensity of certain firms as reported earlier. A related issue is the limited use of local suppliers, although previous evidence has shown that this is due as much to the inadequacies of local component manufacturers as to multinational sourcing policy. Certain employment practices of foreign-owned firms in the industry have been criticised, including anti-unionism, the sex and skill composition of employment and the employment of a 'core' and 'periphery' workforce. In the longer term, the balance of costs and benefits associated with foreign investment in the industry will depend on the extent to which UK subsidiaries shift from being Rationalised Manufacturers towards Product Specialists or Strategic Independents.

Other manufacturing industries

Not surprisingly, the recent behaviour and performance of MNE subsidiaries (and their impact on the economy) in other manufacturing sectors varies enormously.

In chemicals, several foreign-owned companies have rationalised their UK operations in response to the recession in the industry (e.g. Du Pont; Monsanto). Overall, however, the multinational sector of the chemical industry has shown a considerable degree of stability in recent years with few examples of large scale redundancies or plant closures. Other aspects of the operations of MNE chemical subsidiaries (e.g. export propensity, local R & D, etc.) vary widely on an individual company basis. In general, the export propensity of the sector is substantially lower than in the industries discussed above. Important exceptions to this generalisation, include companies such as Monsanto, Esso Chemicals, Du Pont, Merck Sharp and Dohm, Ciba-Geigy, May and Baker, and Akzo, which regularly export between 30 and 40 per cent of UK output. Such differences are partly related to nationality of ownership, with US chemical subsidiaries being more export oriented than the subsidiaries of European MNEs (see later). R & D within the majority of foreign-owned chemical companies is highly centralised at corporate level, thus providing little direct benefit to the UK in this respect. Moreover, several of the leading pharmaceutical companies in the industry have claimed that the UK has become less attractive as an R & D location with the introduction of the NHS restricted list.

As Chapter 3 suggested, subsidiary level R & D can be of great significance and in pharmaceuticals the benefits to the UK economy can be illustrated clearly in the case of SKF. This Swedish subsidiary's Research Centre at Welwyn Garden City was responsible for the development of 'Tagamet' — a revolutionary new drug used in the treatment of peptic ulcers. The new drug, which took more than ten years to develop at a cost of £20 million, completely changed the. fortunes of both the parent company and the UK subsidiary. Between 1974 and 1978 worldwide sales and assets of the parent company doubled, while profits trebled. The effects on the UK subsidiary were even more profound. Not only did the UK subsidiary develop the drug, it also manufactured it for domestic and worldwide markets. Total UK turnover doubled from £24 million in 1976 to almost £60 million in 1978. Exports and profits more than trebled from £7 million and £3 million respectively in 1976, to £21 million for both in 1978. There was also an increase of 30 per cent in the number of employees in the UK (from 1,000 in 1976 to 1,200 in 1981) while a new R & D laboratory has been established with the aim of developing a replacement for Tagamet, once the patent expires, in order to secure the company's market position.

MNE subsidiaries in the food, drink and tobacco industry have shown a considerable degree of stability of output and employment in recent years. In 'other manufacturing' industries, by contrast, the recent performance of overseas-owned firms has been less satisfactory, with substantial job losses and plant closures resulting from corporate rationalisation and restructuring. Examples would include Gillette, Alcoa, Englehard, and Alcan in metal manufacturing, while in textiles, plant closures have occurred at Levi-Strauss, Blue Bell, and British Enkalon as well as rationalisation of UK fibre production by Du Pont and Monsanto.

Nationality of ownership

The nationality of ownership dimension of MNE impact has attracted a considerable amount of attention in the UK in recent years. In particular, the impact of Japanese direct investment has been debated extensively following the announcement of large investments by Nissan and Komatsu, amongst others, with most attention focusing on the impact of such investments on existing firms in the industry (Austin Rover, JCB, Caterpillar, etc.), on local content, and the distinctive personnel management approach of the Japanese (single union representation, no-strike deals, etc.). Although the concern with Japanese investment is understandable, it is also important from a promotional perspective to distinguish between the net benefits and costs associated with US and European direct investment.

Attempts to identify the precise effects of country of origin on MNE impact are complicated by the fact that certain other operating characteristics of MNE subsidiaries in the UK are linked to nationality of ownership (e.g. length of establishment, entry methods, subsidiary size, sectoral distribution). Despite such complications, it is still possible to identify a number of important differences in the behaviour and performance of MNE subsidiaries which are due specifically to nationality of ownership differences. The following paragraphs examine such differences in relation to US and European MNEs, while the case of Japanese direct investment is considered later.

US/European multinationals

A recent survey of 140 MNE subsidiaries in the UK highlighted a number of important differences between US and European-owned plants, with significant impact implications.[17] One of the most important differences was the restricted product and market roles of the latter, with a much higher proportion of European-owned plants supplying mainly the UK market. Overall, nearly 70 per cent of the output of European-owned subsidiaries was destined for the UK market, compared with less than 50 per cent for US-owned plants.

Other important differences between the two groups emerged from the host-country–oriented strategies of European-owned plants. Thus, European subsidiaries employed less advanced product and process technologies than their US counterparts. This was explained in terms of the narrower range of markets supplied by the former, such that competition was less severe, thereby reducing the necessity for the transfer of advanced technology from the parent company. The lower plant status assigned to European-owned subsidiaries was supported by other evidence in the study. Subsidiary level R & D activity was less in evidence in the European sample, and the proportion of managerial/professional employees to total employment was much smaller. Taken together with other factors such as industry mix and entry methods, the contribution of European MNEs to the UK economy would seem to be less obviously positive than in the case of American companies, providing always that the latter can survive at all in the face of the Japanese competitive onslaught and their slippage from the commanding technological heights.

The chemical industry can be used to illustrate many of the differences in subsidiary strategy between US and European MNEs in the UK. Most US-owned subsidiaries in the industry are highly export-oriented, with exports regularly accounting for approximately 50 per cent of output. As noted earlier, several European subsidiaries are also highly export-oriented; but for the most part, the UK operation has been established to supply the UK market, with exports representing an insignificant proportion of UK output. Hoechst UK Ltd is the largest foreign-owned firm operating in the industry, with 1985 sales of £584 million. Exports from the UK subsidiary (which is wholly-owned by Hoechst A.G. of West Germany) account for less than five per cent of total UK output. Other European-owned chemical companies with an extremely low export propensity (zero-to-five per cent of sales) include BASF, Siemens, Bayer, UKF and AGFA. Indeed, some of these subsidiaries have been established largely as marketing or distribution centres to sell the parent company's products in the UK, with actual production or manufacturing activity remaining at a low level (i.e. Marketing Satellite subsidiaries). To illustrate the point, Bayer UK Ltd and AGFA-GEVAERT Ltd are both subsidiaries of the West German-owned Bayer A.G., with combined UK sales in 1983 exceeding £300 million, and UK employment standing at approximately 2,000 employees. Neither company undertakes manufacturing or exporting from the UK. AGFA markets and sells sensitised materials and related equipment produced at other locations in Europe, while Bayer UK Ltd markets and sells the parent corporation's chemical products. A similar strategy has been adopted by BASF A.G. of West Germany, whose UK subsidiary BASF UK Ltd, imports and distributes chemical products manufactured in Europe. Total sales of BASF UK Ltd in 1985 were in excess of £170 million.

A somewhat similar situation exists in the electrical engineering industry where several European-owned companies such as Olivetti and AEG-Telefunken have established UK subsidiaries to market and distribute the parent corporation's products. This contrasts with the situation for most American MNEs in the industry which have established strong manufacturing and export bases in the UK.

Japanese multinationals

Although there are more than 400 Japanese companies operating in the UK, the volume of Japanese direct investment in UK manufacturing industry remains limited. By mid-1983, there were only 26 Japanese subsidiaries in the manufacturing sector, employing fewer than 6,000 workers. Since then the Japanese manufacturing presence has increased significantly, with the announcement of large, greenfield investments by Nissan (vehicles), NEC (semiconductors), Shin-etsu Handotai (silicon wafers), Honda (vehicles), Ricoh (photocopiers), Sharp (VCRs), and Komatsu (construction equipment); together with Sumitomo's acquisition of Dunlop's tyre interests, and expansions of existing facilities by Sony, Matsushita and Toshiba, amongst others.

Japanese manufacturing plants in the UK exhibit a number of distinctive characteristics in comparison with their US and European counterparts. Average plant size is extremely small, with 16 of the 26 Japanese manufacturing subsidiaries in 1983 employing fewer than 100 workers. At the other extreme, only Sony and Hitachi employed more than 1,000 employees. Japanese plants are of more recent origin than their US and European counterparts, with most being established in the late 1970s or early 1980s. And Japanese investment is significantly more concentrated by sector, with over 70 per cent of all employment in Japanese subsidiaries being accounted for by consumer electronics — although sectoral concentration is being reduced, given the recent truck and automotive investments. In terms of ownership patterns, on the other hand, Japanese manufacturing investment in the UK differs little from US and European investment, since most plants are wholly-owned. This contrasts with the situation for all Japanese foreign direct investment worldwide, of which only ten per cent is in wholly-owned subsidiaries.

As regards the impact of Japanese direct investment on the UK, it is perhaps too early to reach definite conclusions, given the recent entry of most firms. In the longer term, much will depend on corporate policy regarding expansion, the product and market roles assigned to UK subsidiaries, and firms' responses to governmental pressures to increase local content. However, two recent studies do allow some interim conclusions to be derived. Brech and Sharp

182

studied the impact of Japanese manufacturing subsidiaries in the UK consumer electronics industry, with both positive and negative influences being postulated.[18] On the negative side, the study concluded that competition from Japanese affiliates in the UK had resulted in reduced sales, plant closures and employment losses in the indigenous sector. Production capacity in the indigenous colour TV industry, for example, declined from 2.2 million units in 1973 to 1.5 million in 1982. Despite this, Japanese investment was seen as perpetuating a fragmented industrial structure which resulted in the establishment of too many plants of sub-optimum scale and considerable excess capacity. As at the mid 1980s there were 13 colour TV producers in the UK serving a domestic and export market of 3.25 million sets. Optimum plant size in the industry, on the other hand, has been estimated at approximately 500,000 sets per annum. Japanese firms were criticised, in addition, for their high imports of component materials.

On a more positive note, the study identified several major advantages arising from Japanese involvement in the industry. The most important of these included the improvement of industrial competitiveness arising from the Japanese emphasis on quality control, the introduction of advanced production techniques, and the superior organisational and industrial relations practices of the Japanese. Such practices were seen as improving the competitiveness of those indigenous firms remaining in the industry through the demonstration effect; while the Japanese emphasis on reliability was regarded as improving the performance of local component manufacturers supplying the Japanese subsidiaries. The second study, by Dunning, argued that such positive effects strongly supported 'the continuation of a liberal policy towards Japanese participation in UK industry'.[19]

The long-term intentions of Japanese firms operating in the UK have been an issue of considerable debate in recent years. It has been argued that most Japanese investment in the UK has occurred in order to defuse political opposition with respect to Japanese imports (e.g. Nissan) and that such investment could easily be withdrawn if import restrictions were abolished. The optimistic view, on the other hand, points to the potential long-run benefits to the UK from the natural evolution of Japanese subsidiaries from marketing/distribution subsidiaries through local assembly operations towards fully-fledged manufacturing operations with a widened product range and the establishment of local design and development capabilities. In addition, the optimistic view stresses the possibility of initial

investments resulting in further investments by component manufacturers. Developments during the late 1970s and early 1980s lend
some support to this viewpoint, with several Japanese companies,
including Sony and Matsushita, expanding their UK operations,
mainly by widening their product ranges. Again recent major investment projects by NEC and Shin-Etsu Handotai have included the
establishment of local R & D centres. Dunning has argued that the
evolution of Japanese subsidiaries in the UK will be accompanied by
greater local content, thereby creating opportunities for UK
suppliers.[20] And a similar conclusion was reached by Turner in his
work on industrial collaboration with Japan, the view being that
Japanese companies will deepen their overseas investments in the
process of becoming fully-fledged multinationals.[21]

Entry methods

The impact of inward direct investment will vary with the entry
methods used by foreign MNEs, the general consensus being that
greenfield establishments are preferable to entry through the acquisition of UK enterprises. Greenfield entry, it is argued, results in a
greater transfer of technology and capital, increased exports and
employment, and improved competitiveness. The impact of foreign
acquisition, on the other hand, is more problematic, with potentially
negative effects arising from rationalisation, plant closures, and the
possible transfer or closure of indigenous R & D units. Acquisitions
may result in a less competitive market structure through increasing
the market power of the acquiring firm. There may be some positive
effects deriving from acquisition including technology transfer
through access to the acquiring firm's R & D and the stimulus
provided to exports through the parent's international marketing
network. In some cases, the alternative to acquisition may be
complete closure and this substantial opportunity cost must be taken
into account when considering foreign takeovers in the UK.

The relative benefits and costs associated with foreign acquisitions have attracted a considerable amount of public attention in the
UK in the recent past, especially in the vehicle industry where an
indigenous presence is still regarded, rightly or wrongly, as an
indicator of industrial virility. In each case, the issue of national
sovereignty was high on the agenda in addition to the economic costs
and benefits of the proposed acquisitions. The controversy surrounding these cases must be seen in the context of the wider debate

regarding the recent takeover boom in the UK which has involved mainly domestic companies rather than foreign MNEs. It is also worth noting that the issue of foreign acquisitions is a double-edged sword, with an extremely large number of British companies being involved in large scale acquisitions in the US in recent years.[22]

Recent empirical work supports the view that foreign acquisitions in the UK contribute less to the economy than the establishment of greenfield plants. The DTI study quoted earlier arrived at two main conclusions regarding the acquisition mode of entry.[23] Firstly, few substantial benefits accrued to the UK company in the post-acquisition period. Secondly, the performance of acquired subsidiaries was significantly poorer than their greenfield counter-parts across a range of measures including sales growth, export propensity, employment and technology employed. Overall, the survey concluded that many of the proposed advantages of acquisitions were illusory.

The two case studies presented below illustrate many of the issues surrounding the impact of foreign acquisitions. In both cases, the long-run benefits of the acquisition were significantly less than suggested at the acquisition date.

Kelvinator Ltd

In 1980, this company was purchased by the Italian domestic appliance manufacturer, Industrie Candy S.p.a., a fairly small multinational with sales of only £100 million and a worldwide workforce of fewer than 4,000. The UK company, which was previously owned by White Consolidated Industries of the USA, manufactured a range of up market refrigerators, domestic freezers and cabinets for the ice cream industry, at its plant in Bromborough, near Liverpool. Under its previous US owners, Kelvinator had experienced several lean years during the latter half of the 1970s. Between 1978 and 1980 sales fell from £11.7 million to £5.5 million as a result of high imports. Total losses over the same period amounted to more than £1 million. The takeover by Candy in 1980 was aimed at halting the decline of the UK subsidiary (which was renamed Kelco Ltd after the takeover). In particular, the UK opera-tion was to benefit in three major ways from the takeover. First, Candy was to invest in new plant and machinery to upgrade the almost obsolete machinery at the Bromborough plant. Second, exports from the UK subsidiary were to be increased by utilising the new parent company's European distribution network. Finally, new products bearing the Candy name, were to be manufactured in the UK.

The recent performance of Kelco raises doubts regarding the realisation of these intended benefits. Turnover has increased significantly (£17 million in 1984) and the operation made a small profit in 1983 and 1984 (approximately £500,000). Employment increased from 262 in 1981 to 386 in 1984. What is particularly worrying from an impact perspective is the export performance of the plant. Prior to the acquisition, the plant had exported almost 40 per cent of its output. By 1982, exports had fallen to less than five per cent of output and by 1984 to less than one per cent. This would be of little concern if due to a lack of competitiveness which would improve over time, consequent on the other actions taken by the parent company. What may be more serious is that the reduction in exports may be the result of a conscious decision by Candy to confine the UK plant to producing for the domestic market only, with the European market being supplied from its Italian operations. A significant part of the apparent improvement in UK subsidiary turnover may also be due to the resale of machines imported from Italy, rather than an increase in UK production levels.

Terex and Hymac

The acquisition of Terex Ltd and Hymac Ltd by IBH Holdings A.G. of West Germany further illustrates the difficulties of realising the intended benefits of foreign acquisitions in mature industries. IBH Holdings was established as recently as 1975 when Horst-Dieter Esch, a West German entrepreneur, acquired control of three privately owned German construction equipment enterprises — Zettlemeyer, Hamm and Duomat. The ultimate objective in acquiring these companies was to establish a strong European presence in the construction equipment industry to compete with the large US and Japanese MNEs, such as Caterpillar and Komatsu, which dominate the industry. To achieve this objective, IBH set out on a course of rapid expansion through the acquisition of existing construction equipment companies including three French-based concerns — Derruppe, Maco-Meudon, and Manubat-Gingon; in the UK, Hymac, Terex, and Blau Knox; and the Terex subsidiary of General Motors in the USA. The company also made an unsuccessful bid to acquire control of the construction equipment part of International Harvester's operations. By 1982, IBH had become the world's third largest manufacturer of construction equipment with an annual sales volume of approximately DM 2.5 billion.

The acquisition of Hymac and Terex in the UK had two major advantages for IBH. Firstly, it expanded the parent corporation's product range. Hymac was a market leader in the manufacture of hydraulic excavator equipment, while Terex was a major manufacturer of dump trucks, wheeled loaders, scrapers and dozers. Secondly, both Hymac and Terex had well established distribution networks which could be used to sell other IBH products in both the UK and abroad. It was suggested at the time that the acquisitions would result in major benefits for both UK companies by shifting some European production to the UK and by providing a Continental European outlet for the products of both Hymac and Terex.

As in the case of Kelco, these benefits largely failed to materialise, with the acquisitions being followed by substantial job losses and rationalisation in both companies. In 1983, IBH itself was forced into a major restructuring plan, following the collapse of its major creditor, the SMH Bank of West Germany. The company announced the closure of its Hymac plant in South Wales and the possible closure of the Terex plant in Scotland unless a buyer could be found. At the time of writing, the future positions of the two UK companies remained uncertain. Terex was re-acquired by its former parent company — General Motors — but there were prospects of a sell off to Northwest Engineering of the USA during 1987, with the transfer of both manufacturing and engineering from America. Hymac was acquired by NEI and resold to the BM Group in 1986.

CONCLUDING REMARKS

The purpose of this chapter was to review the role of multinational operations in Britain within a corporate strategy framework. From a time perspective the strategies of American corporations, and thus the roles of their UK subsidiaries, have shown radical change; and some of the turbulence which was highlighted in Chapter 4 in particular can be seen as the outcome of this fundamental strategic change. There is little question that rationalisation and divestment among American MNEs remains a prominent cause for concern at the UK level: US management and technology is no longer unchallenged and therefore UK subsidiaries cannot rely on a continuing flow of innovations from America to support their profitability and growth. Furthermore, environmental problems which caused major upheavals from the middle 1970s have continued, albeit in different form, through the 1980s. For example, the oil price slump of 1986 led to divestment among engineering suppliers to the North Sea oil industry, and among heavy equipment manufacturers as developing countries' oil revenues plummeted and development plans were shelved. And it is not only US manufacturing firms which have been beset by internal weaknesses and environmental threats at the UK level — famous names in services such as Kentucky Fried Chicken have disappeared too. Environmentally at least the future seems likely to see more of the same, for anxieties about cutting the trade imbalance will see continuing pressures for a dollar depreciation and thus reducing incentive for foreign direct investment. So more American companies are likely to fall into the 'divestment' category in Figure 5.2.

The representation of US multinational activity in Britain shown in Figure 5.2 is interesting in another respect in that it illustrates a subsidiary life cycle spanning 40 years or more. The discussion in earlier chapters, confirmed again here, is that more recent phases of inward investment will be subject to greater life cycle volatility and probably shorter life spans.

The Japanese companies are at a much earlier — but growing — stage of their strategic development in Europe. Dunning, indeed, has compared and contrasted the role of US manufacturing affiliates in the UK in the early 1950s, with that of their Japanese counterparts in the early 1980s.[24] It was concluded that while both were import substituting, rather than rationalised in character, the Japanese investments are part of a consciously planned regional strategy. If this is so then the strategy upheavals which occurred in many American companies to take them from the country-by-country approach of the 1950s and 1960s to the European approaches of the 1970s will not be necessary in Japanese firms. But this is for the future. What is also interesting is Dunning's comment concerning the nature of the firm-specific advantages possessed by the two groups: 'While US MNEs in the 50s were essentially transferring innovatory advantages to their UK affiliates, their Japanese counterparts in the 80s were exporting the advantages of an imitator, whose competitive edge rested on the introduction of differentiated products . . . and greater productive efficiency. It is these which Japanese companies have transmitted so effectively to the UK, in a way which has not only taken away markets from indigenous companies but from some of the earlier innovating US subsidiaries as well.'

This chapter has shown that subsidiary roles in Britain may vary considerably and that equally the impact on the UK economy can be very different. There is as yet no evidence available on the proportion of MNE subsidiaries in Britain within the six categories specified in Figures 5.3 and 5.4, but the suggestion must be that Miniature Replicas and Rationalised Manufacturers are predominant. This links back to the discussion on the subject of the weaknesses of 'branch plants' in Chapter 4. Before concluding this chapter, it will be useful to draw again on the Canadian literature relating to subsidiary roles, where the problem of Miniature Replicas and Rationalised Manufacturers has sparked off a lengthy debate on the desirability of attracting Strategic Independent affiliates with World Product Mandates. The arguments in favour of World Product Mandates for Canadian subsidiaries may be summarised as follows:

> There are dangers in relying on a continuing flow of new products and processes from US parent MNEs (as noted above)
> The granting of a World Product Mandate (WPM) means that subsidiary autonomy is enhanced through greater control over product design and development; and there are other benefits, both direct and indirect, associated with subsidiary level R & D.
> The subsidiary will become a division or strategic business unit (SBU) within the MNE
> There is likely to be higher value added in production activities, as well as greater subcontracting and productivity spillover
> The quality of management is higher and more internationally oriented; international marketing skills are required even if the subsidiary is granted access to the parent's global marketing and distribution network.[25]

The various authors have also drawn attention to possible problems associated with WPMs. The first three points listed below represent subsidiary-level difficulties and the remainder possible parent-level objections to WPMs:

> For the subsidiary, a substantial change in management culture and expertise will be necessary to enable the firm to develop from being an implementer to an innovator, and to progress from routine to entrepreneurial decision making
> In particular the development of international marketing skills will take time to achieve, meaning a slower build up of exports than under rationalisation; and the subsidiary will be subject to higher risks from exposure to overseas market changes
> To remain internationally competitive the mandated product and technology must be subject to development and innovation

The adjustment costs for the MNE parent in implementing WPMs may be very high

The MNE parent must surrender some control over R & D and proprietary know-how to the subsidiary, raising internal organisational costs and the danger of dissipation of technological advantages

Global competitiveness may require centralised planning and operations to exploit economies of scale or economies of scope; and facilitate rapid and efficient response to changes in environmental and internal factors.

Reflecting the previous two points, the number of potential WPMs may be quite limited. They may be niche businesses, where market size is small and the activity is outside the mainstream business of the MNE; as well as facing threats from the focused strategies of larger competitors.

On balance the arguments lie in favour of Strategic Independent subsidiaries and WPMs in Canada, and the same conclusion would tentatively be drawn from the perspective of the UK economy. Autonomy does matter.[26] It must be admitted, however, that detailed investigation of WPMs in a UK context is necessary, not least because the principal problem lies in persuading or cajoling the parent MNE to go down this route, in turn requiring policy changes. There is beginning to be evidence of the parent multinationals themselves seeing the benefits in permitting national subsidiaries to achieve global scale by making them the company's world source. Such decentralisation, however, goes hand in hand with close control and coordination to ensure that dispersed production facilities, R & D labs and marketing facilities work together. If this can be achieved it eliminates a number of the problems with WPMs cited above. MNEs such as NEC and Philips are quoted as examples of firms which have made considerable strides in these directions, but it is doubtful whether many others exist.[27]

NOTES

1. White, R.E. and Poynter, T.A. (1984), 'Strategies for foreign-owned subsidiaries in Canada', *Business Quarterly*, summer; see also, Etemad, H. and Dulude, L.S. (eds) (1986), *Managing the multinational subsidiary*, Croom Helm, London

2. Science Council of Canada (1980), *Multinationals and industrial strategy: the role of world product mandates*, Ottowa, September

3. Rugman, A.M. and Bennett, J. (1982), 'Technology transfer and world product mandating in Canada', *Columbia Journal of World Business*, 17(4), pp. 58–62.

4. Young, S. and Hood, N. (1976), 'The geographical expansion of US firms in Western Europe: some survey evidence', *Journal of Common Market Studies*, 14(3), pp. 223–39

5. Hood, N. and Young, S. (1982), *Multinationals in retreat: the Scottish experience*, Edinburgh University Press

6. Young, S. and Hood, N. (1980), 'The strategies of US multinationals in Europe: a host country perspective', *Multinational Business*, 2; see also Doz, Y. (1986), *Strategic management in multinational companies*, Pergamon Press, Oxford

7. The quotation is from a company brochure of Hewlett-Packard Ltd

8. Digital Equipment Corporation (1985), 'The strategic role of European manufacturing', *DECWORLD*, 9(1), February

9. Dunning, J.H. (1986), *Japanese participation in British industry*, Croom Helm, London, p. 45

10. Hood, N. and Young, S. (1983), *Multinational investment strategies in the British Isles: a study of MNEs in the assisted areas and in the Republic of Ireland*, HMSO, London, pp. 297–300

11. Buckley, P.J., Berkova, Z. and Newbould, G.D. (1983), *Direct investment in the United Kingdom by smaller European firms*, Macmillan, London

12. House of Lords (1985), *Report from the Select Committee on Overseas Trade*, 238-I, Session 1984–5, HMSO, London, 30 July, p. 484.

13. The case examples quoted have been extracted from company accounts, the Extel Statistical Service and Press reports

14. The decision to locate production of the first generation PC at Greenock is analysed in detail in Young, S., Hood, N. and Hamill, J. (1985), *Decision-making in foreign-owned multinational subsidiaries in the United Kingdom*, ILO working paper 35, International Labour Office, Geneva.

15. Ronstadt, R. (1977), *Research and development abroad by US multinationals*, Praeger, New York

16. IBM's personnel approach is discussed in detail in Incomes Data Services (1980), 'Staff status', *IDS study 227*, October; and Incomes Data Services (1984), 'Employee communications', *IDS study 318*, July

17. Hood and Young, *Multinational investment strategies*, Part 4, Chapter 1

18. Brech, M. and Sharp, M. (1984), *Inward investment: policy options for the United Kingdom*, Chatham House papers 21, Routledge and Kegan Paul, London

19. Dunning, J.H. (1986), *Japanese participation*, Croom Helm, London, p. 193

20. Ibid., p. 104

21. Turner, L. (1987), *Industrial collaboration with Japan*, Chatham House papers 34, Routledge and Kegan Paul, London

22. See *Management Today* (1981), 'Britain's American invasion', February; and (1986), 'Britain's sundown billions', April

191

23. Hood and Young, *Multinational investment strategies*, Part 4, Chapter 2

24. Dunning, J.H. (1985), *US and Japanese manufacturing affiliates in the UK: some similarities and contrasts*, University of Reading discussion papers in international investment and business studies, 90, October

25. Etemad and Dulude, *Managing the multinational subsidiary*

26. This is the answer to the question posed in the concluding section of Chapter 3, 'Does the loss of autonomy at subsidiary level in the UK matter?'

27. Bartlett, C.A. (1987), 'Building and managing the transnational: the new organisational challenge', in Porter, M.E. (ed.), *Competition in global industries*, Harvard Business School Press, Boston, Massachusetts

6

The UK Policy Response

INTRODUCTORY ISSUES

Several of the previous chapters, especially Chapters 3, 4 and 5, have touched on some aspects of policy, whether in the corporate, regional or technological context. While this chapter pulls these various threads together by way of introduction, it is primarily concerned with an overview of UK government policy towards the foreign-owned sector over the past decade or so. It identifies the principal foundations upon which it has been built and the dominant influences which have contributed to the UK policy stance. This stance has evolved over an extended period and the basis for changes within it are considered. Given the diffuse nature of the policy and the widespread data problems identified in earlier chapters, any evaluation of effectiveness is difficult. Whenever possible this is, however, attempted. While the chapter contains a number of pointers on the future directions which UK policy might take, these matters are primarily dealt with in the final chapter.

Corporate and governmental perspectives

Throughout this book, the twin threads of MNE corporate strategies and governmental policy dimensions have been present. Indeed the interface between the two has been either explicit or implicit at several points, starting from Chapter 1. In that chapter the scene was set in a wide-ranging discussion of the features of international competitiveness, especially of globalisation and technological change, as these impacted on MNEs. Many of the suggested outcomes for the UK economy have been examined in subsequent chapters, although heavily conditioned by the availability of research and statistical data on the issues for the future. Thus, Chapter 2 interpreted these trends in the global environment for the UK economy and particularly for the investment attraction process, while at the same time taking into account the corporate impact. Chapters 3 and 4 respectively considered overall UK economic and regional impact and were primarily concerned with outcomes which would in turn become inputs for policy formulation. In both these chapters the important dimension of the interaction of the foreign-owned sector and indigenous business emerges. This particular 'impact zone' is one where governmental and corporate perspectives are not readily reconciled, yet it is vital in the determination of a positive or negative effect on UK competitiveness.

As subsequent paragraphs will show, it has not exerted a pervasive influence on UK policy and even if the improvement of UK competitiveness had been the primary objective of having foreign direct investment in the UK, the interactions in this zone could not be said to give unequivocal signals for policy. So there may be sound long term economic reasons for encouraging foreign investment in an industrial sector where domestic performance has been laggard, even if short term market share is lost and the level of initial value added is poor due to a weak industrial infrastructure. Equally, by way of an import substitution strategy, a strong foreign-owned company might be induced into the UK market where existing UK companies have, by their performance, almost forfeited the right to be sheltered in any way. Having observed the difficulties, however, there was a clear suggestion in Chapter 1 that there were new items appearing on the policy agenda, one of which was precisely if and how MNEs could play a greater role in enhancing UK competitiveness. This raises key questions such as the relationship between MNE integration or globalisation strategies and the nature of activities in host economies; and the mechanisms by which the desirable operating characteristics of foreign firms have been transferred to domestic enterprises — or indeed whether some of these are at all transferable.

Interesting and important as these questions are for the construction of policy and the reconciliation of the twin perspectives of MNEs and governments, it is necessary to start at a more mundane level by setting the UK policy context and acknowledging the constraints within which it has evolved. The more open ended questions associated with the future policy arena are, therefore, postponed to Chapter 7.

The conclusions drawn from the evaluations of the earlier chapters are in themselves important inputs into any policy review. From the evidence of Chapter 2 there would be an expectation of more effective attraction policies and constant organisational review, in the light of the more competitive environment which has emerged for direct investment. Equally, policy might be expected to be adjusting to reflect the changing mix of trading method and country balance, given a continuation of UK intentions to remain a strong force in this business. Both Chapters 3 and 4 conclude that there is much more scope for innovation in the search for higher net benefits to the local and national economy, although the weakness of local infrastructure remains an inhibiting factor at assisted area level. We have already referred to the 'impact zone', and it is reasonable to assume that this might be a focus for some policy attention, if some of the more exalted aims accruing from a healthy foreign-owned sector are to be realised. The general drift of these findings is perhaps best characterised as reflecting an interest in nudging direct investment policies away from the purely environmental level to that closer to the sectoral or regional level. Put in another way, it implies a closer link between industrial policy and policy towards the foreign sector, where the latter is regarded as but one instrument of the former. Having looked at the realities of the UK's policy position in subsequent sections, the desirability and practicability of this trend can be reassessed.

Policy context

The previous section recognised that there were many issues which could be an appropriate focus for policy, while earlier chapters have highlighted a number of the problems faced when attempting to measure the impact of foreign direct investment in the UK. It is important to recognise that such difficulties are of significance when it comes to policy formulation. However, they are only one of the group of factors shaping UK policy. In the strictest sense it is not possible to talk of a British foreign direct investment policy, since it consists of many strands and of policy components implemented by a wide variety of departments. Moreover, while the general posture of UK industrial policy has been ownership-neutral, there are a variety of ways in which the policy impact has not been neutral as regards inward investors. So, policy measures taken with no specific thought for their effect on inward direct investment are inevitably part of the policy environment in which such investment has taken place. The matter is further complicated in that a distinction has to be drawn between the broad policy parameters and practice in specific cases. For instance, there are rarely used enabling pieces of legislation which might be employed to block a foreign takeover within a particular industry as a matter of principle, such as has protected a leading capital goods exporter like Davy Corporation from foreign acquisition. There are also cases, apparently applying to some Japanese investors, where unwritten performance requirements have been invoked and others where public purchasing preferences can shape the activities of a multi-national enterprise. The use of performance requirements has been frequently associated with the application of Voluntary Restraint Agreements, one of whose aims is to replace direct imports by inward investment. UK policy in this whole area is, in short, highly fragmented and it is to the identification and evaluation of these fragments that much of the early part of this chapter is devoted.

Previous comments in the book have shown that policy towards foreign direct investment does not exist in a vacuum and that it is highly constrained. Both these issues should be reinforced at the outset in this chapter. As noted above, policy towards multinational enterprises investing in the UK has to be seen as a part of the overall policy stance towards industry. The latter has gone through many phases[1] and has been subject to dramatic reappraisal since 1979. By the mid 1980s, it was operating with the central aim of 'a profitable, competitive and adaptive productive sector in the UK'. Inward investment (in both direct and collaborative modes) features quite specifically within these aims. It is regarded as primarily making its contribution through the enhancing of industrial efficiency in many of the forms discussed in Chapter 1 and which underlie Chapter 3. Its role is not, however, confined to the generation of improved efficiency, but rather to aims associated with employment, exports and local development impact — all of which are central elements in the political process. In practice, therefore, successive UK governments have demonstrated the pragmatism associated with different benefit/cost relationships related to different projects. While implementing a policy of privatisation, the government indicated its desire to limit the potential transfer of control of Jaguar plc shares to foreign owners in 1984 and expressed great concern when the flotation of Enterprise Oil resulted in a substantial (British) MNE stake in the form of Rio Tinto Zinc in the same year. Equally, in pursuit of the use of public purchasing to promote innovation,

196

successive UK governments have fallen foul of international agreements in computer cases involving IBM and ICL, where preference has been shown for a British supplier.[2] In aggregate, inward investment would be viewed as making a net positive contribution to many of these stated industrial policy ends. It is hardly surprising, thus, that consistently restrictive policies over the past decade or so have been largely confined to the special case of North Sea oil exploration (which is the subject of later consideration).

Policy determinants

In the early 1970s UK policy towards foreign companies was aptly described by one author as one of *'benign neglect'*.[3] Such a description is now much less accurate, in that the ensuing period has been associated with a renaissance of national interest in a variety of forms which affect mobile investment. Given the creation and formalisation of more aggressive UK foreign investment attraction agencies at both national and regional level since the late 1970s, the removal of exchange controls and the specific cases of intervention on a company and sector basis, a more apt summation of the position might be that the policy is one of *'bounded prejudice'*. Having said that, the UK action is mirrored in many other European countries, as economic self-interest in industrial matters has gained momentum. There are, even so, some quite fundamental factors which ensure that any policy movement in this whole area is relatively slight and its application somewhat veiled. A number of these emerge in Figure 6.1. Reference was made in Chaper 2 to the. UK as a competitor for inward direct investment and this is undoubtedly an overriding factor in the determination of negotiating strength. The three market areas in Figure 6.1 are potentially quite distinct, with UK bargaining power being higher for domestic markets and progressively weakening as the project incorporates global product responsibilities. While the principal effect of such project differences falls in the application of the attraction instruments (chiefly financial packages) rather than in their design, the very existence of intense competition for EEC projects and global products governs both the shape and strength of UK policy.

As Figure 6.1 shows, the competitive dimension combines with an extensive set of national, and a growing list of international, constraints. At national level, the existence of a substantial net balance of outward investment acts to establish narrow boundaries within which any UK government can act. Taken with considerations arising from the need for job generation at national and

Figure 6.1: Determinants of the UK's strategy to attract and control foreign direct investment

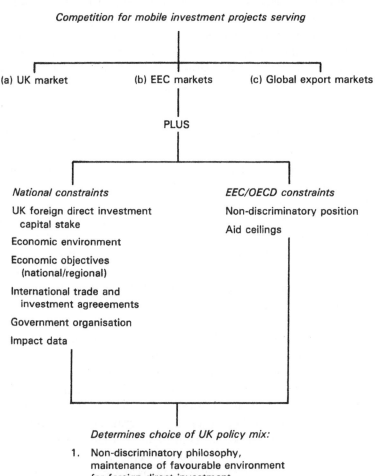

Competition for mobile investment projects serving

(a) UK market   (b) EEC markets   (c) Global export markets

PLUS

National constraints

UK foreign direct investment
   capital stake

Economic environment

Economic objectives
   (national/regional)

International trade and
   investment agreeements

Government organisation

Impact data

EEC/OECD constraints

Non-discriminatory position

Aid ceilings

Determines choice of UK policy mix:

1. Non-discriminatory philosophy,
   maintenance of favourable environment
   for foreign direct investment

2. Attraction-dominated; incentives, few
   disincentives

3. Performance-monitoring at minimum level

4. Limited sector-specific emphasis

5. Minimum exercise of enabling legislation

6. Constrained self interest by case law

regional level, the other constraints listed in the figure constitute a formidable array. Limitations at the national level have been the more demanding, although technically EEC policies take precedent. Together they result in UK policy interest being primarily attraction-based and only marginally concerned with regulation. Figure 6.1 outlines some of the basic tenets which have implicitly influenced the policy mix. While not all of these could be consistently applied to all circumstances, they represent a liberal policy stance with, at times, a strong hint of chauvinism. Since the latter is subtle and not always visible, there are several instances in this chapter where comments have to be interpretative rather than based on hard data.

Policy types

In categorising government policies towards multinational enterprises, a distinction is often made between incentives and performance requirements. Into the first category would fall any government action or policy which increases the net cash flow of an investment over what would have been anticipated without such intervention. Some of the effects of their application have been considered in other chapters. The second category includes any requirements placed on the firm by the host government, including minimum local content and export levels, maximum import levels, and so on. Generally speaking, developed countries offer incentives much more frequently than they impose performance requirements; the reverse is often, but not always, true of developing countries, since a high incidence of performance requirements can have negative effects on investment flows. As was noted above, the focus of UK policy is towards incentives and this is evidenced by partial data such as are presented in Table 6.1. Of equal interest is the suggestion that a higher proportion of US affiliates in the UK receive incentives than in other major European locations for US affiliate stock — such as France and West Germany. This may be in part accounted for by the UK regional distribution of affiliates outlined in Chapter 4, although several other European countries have regarded foreign direct investment as of considerable importance in correcting regional economic disparities. In the matter of performance requirements, the UK position is not markedly different from its main European competitors, with the exception of Republic of Ireland, where the 1977 Benchmark Survey reported some 20 per cent of affiliates reporting their imposition. While commenting on these, it is important to remember questions of definition. Although included in principle within the broad definition outlined above, the achievement

Table 6.1: Country concentration of low to moderate incentives and low performance requirements towards US affiliates

Country[a]	% of US affiliates receiving incentives	% of US affiliates subject to performance requirements
Australia	37	8
Belgium	26	7
Canada	18	7
France	18	7
Germany	20	2
Italy	29	6
Japan	9	8
Netherlands	29	2
Switzerland	12	7
United Kingdom	32	3

Note: a Ten of the twelve countries with largest stock of US foreign direct investment at year end 1977. Data for Brazil and Mexico not available. Table based on data from BE-10 benchmark survey of US direct investment abroad — 1977.
Source: US Department of Commerce (1981), *The use of investment incentives and performance requirements by foreign governments*, Investment Policy Division, Office of International Investment, International Trade Administration, US Department of Commerce, Washington, D.C., October, Table 5.

of employment targets associated with the granting of government incentives is normally excluded from lists of performance requirements. A considerable proportion of the investments in the US affiliates cited in Table 6.1 will have been subject to these in the UK. Perhaps the fact that they are not regarded as a requirement in this context is in itself an indication of their effectiveness!

Industrial policy and the foreign-owned sector

Although inward investment policy will be considered as free standing later in this chapter, it is in reality merely one component of industrial policy. Some of the discontinuities which have been evident in British industrial policy over the past two decades could have had negative effects on foreign investment. National planning experiments in the mid 1960s; disengagement from 1970 onwards (with its reversal in 1972); the efforts to give government a more central role in industrial performance from the mid 1970s; the subsequent period of 'industrial strategy'; and the renewed focus on disengagement from 1979 are all components of the change over this period. Yet it is debatable whether this, on balance, has discouraged inward direct investment. Such investment was towards Europe, where many of the alternative locations had other disadvantages. Moreover, there was probably a greater degree of underlying continuity than is perceived, especially in policy instruments, which had a major impact on MNE operations. The systems of capital incentives, regional and competition policies, R & D support and so on would all fall into this category. The changes which have occurred in these areas have been broadly within the boundary conditions which most international companies would regard as acceptable — in spite of short term criticisms to the contrary. Frequent detailed changes in provisions and the varying extent to which some measures have been implemented are both negative factors. So too are the discontinuities introduced by the new directions taken since 1979, including the move towards greater selectivity which was discussed in the regional context within Chapter 4.

All of this makes the establishment of measurable effects and links between industrial policy and the foreign sector extremely difficult. Figure 6.2 provides a brief overview of the identifiable areas of impact and the direction in which the weight of evidence lies. Paradoxically, the characteristics of the foreign-owned sector outlined in Chapter 2 enable it to be a major net beneficiary from many industrial policy measures. The downside risks for the foreign investor arising from industrial policy are of two types. At a tactical level there are the costs associated with short term changes in support schemes, legislation and so on. In aggregate these are probably small. At the strategic level they have been of greater and more lasting significance in matters of acquisitions and public ownership; but the effects are confined to a small number of specific cases. It remains an open question as to whether a more selective approach will be of greater benefit to the foreign investor. In recent years around one quarter of industrial aid has been selective and the signs are that it will increase proportionately. Since the foreign-owned sector as a whole possesses so many of the characteristics which governments wish to encourage, it is difficult to conceive that it would not benefit substantially from more targeted aid regimes. Specific new projects may, however, be less favoured by the nature of the selectivity towards job attainment, cost per job limits and so on.

The overview presented in Figure 6.2 suggests that it is possible to claim that UK industrial policy stances have been generally supportive of inward direct investment over the past decade. The fine print of the operation of some of these instruments are, of

Figure 6.2: UK industrial policy and the foreign-owned sector
(1975–86)

Police area	Instruments[a]	Impact area	Evidence on net effects on inward investment
Competition	Monopolies and Mergers Commission[b]	Acquisitions, anti-competitive practices	12 references, 5 found against public interest. Marginal constraint
	Price Commission	Price controls	Small number of referred cases, marginal constraint overall
Investment incentives	Tax allowances, investment grants, etc.	Cash flow, profitability, etc. depending on location and project	Positive effects especially in assisted areas. Higher uptake levels in optional schemes
Manpower policy	Industrial Training Boards	Labour skills	Positive where high skill intensity and labour shortages
	Manpower Services Commission	Efficiency of labour market in general	No direct evidence, but pressurised to be positive
Industrial innovation	Sectoral schemes	R & D costs: investment costs	High uptakes in selective schemes, positive effects
	Alvey Programme (from 1983)	R & D costs	Potentially negative if indigenous company focus maintained
Public ownership	Company-specific rescues	Total business operation	Negative in areas of direct impact (e.g. car industry, computers), elsewhere neutral

Notes:a In addition it should be acknowledged that Industrial
Development Act powers, Banking Act powers and insurance regulation
requirements might be among the many different factors which could
deter foreign involvement in UK.

b The number of references is in itself a poor indication of the
strength of policy in that company advisers and the Office of Fair
Trading may deter much foreign bid activity.

202

course, matters for detailed consideration later in this chapter. For these purposes the following sections distinguish the two basic dimensions of industrial policy which are designed to impact on the foreign sector as such. These are, firstly, policies to attract investment and, secondly, those concerned with its evaluation and control.

ATTRACTION AND REGULATION OF INWARD INVESTMENT IN THE UK

The objectives of these two policy elements differ substantially and are almost inherently contradictory. Attraction policies aim to maintain a continuing flow of direct investment from an ever-widening number of host countries; while policies linking evaluation and control are governed by the potentially negative impact on the economy. In the UK context, the policy stance in both has been traditionally passive at national level and only active at regional level as regards attraction. To illustrate, regulatory activity directed to the foreign-owned sector has principally been to establish general boundary conditions. A comparison of the impact issues of Chapter 3 and the policy components of this chapter reveals the mismatch between the two. Such disparities are not confined to this policy area. In this case the divergence is a measure of how the constraints in Figure 6.2 actually operate. But it also reflects the paucity of impact data and the lack of overall coherence in policy towards the foreign-owned sector.

UK attraction and regulation policies in the late 1980s can no longer be styled as passive. The principal pressures for change since the late 1970s have been competition and self-interest, with the most visible evidence accruing on the attraction side. Harbingers of a more active posture include the formation of a centralised agency, in the form of the Invest in Britain Bureau (IBB) from 1977; and the push towards the formation of more effective regional coordinating bodies in Scotland (Locate in Scotland [LIS]), Wales (Wales Investment Location [WINVEST]) and Northern Ireland (Industrial Development Board [IDB]) — all of which were formed in the early 1980s. The shift on the regulation side is more related to case law than statute; to operational behaviour rather than organisational structures.

Attraction

A distinction has been drawn between the institutions involved and the instruments employed in this process in the UK. At the outset it should be recognised that many of the institutions have remits which extend well beyond inward investment, or indeed beyond industrial development as a whole. Equally, neither are the institutions nor the instruments designed to discriminate between sectors or between investing firms on the basis of ownership. In effect, however, several of the institutions devote most of their resources to attracting firms from outside the UK and hence a veiled form of operational discrimination emerges.

The UK does not have a single national system for attracting inward investment and is unlikely ever to have one. The pattern of institutions involved remains complex, in spite of the rationalisation process of recent years. *Four tiers of activity can be distinguished*, in each of which lies some measure of financial discretion and statutory responsibility for the promotion of industrial development through inward investment.

At the *first* level, are local authorities (districts and regions) and new town corporations, all of which are active in promoting the development of their respective areas. This promotion necessarily includes inward investment, although in this sphere their activities are constrained. So, for instance, changes in local government legislation on industrial development matters in recent years have placed more coordination responsibilities on regional authorities; while new towns are subject to direct ministerial influence through government sponsoring departments. Not all of the bodies within this tier are active in overseas promotion, their scale being often (but not always) a governing factor. Even with the drive towards co-ordination at this level, it is still open to the criticism of creating confusion in the minds of overseas investors, while the inter-authority relationships continue to show tensions. It is probable that its role in inward investment attraction will continue to be eroded.

At the *second* level, are government agencies and allied bodies which have some substantial regional responsibility to lead on inward investment. These have grown in number and in stature since 1980, driven primarily by a desire to eliminate the disbenefits arising from the operations of the first tier. Some of the ensuing criticisms were the subject of damning indictment by Parliamentary committees,[4] which have attacked the absence of a professional marketing approach to attraction, lack of coordination and duplication of effort (both between national and regional bodies and between regional bodies themselves). The two classic illustrations of the new breed of organisation designed to take these criticisms on board are LIS and WINVEST. LIS was set up in April 1981 as a joint venture of the Industry Department for Scotland (then the Scottish Economic Planning Department) and the Scottish Development Agency. Two years later, WINVEST was formed in April 1983 to bring together the promotional work of the formerly independent Development Corporation for Wales, and the inward investment responsibilities of the Welsh Office Industry Department and the Welsh Development Agency. Both have offices, full-time and part-time representatives overseas, mainly in the United States, and are designed to act as close to a 'single door' approach to their respective regions as possible. While it is rather early to assess the long-term effectiveness of such bodies, the early signs are sufficiently encouraging to be a source of envy in other UK regions.

The *third* level introduces government departments as such, although they are never far from the surface at both previous levels. This is inevitable since they are distinguished not only by their wider geographical remit but also by their financial negotiating powers. While in the LIS and WINVEST cases these powers are directly related to promotional bodies, this is not the norm. Thus, in the English regions, the regional offices of the Department of Trade and Industry have a lead role in the administration of financial support but make no contribution to the other stages in the inward investment attraction process. It is unlikely that this functional separation can be allowed to continue, especially if the level-two bodies continue to impress. In short, this tier has the seeds of destruction within it. Integration with promotional bodies and coordination at national level, would respectively lead to its absorption within level two or the emergent *fourth* and final tier.

IBB, based in the Department of Industry, is the only national body in the UK which attempts to coordinate promotion. It was established in 1977 from a variety of individuals and groups already in different Ministries involved in inward investment work. Its first Annual Report for 1983 emphasised its all-embracing responsibilities which were seen as stretching far beyond promotion as such: 'The IBB can therefore call on the total resources available within government to provide a comprehensive service, including specialist advice within the DTI, and all other Departments, plus organisations such as the British Technology Group and English Industrial Estates.'[5] Figure 6.3 presents its central position

Figure 6.3: IBB: the one-stop shop

IBB: THE ONE-STOP SHOP

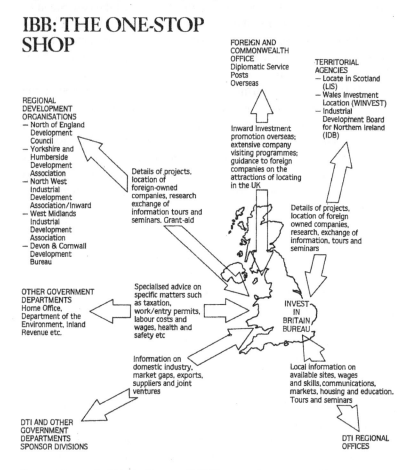

REGIONAL
DEVELOPMENT
ORGANISATIONS
— North of England
  Development
  Council
— Yorkshire and
  Humberside
  Development
  Association
— North West
  Industrial
  Development
  Association/Inward
— West Midlands
  Industrial
  Development
  Association
— Devon & Cornwall
  Development
  Bureau

FOREIGN AND
COMMONWEALTH
OFFICE
Diplomatic Service
Posts
Overseas

TERRITORIAL
AGENCIES
— Locate in Scotland
  (LIS)
— Wales Investment
  Location (WINVEST)
— Industrial
  Development Board
  for Northern Ireland
  (IDB)

Inward investment
promotion overseas;
extensive company
visiting programmes;
guidance to foreign
companies on the
attractions of locating
in the UK

Details of projects,
location of
foreign-owned
companies, research
exchange of
information tours and
seminars. Grant-aid

Details of projects,
location of foreign
owned companies,
research, exchange of
information, tours and
seminars

OTHER GOVERNMENT
DEPARTMENTS
Home Office,
Department of the
Environment, Inland
Revenue etc.

Specialised advice on
specific matters such
as taxation,
work/entry permits,
labour costs and
wages, health and
safety etc

INVEST
IN
BRITAIN
BUREAU

Information on
domestic industry,
market gaps, exports,
suppliers and joint
ventures

Local information on
available sites, wages
and skills, communications,
markets, housing and education.
Tours and seminars

DTI AND OTHER
GOVERNMENT
DEPARTMENTS
SPONSOR DIVISIONS

DTI REGIONAL
OFFICES

Source: Invest in Britain Bureau (1985), annual report, p. 16.

graphically and somewhat optimistically. The optimism stems from several directions, but chiefly in the assumption of effective investment representation through the Foreign and Commonwealth Office (FCO) and in the quiescence of competitive, territorial agencies designed to coordinate at the regional level. The FCO has quite different functions and can be regarded as capable of making only a marginal contribution to foreign investment attraction in an era of detailed sectoral and corporate targeting. Equally, there are inherent tensions between IBB and an effective territorial agency. These were evidenced in 1982 and 1984 over the maintenance of regional offices by Locate in Scotland.

Figure 6.4: Institutions and the inward investment attraction process in the UK

Stages	Operations involved	Major actors		Contested areas
		National	Regional	
1. Information	Analysis of trends in direct investment by sector and company; general intelligence gathering	IBB; FCO	IDB; SDA/LIS; WDA/WINVEST; DTI offices	Minimum IBB involvement; main initiatives in N. Ireland, Scotland and Wales; negligible involvement in DTI regional offices
2. Planning and targeting	Setting of plans and targets for countries, sectors and companies	IBB	Ditto	Major area of contention regarding overseas offices (N. Ireland, Scotland and Wales) and other direct representatives. No direct involvement by English regions
3. Promotion	Advertising, investment seminars, overseas missions	IBB	IDB; SDA/LIS; WDA/WINVEST	National vs regional image promotion, information-flows between IBB and regional bodies
4. Negotiation	Development and presentation of specific financial and allied packages	DTI	As above but with close liaison with sponsoring departments	Controversy here largely at local level in questions of site location and relative roles of regional and local bodies
5. Settlement	Coordination of all relevant bodies to minimise blockages as project is set up	—	'Agencies'; local authorities; new towns, etc.	Absence of appropriate coordinating role through DTI offices
6. After care	Maintaining close contact on operational matters	—	Ditto	—

The origin of some of these difficulties can be seen to exist at different parts of the attraction process, as Figure 6.4 shows. Some of these disputed areas are transitory, others are endemic in the present system. Figure 6.4 represents the authors' view of the reality of IBB operations. It represents a sharp contrast to the official and untrammelled view of Figure 6.3. IBB cannot effectively operate across many aspects of the attraction process, by definition: but effective attraction policies require all six stages in Figure 6.4 to be in balance. In short, there is no evidence that UK centralisation for its own sake will make for an efficient attraction system. Equally, a distinction has to be drawn between a bureaucratically rooted institution and one which can integrate with managerial decision making. The IBB has found difficulties in breaking free from the former classification and does not have the capability to operate flexibly across all stages of the process shown in Figure 6.4. The optimal solution might well be the restriction of IBB to promotion and overall coordination, plus the extension of level two bodies to other parts of the UK in order to maintain an overall attraction package which is sufficiently flexible to be competitive, yet sufficiently integrated to be steered.

Many of these pressures have remained beneath the surface since IBB was formed and have only been brought to the public attention through the information leaks associated with bitter internal policy reviews. More visible has been the criticism of a fragmented attraction effort. It was in reaction to this that the Committee on Overseas Promotion (COP) was set up in 1980, chaired by the IBB Under Secretary. Bringing together the key national (Foreign Office, Industry and Environment) and regional departmental interests, this body is designed to coordinate by consensus without any formal inter-departmental authority. The coordination is principally of promotion, only part of the process as Figure 6.4 shows; nor, of course, do IBB or COP have any monitoring function.

As will be clear from Chapters 3 and 4 and the comments earlier in this chapter, the UK has no specific attraction instruments. Britain's long standing commitment to 'national treatment' involves no discrimination in principle between nationality of investor. Moreover, such commitments are inherent in the Treaty of Rome and in OECD Guidelines to which the UK subscribes. Added to this are EEC constraints on public sector contributions, varying on a regional basis, the application of which is the subject of EEC scrutiny. However, by making maximum use of discretionary finance under national legislation; employing a variety of local aid schemes which impact on infrastructure and associated costs; utilising the powers conferred on regional development agencies where they exist, the UK has continued to maintain the facility to construct competitive 'packages' where necessary. In recent years this has come closer to the merchant banking approach to foreign investment, exploring every alternative combination of existing instruments and interpreting their applicability to the limit. The UK is not alone in being drawn in this direction by intra-European competition as every attempt is made to ensure that financial incentives are allowed to play as much of a role as the prospective inward investor would seek.

Evaluation and control

Over an extended period of time, the UK has developed a number of mechanisms which are used to evaluate inward foreign investment. They are principally designed to establish limiting conditions or take into account specific negative effects which are likely to accrue to the economy. The situation has been characterised as one where there are 'no more than residual elements of monitoring and control'[7] but there is some evidence of a change in particular circumstances. However, because many of the measures apply in limited cases and due to the overall UK policy posture, they cannot be effectively described let alone evaluated. Almost all the major government departments have some involvement with matters pertaining to inward investors, invariably by coincidence rather than by design. To take one example, the Department of Trade and Industry has interests in grants, disclosure, monitoring (with a low profile) and, in the past, in planning agreements; Treasury interests include international tax practice, revenues, exchange control, customs and excise; while monopoly, merger and price policies have straddled a number of departmental responsibilities. Far from regarding this situation as undesirable, almost all UK governments over the last 20 years would have viewed it as essential, contesting that moves towards coordination might in themselves be interpreted either as a retreat from a permissive British policy stance or offending 'national treatment' undertakings.

While it was indicated earlier in this chapter that UK policies in this area do not bear a very direct resemblance to the impact framework and evidence in Chapter 3, a number of themes have been selected to illustrate the principal policy constituents. These include regulations governing ownership, financial and fiscal affairs, sectoral policies and emerging performance requirements — each being examined over the past decade.

Ownership

Like many other countries, the UK has no prescribed list of industries where foreign direct investment is either forbidden or discouraged. Powers exist under the Industry Act (1975) to prevent 'an important manufacturing undertaking' passing into foreign control where this is against the national interest. In this context, control would constitute at least 30 per cent ownership. Government action in this category would be either by forbidding a takeover or by compulsory acquisition of the assets or shares which are threatened with takeover. This has been regarded as a reserve power under the Act and it does not, and cannot under treaty, apply to companies based in EEC countries. The letter of this Act has not been applied to inward direct investors from other sources, although its spirit probably has through the discouragement of potential investors at the early stages.

By far the most visible aspect of official UK policy are the operations of the Monopolies and Mergers Commission (MMC). Its responsibilities are directed to anti-competitive activity irrespective of company nationality and there are no special criteria applying to the acquisition of UK-based companies by foreign-based enterprises. Indeed there are no statutory criteria for references to the MMC in any given case. There is perhaps a tendency to give too much weight to the relative importance of the MMC within discussions of inward investment regulation policy, simply because the reports of that body are publicly available. The very existence of the MMC and Office of Fair Trading (OFT) doubtless screens off many other potential foreign bids, and so in some ways the actual reference cases are not truly representative. They also constitute one of the few sources of data on the application of UK policy, even although the MMC itself cannot be expected to mirror government policy with any accuracy. In the period between 1975 and 1986, there were ten major references involving inward investment via acquisition routes, of which four were rejected. Although visible and often controversial, these references represent a very small percentage of total acquisition cases involving multinational companies. The greater interest often lies in the type of evidence which government departments submit in individual cases and the interpretations which are placed on this by other potential foreign acquirers.

Figure 6.5 summarises the ten MMC references involving foreign companies from 1975 to end of 1986, a figure representing under 20 per cent of all references during that period. The table is structured in order to draw attention to the impact areas which were regarded as dominant in each case. For this purpose the criterion of 'public interest' overlaps with some of the impact dimensions which were considered in Chapter 3 but by no means totally. As the figure suggests, the positive issues are largely macro, with productivity, employment, balance or payments and so on dominating. In no way does the MMC apply a benefit/cost approach to the specifically international dimensions of foreign references; in fact in some cases it is quite difficult to find traces of any mention of such matters. The reason for this lies in the legislation itself, which charges the MMC to find specific effects which are adverse to the public interest. Where these are found, they might constitute a basis for the potential acquirer to give undertakings to the Secretary of State to offset the damage to public interest.

The central concerns of the MMC are not about the inter-nationalisation of business, or the operations of multinational corporations. Wider questions about the consequent effectiveness of UK monopoly legislation as regards international companies have thus emerged over a number of years. It was, for example, a sentiment reflected many years ago in the report of Steuer *et al.* 'The practice of securing undertakings in important takeover issues has not developed into an accepted policy for countering possible ill-effects from inward investment nor is it clear that in its absence the companies concerned would have acted differently in any important respects.'[8] It is precisely in this area that the absence of impact data proves telling in inward investment cases which come before the MMC. The onus is not on the establishment of benefit or lack of benefit accruing from such an association but rather on the existence of the disbenefits which might be deemed to be against the public interest. The paucity of impact data to defend the case as stated is frequently only too obvious when set against apparently tangible benefits such as further investment, wider international market opportunities and so on. This dearth is reflected in evidence submitted to, and perhaps therefore in the decisions recommended by, the MMC.

One recent set of evidence[9] on the effects of inward acquisition highlights both the issues and the problems of accumulating the relevant impact data (see Chapter 4, pp. 131–2). This work concluded that in terms of internal company effects (such as on sales, employment and profitability) no great harm was being done by inward mergers to the Scottish economy. The picture was

Figure 6.5: Foreign takeovers referred to the Monopolies and Mergers' Commission (1975–86)

Case/year	Decision	Positive	Negative
			Dominant issues
1975			
Proposed takeover of AD International Ltd (dental supplies) by Dentsply International Inc, USA	Merger would benefit the public interest and should be allowed to proceed	Merger would benefit ADI's R & D	Some adverse effects on competition possibly resulting in higher prices
Proposed takeover of B.S. & W. Whiteley Ltd (manufacturers of electrical insulating pressboard) by H. Weidmann A.G. of Switzerland	Merger would benefit the public interest and should be allowed to proceed	1) Productivity and efficiency would be improved 2) Employment would increase 3) Positive effects on the balance of payments by reducing imports and increasing exports	Some increase in market power possibly resulting in higher prices, but market conditions would prevent this in the near future
1976			
Proposed takeover of two UK shipping lines (Furness, Whitby & Co Ltd and Manchester Liners Ltd) by the Bermuda-registered but Canadian-headquartered Euro Canadian Shipbuildings Ltd	Merger would be against the public interest and should *not* be allowed to proceed	Cost savings and improved efficiency through integration and rationalisation, but outweighed by disadvantages	1) Loss of national control of decision making 2) Adverse effects on employment and the balance of payments 3) Reduced service to UK exporters and shippers 4) Adverse effects on the Port of Manchester, creating regional difficulties

Year	Case	Recommendation	Benefits	Adverse effects
1977	Proposed takeover of Crane Fruehauf Ltd by Fruehauf Corp of the USA. The former was already partly owned by the latter	Merger would not be against the public interest and should be allowed to proceed	1) Some long-run improvement in employment prospects 2) Overall positive effect on the balance of payments	Some adverse effects on competition — but negligible
1979	Proposed takeover of Alginate Industries Ltd by either FMC Corp, USA or Merck & Co Inc, USA	A takeover by either company would result in substantial benefits to Alginate, therefore, the proposed merger should proceed	1) Improvement in output and employment 2) Advantages arising from FMC's and Merck's worldwide marketing network and R & D	None
1980	Proposed takeover of The Highland Distilleries Co Ltd by Hiram Walker — Gooderham & Worts Ltd, Canada	Proposedd takeover was found to be against the public interest and should *not* be allowed to proceed	No major benefits could be seen from the proposed merger	Merger would result in a substantial increase in concentration of distillery ownership resulting in reduced competition

Figure 6.5: Contd.

Case/year	Decision	Dominant issues Positive	Negative
1981			
Proposed takeover of the car rental firm Godfrey-Davis Ltd by Compagnie Internationale of France (owned by Renault)	Advantages of the proposed merger outweigh the disadvantages and should be allowed to proceed	Merger would allow Godfrey Davis to compete more effectively in international car rental markets by utilising the French group's European marketing network	Some adverse effects on competition in the UK but not thought to be too significant given the relatively small size of Godfrey-Davis Ltd
Proposed takeover of the UK based Davy Corp Ltd (process plant contractors) by Enserch Corp, USA	Merger would be against the public interest and should *not* be allowed to proceed	Certain advantages arising from access to Enserch's financial resources, R & D, and overseas markets, but outweighed by disadvantages	1) Loss of national control 2) Reduction in both exports and employment as a result of 1) 3) Adverse effects with respect to US legislation and the centralisation of decision making

1982 Proposed merger of the Royal Bank of Scotland with either the Standard Chartered Bank (UK) or the Hong-Kong and Shanghai Bank	Both proposed mergers would be *against* the public interest	Some advantages arising from access to extensive branch networks outside the UK; increased financial resources; and stimulating competition in the retail banking sector by creating a 'fifth force' to compete with the "Big Four"	1) Main disadvantage was the loss of decision making power from Scotland which was seen as increasing the process of economic centralisation contributing to the economic problems of the region 2) Other disadvantages related to 1) were reduced career opportunities and an increase in emigration from Scotland
Proposed takeover of Huntley & Palmer Foods plc by Nabisco Brands Inc, USA	Merger would not be against the public interest and should be allowed to proceed	Fall in employment will be less severe than if the proposed merger had not taken place	1) Merger would increase concentration levels in the snack food industry, but should not result in serious adverse effects 2) Some reduction in employment is inevitable

Note: There were no references involving foreign companies in 1978 or 1983 and 1986.

significantly different when external effects were considered. Although difficult to measure, the derived demand and organisational effects emerged as the most important of all external effects — which were generally both pervasive and adverse. Among their conclusions, these researchers argued that a change in the bias of merger legislation would be helpful to avoid such negative effects, including a switch in the onus of proof towards the acquiring company.

Some guidance is given to successive governmental thinking on these matters by the substance of departmental evidence to the MMC. Consider this in the four 'found against' cases since 1975. In the case of Euro Canadian Shipbuildings (ECS) and Furness, Withy & Co and Manchester Liners (ML) in 1976,[10] negative effects included those on the balance of payments emerging from ECS having a less UK-centred purchasing policy for both ships and containers. Addressing this referral, the Department of Trade evidence indicated that any movement (of ships) away from the British flag on a major scale could give cause for concern, but that no view had been taken on the optimum size or shape of the British Merchant Marine. Such observations reflect the difficulties faced by any one department commenting on inward investment in the absence of an overarching industrial policy framework.

Similar types of concern have been voiced over the strength of the Scottish regional factor in the two rejected cases of Hiram Walker and Highland Distillers (1980) and Royal Bank of Scotland (1982).[11] The strength of the arguments advanced by the Scottish Development Agency and the Scottish Economic Planning Department (now the Industry Department for Scotland) in both cases is to be seen as more a reflection of healthy regional institutions than of a UK decision to have MMC policy sensitive to regional concerns. Yet, however difficult it was to quantify negative effects on local managerial opportunities, loss of decision-making authority, reduction in regional dynamism and so on, these arguments prevailed with the MMC in these cases. In most other UK regions the same arguments would not have been heard with such force, let alone prevail.

There would appear to be relatively few MMC cases where the nationality of the bidder is deemed to be material to the acceptability of the bid. The fourth 'found against' case in Table 6.2, namely that of Enserch and Davy Corporation[12] is in this category. Davy Corporation is the flagship of the UK international engineering contracting industry operating in an area where trade, aid and foreign relations are closely linked. As such, it operates very closely with various UK government departments in a manner which the

MMC were convinced would be damaged if it were to be taken into American ownership. The consequent negative effects on the UK export effort in this area were considered to be important. That this adverse finding was case-specific and not an application of any unwritten principle is evidenced by the fact that two years later Enserch acquired Humphreys and Glasgow, a much smaller UK process plant contractor (about ten per cent of the size of Davy) without referral to the MMC.

In a setting where under three per cent of all proposed UK mergers and acquisitions are referred to MMC and where about two per cent of all proposals have been directly stopped (those abandoned plus those against the public interest) since the mid 1960s, it is unlikely that much could be made of the impact of the MMC on the foreign-owned sector. The general stance remains liberal and the outcome of reference cases normally quite predictable. The general problems of assessing future consequences which beset all merger policy is often compounded when an international dimension is added.

Fiscal and financial

Under this general heading are a variety of regulatory measures, the effects of which are almost entirely indeterminate due to either data problems or secrecy, or both. Taking the fiscal side first, the principles of national treatment again prevail. There is no general evidence to suggest that the UK practice on the levels of corporate taxation applying to inward investors is markedly different from its European neighbours, with the exception of the Republic of Ireland. Such taxation is certainly not used as a regulatory device in the UK, indeed quite the contrary. The effective rates of corporation tax in the UK in general have been affected by the low profitability of UK business, while the generous allowances under the (pre-1984) regime with regard to depreciation and stock appreciation, together with assessment of tax based on post-interest profits rather than pre-interest surpluses, have often worked in favour of the successful foreign sector. At the personal level, foreign nationals have traditionally been generously treated by UK legislation, although somewhat less so for those in senior posts following changes announced in 1984.[13]

More important but no less illusive are UK stances towards tax avoidance via transfer pricing, the use of tax havens and so on. Data on international tax avoidance are almost non-existent. Information known to one fiscal authority is often not shared with another, still less published. It has often been suggested[14] that the scope for international tax avoidance relative to the size of a national economy is indicated by measures such as the ratios of two-way trade and inward investment income (i.e. from outward investment) to gross domestic product. By the former measure, the UK could be somewhat more prone to gain or loss by such avoidance than other OECD countries, although, of course, such a crude measurement does not take into account distortions in international trade caused by existing tax systems. That said, it is not known whether the UK avoidance picture actually differs from that of other major host countries in Europe. In 1976 the Inland Revenue did establish a special unit to deal with the transfer pricing policies of transnational companies, presumably, of both UK and foreign ownership. Almost nothing is known of its operations and hence of its effectiveness.

The UK tax legislation has provisions for regulating transer pricing. Under Section 485 of the 1970 Taxes Act the Inland Revenue can impose a commercial price 'at arm's length' to prevent profit being extracted from the UK to an overseas company by artificial pricing arrangements. In this whole area, some of the most active legislative debates since 1979 have in fact surrounded international tax avoidance by UK companies in the 'controlled foreign companies' category[15] where these companies make extensive use of tax havens. The removal of exchange controls in that year prompted much of this action. From a legislative perspective, the inward investment sector has thus attracted relatively little attention in the UK.

Before leaving some of these contentious areas, it is important to remember that there are fiscal dimensions to attraction as well as to regulation. The former most directly occur within financial packages. Less obvious, however, is the contribution made by the British Isles tax havens to international trade with inward investment in the UK.[16] The islands of Jersey, Guernsey and Isle of Man are extensively used as financial support areas in the three related roles of deposit centres for international lending and investment, flotation centres for indigenous offshore funds and as centres for external company registration. Initially characterised by the entry of a wave of UK merchant banks in the 1960s, the 1970s witnessed a substantial inflow of foreign banks from the US, Europe and the Far East. While there are no data to quantify the exact contribution of these centres to the inward investor in the UK it can be reasonably assumed to bring support and net benefit to their operations. Further, they are a part of the overall package which makes the UK an attractive host country for international 'treasury' managers.

Since exchange decontrol in 1979 the rate of development in these centres has been particularly dramatic, with rapid rises in bank deposits and external non-UK company registrations both surging ahead. Some indication of the relevance of the latter to international trading, is demonstrated in the fact that in Jersey only some 25 per cent of the companies registered were UK-owned in 1982. Of all the forms of investment associated with such tax havens, a limited number are of direct relevance in supporting inward investment in the UK. Among these are investment holding companies and captive insurance companies. Successive UK governments have clearly regarded these havens as aiding both the UK balance of payments and currency reserves; at the same time, it has been necessary to ensure that UK tax evasion and legal avoidance are continually contained.

The only sustained financial control regulating inward investment in the UK in the post World War Two period has been exchange control. Operating from 1947 until its final abolition in October 1979, its actual influence varied considerably and in its latter years it was largely a formality. All inward investment did however technically require permission from the Bank of England working closely with the Treasury, principally through the Foreign Exchange Committee. Policy was primarily motivated by reference to the UK reserves, the need for self-financing, and the payment of a 'fair price' in takeover situations. Even within the many periods during which UK reserves were under pressure, there would appear to be little tangible evidence that this process was applied with much zeal and approvals were invariably swift. The high reliance on undistributed profits among the US foreign-owned sector and the ubiquitous desire to facilitate inward investment, combined to remove the strength of such measures long before their substance was removed.

Sectoral

There are a number of sectors where UK policy has had a particular impact as it has been directed towards tackling specific problems. Two of these are the subject of illustration in this section.

Some of the most consistent and overt control mechanisms directed towards inward investment in the UK have been in the *North Sea oil industry*, principally those calculated to influence the purchasing policies of the oil companies. Although strictly in adherence with 'national treatment' policies it was always recognised that the desired changes in traditional patterns of supply would largely occur within the foreign-owned companies. The initiative for such action dated from an influential report in 1972[17] which called for a quarterly system of confidential returns to government on offshore purchases. From that year a system of purchase auditing was progressively developed and supplemented by teams of audit engineers to monitor the actual purchasing decisions of the oil companies. The prime motives for this system and the ground rules were both incapsulated in a formal Memorandum of Understanding and Code of Practice between the Department of Energy and UK Offshore Operators Association Ltd in 1975. The responsibility for its implementation to ensure an increasing share of the offshore market for British companies was placed in the hands of the Offshore Supplies Office (OSO).

In their first survey of 1974, British firms had reportedly gained 40 per cent by value of the total offshore market, whereas in the five yeras to 1983 the reported average was 72 per cent.[18] Setting aside the considerable definitional and monitoring difficulties behind these figures, the overall evidence points to a marked change in purchasing patterns arising from OSO's ensuring 'that UK organisations are given a full and fair opportunity on each and every contract'.

A number of the difficulties faced by OSO in implementing this auditing procedure are inherent in such forms of regulation. Initially there were considerable problems of staff expertise in a complex sector where few had oil backgrounds. Further, the code of practice has no legal standing and is a system of moral suasion. Such sanctions as exist have been in the threat of legislative action of various types and in the potential damage to future licensing prospects — both of which are admittedly powerful! From the perspective of the inward investor, this procedure has undoubtedly led to changes in practice, although to what degree and with what level of permanence is open to question.

The OSO effect is probably at its best where the competitive margin between a UK and foreign supplier is small. The operators concerned are moreover familiar with regulated environments. By establishing wholly-owned or joint venture operations many have managed to become sufficiently British for the purpose of this auditing. On the other side, the operators have become more receptive to UK suppliers, who themselves have responded more effectively to the market opportunities by increasing capacity and developing appropriate skills. Perhaps the major benefit from this exercise has been in the host government formally declaring its interest in purchasing patterns, thereby requiring the reconsideration of benefit accruing from this major investment programme. These measures have also to be seen in their political context in that when they were introduced the operators were much more concerned with the new Petroleum Revenue Tax, the administrative controls on oil production and depletion contained in the Pipelines Bill and the possibility of participation, than about the introduction of procedures concerned with offshore supplies. In effect then, the first three years of auditing (1973–6) were ones where there were considerable incentives to be cooperative in the supplies area in order to improve future bargaining positions regarding taxation and participation.

Before leaving this rather special case of sectoral intervention, one other important aspect of regulation policy should be noted. In contrast to early licensing policies in the 1964–71 period which were primarily directed towards ensuring a high level of exploitation and extraction, later rounds have reflected other concerns. These are of interest in the light of the impact issues considered in Chapter 3. Thus for example in the Ninth Round of Offshore Licensing (1982–3) considerable emphasis was placed on contributions to the UK economy and the generation of new technology. The latter specifically dealt with the estimation of assistance to UK concerns on matters of R & D, demonstration and test, commercialisation and exporting. It also required comments on the ownership of technology developed and estimates of the benefit of the payouts to UK offshore capability. However tentative, moves in this direction begin to redefine the ground rules for international oil companies and in the UK context show a willingness to employ negotiating muscle within an overall liberal policy stance.

Pharmaceuticals are among the other UK sectors where regulatory policies can be deemed to have exerted an important influence on inward investment. Drug prices are a subject of concern ·in most countries. Some of the earliest price scrutiny was in the UK simply because of the existence of the National Health Service. Inward investors in this sector have, therefore, been dealing with a virtual monopsonist for the past four decades, as have UK suppliers. Successive government reports have focused on pricing questions, including Hinchcliffe (1959), Sainsbury (1967) and the MMC consideration of Hoffman-La Roche in 1973.[19] The latter was particularly influential as the company was ordered to cut the 1970 prices of its two main products (Librium and Valium) by 60 per cent and 75 per cent respectively.

On the administration side, two price regulation schemes have dominated the last few decades. In one form or another a Voluntary

221

Price Regulation Scheme (VPRS) existed since 1957. This was amended in 1977 to the Pharmaceutical Price Regulation Scheme (PPRS). The scheme has been reorganised fairly frequently and since it is not statutory, it can be modified as conditions change. PPRS at its simplest provides a framework for negotiation between the Department of Health and Social Security (DHSS) and the firm marketing a medicine. Companies with sales to the NHS of around £1 million must supply the DHSS with a standardised Annual Financial Return (AFR) which gives details of sales, costs and capital employed in the previous years. By controlling profits, effective prices are kept in check.

The system has given drug companies considerable incentives to develop and launch new products in this country. Important components of the scheme include the setting of targets for each firm in terms of return on historic capital employed. In 1984, for example, this reportedly varied up to 21 per cent,[20] compared, for instance, to defence contractors target of 17 per cent. In assessing the 'reasonableness' of profitability, the DHSS is specifically required to take into account the contribution which the company makes to the economy, including foreign earnings, investment, employment and research. There is thus an incentive to expand research and an effective reward mechanism in profits attainable. Since UK prices are used as base prices in many other markets, the profitability effect goes far beyond the UK market. In short, the PPRS might be deemed to provide a built in incentive for MNEs to expand in the UK.[21]

There is no substantial evidence to suggest that these regulatory systems have differentiated against foreign investment, in spite of some fears to the contrary expressed over many years. For example, in 1972 it was observed by the National Economic Development Office that UK drug prices were not only relatively low by international standards but that they were drifting lower owing to continuous governmental pressures.[22] If this state of affairs continued then 'both the incentive to invest in the UK and the supply of necessary funds would be reduced'.[23] Offsetting this, there are many other factors which make the UK an attractive location for inward investors in the pharmaceutical industry, including its highly regarded medical and scientific establishment, its patent system and rapid and professional system of drug registration.[24] The record of investment flow would seem to suggest that the latter outweighs the former. Moreover, there is evidence[25] to suggest that the presence of foreign companies has acted as a major stimulus to competition

222

within the UK industry, affecting research volume and quality in a positive manner. From the host country's perspective, some concerns have been expressed in the opposite direction, namely that the present target rates of return are too high and that PPRS does not give enough incentive for research into new products, although the latter is doubtful when all the evidence is considered. Most recently, the introduction in 1985 of a limited list of drugs available for NHS prescription has had a direct impact in some closures and reduction in investment in the UK. This delisting of established products was regarded by international drug corporations as a breach of trust and as introducing long-run uncertainty into the UK environment. While the assertion is valid to a degree, the general attractiveness of the UK remains.

Performance requirements

As observed earlier in this chapter, the UK has no formal policy of placing performance requirements on inward investors. At the same time in certain industries and for particular investors a variety of 'undertakings' and 'voluntary restrictions' have emerged which are directly targeted to inward investors. These have invariably been in industries which have overcapacity in the UK or Europe, those which have a high level of employment sensitivity and those which have strong corporate pressure groups. The inward investors in this group have been largely Japanese, thus prompting one observer to conclude as long ago as 1977 that every Japanese company which had so far invested in Britain had been required to make confidential assurances, mainly about export ratios and local purchasing.[25] It is very difficult to distinguish fact from fiction in this whole area. The restrictions which exist are partly from industry and partly from government sources and are more industry-specific than they are ownership-specific. However, for whatever reason they exist and their presence can be best illustrated in the two examples of colour TV sets and automobiles.

Different transmission systems act as a barrier to international trade in TV sets. The Phased Alternative Line (PAL) system operates in the UK as devised in 1961 by Telefunken from an earlier US system. Until 1980, companies wishing to produce sets for markets in the PAL system had to take out licences from Telefunken. EMI operated the UK licence for Telefunken, a licence which required restraints on the import of sets above 20″, thereby preserving the lucrative larger screen market for local producers. Having initially been unwilling to license Japanese producers to make PAL sets, the licence conditions severely restricted non-local manufacture. In addition to such technical and licensing constraints, Japanese producers had other problems in the form of voluntary restrictions on exports. Since 1973, such restrictions have existed on colour and monochrome sets through an 'orderly marketing agreement' between the UK Radio Industry Council and the Japanese Electronic Industries Association.[27] Given these trading conditions, it was not surprising to find that the Japanese majors wanted to establish manufacturing capacity in Europe, chiefly in the UK. This route was taken by Sony (1974), Matsushita (1976), GEC-Hitachi and Mitsubishi-Tanberg (both 1979) and Sanyo and Toshiba (both 1981). In the Hitachi case, the company first attempted to set up a manufacturing facility in 1977 but withdrew in the face of strong opposition from the indigenous industry and unions.[28] It is widely believed that all these projects were subject to some form of voluntary restraint agreement with the Department of Industry on local sourcing of components, production volumes and exporting, but details are not publicly available. Several of the companies reported particular difficulties in implementing local procurement policies and in the slow build up of production which they were allowed. Nevertheless, the restraints on alternative modes of supplying the UK market have required these costs to be borne.

The classic, and by far the most publicised, case of this type in the UK over recent years was that of Nissan, which announced their intention early in 1981 to establish a UK plant to produce 200,000 cars per annum. It was not until over three years later that a scaled down project was finally given the go ahead. There were many factors behind this delay and change in the project scale, several of which are quite outwith the scope of this chapter. They include the recession in Europe, fear of UK (and Japanese) trade union attitudes, Britain's position in the EEC, internal changes within the company, a heavy investment programme elsewhere, and so on. Among the factors, however, were UK pressures on local content and export ratios. As with colour TV, the industry pressure groups were out in force in the form of The Committee of Common Market Automobile Constructors (CCMC). CCMC stressed the requirement for a 'European' car to have an 80 per cent component value, not purely an 80 per cent added value. UK producers wished to go further by applying agreed monitoring to ensure compliance with these and export requirements. In the plethora of subsequent discussion, it was believed that the UK government was quite unable to achieve its initial objectives on component content and that a figure

224

of under 60 per cent of value added was initially accepted with a time scale over which this would rise to 80 per cent.[29]

Nissan is by no means the only Japanese vehicle producer to experience this form of British pragmatism. In 1978 Mitsubishi's plans to manufacture trucks in the UK were abandoned after two years of negotiations with the Department of Industry;[30] while in 1982 the government discouraged Toyota's proposed £10m equity investment in Lotus, apparently to avoid further antagonising other European governments by allowing another 'Trojan horse' into Europe, but also for fear of prejudicing the prospective Nissan project. Japanese automobile technology has, of course, been transferred to the UK by other routes, as witnessed in the BL/Honda relationship.

Some of the most obvious conflicts between the strategies of multinational companies and UK national interests continue to show themselves in the automobile industry. The system of 'tied imports' has been shown to have dramatically reduced the UK content of the car market from some 90 per cent in 1969 to 34 per cent in 1984.[31] The subsequent net trade deficit of the UK car industry and the contribution of individual firms to this position has thus become an area for close scrutiny by government (see Chapter 3). Ford and General Motors have been subject to considerable pressures as a result. For example, between 1980 and 1983, Ford's contribution to the UK balance of payments moved from a positive £60 million to a deficit of £680 million. While the company's UK content was around 80 per cent, in products built in the UK, it has been running its UK plants well below capacity and depending heavily on imported products to improve market share in the past decade. The General Motors position has been subject to even more severe criticism, since by the mid-1980s, there was only around a 22 per cent UK content in its UK sales. In this case, again the growing UK demand was met by Continental plants. There is much evidence that successive ministers in the Department of Trade and Industry have put pressure on both companies to achieve a better balance of trade, although details in timing and targets are not available.

What then should the inward investor conclude from this dimension of UK policy? If similar sectoral conditions prevail, limited use of performance guidelines (if not explicit requirements) are effectively now regarded as part of the UK portfolio. For some, the best defence will remain that of encouraging their own suppliers to move to the UK in order to meet both the demands of competitiveness and local content, a strategy well tested, for example, by Japanese automobile producers within South East Asia. For others, and perhaps they are in the majority, greater attention will be paid to the real and potential demands for a measure of 'trade balance' in the selection of locations which have well developed supply infrastructures. Such practices were seen in Chapter 4 to be present in the electronics industry.

EEC POLICY AND INWARD INVESTMENT IN THE UK

In the EEC and other international organisations dealing with multinational businesses, UK attitudes have been traditionally cautious, with support being given to voluntarist approaches to international regulation. At this level it is clear that the policy stance has often changed markedly with governmental change. This is witnessed by the strong support of the UK government in 1977 for the EEC code of conduct for European multinationals operating in South Africa; while in contrast the Conservative government in the early 1980s consistently opposed the adoption of measures specifically targeted at international companies, especially in the field of industrial relations.[32]

Like the UK itself, the EEC has no regulatory policies which set out purely to deal with inward investment in member countries. Indeed, relatively few EEC measures address multinational corporations at such, and where they do, the thrust is towards scale and the efficient operation of markets rather than ownership. Community policy towards the MNE has, however, been developing since the early 1970s and has been in a more active phase since the early 1980s. 1970–3 was a preparatory period of fairly general declarations of intent, identifying some key sectors for EEC measures. From then on until 1976–7 relatively little happened in the aftermath of the oil crisis. Thereafter, in part encouraged by parallel OECD work and external UN and allied pressures, a whole series of rules and decisions have emerged with considerable MNE implications in areas such as employment protection, anti-trust and information disclosure. These developments reflected a desire to employ specific measures to contain disbenefits in some sectors, avoiding the route to EEC codes of conduct; the operation of an attempt at investment harmonisation as between MNEs; and a desire to encourage European MNEs by removing obstacles to a single EEC market, an objective often resented by US MNEs operating in Europe. The fact that by 1981 over one third of the 160 or so substantive decisions taken by the Commission on competition policy were directed towards MNEs (of European and foreign origin), gives some indication of the attention paid to them.

There is no reason to suggest that inward investors in the UK are more or less prone to the effects of EEC policies on multinationals than in other member states. But it is necessary to consider both how existing policies have had an impact on MNE practice and how UK governments react to EEC policy initiatives for the future. Thus, ensuing sections briefly pursue these themes.

Anti-trust

EEC anti-trust measures, with their dual thrust against cartelisation and monopoly, have been one of the most aggressively developed policy areas since the late 1970s. Often inspired by US practices, European anti-trust measures have now emerged as capable of cutting deeply into the strategies adopted by both American and Japanese investors in recent years.[33] The EEC's declared aim is to counter the long-term growth of oligopoly which emerged over the 1970–80 period. Specific sectors have long since been identified as oligopolistic or displaying tendencies in that direction. Among them are chemicals, electronics and motor manufacturing. Going further, specific firms have been shown to display high shares in key markets and thus be prone to appear on any EEC hit list. Among these in the UK are inward investors such as Kodak, Roche, Heinz, IBM, Carnation Foods and Hoover. Coming late into this area the EEC has made a mark rapidly, often arriving at quick decisions which· have made a considerable impact on a number of inward investors in the UK as the following examples demonstrate.

Selective distributive systems

These have proved an easy target for EEC regulations in cases where international companies had agreements whose effect is to re-partition the Common Market as part of their own marketing strategy — thus violating Article 85 of the Rome Treaty. As an example, Pioneer Electronic Europe NV, together with its French, British and West German sole distributors, were fined around 5 per cent of Pioneer Europe's annual turnover for preventing parallel imports into France of Pioneer imports from UK and West Germany, where prices were much lower. Another Japanese corporation, National Panasonic (UK) — Matsushita's marketing subsidiary — fell foul of the same legislation by banning exports from Audiotronics, one of its UK dealers. Similarly, in the

continuing saga of European car prices, Ford Werke AG were fined
for protecting their parents' UK market price position by refusing
to supply right-hand drive cars to German dealers wishing to supply
the UK market at prices 30 per cent below those prevailing for Ford
cars in the UK.

Copyright and related rights

Article 85 has also been applied to industrial and commercial
property rights — a key area for R & D intensive inward investors.
The most notable UK case over the recent past was decided in 1983.
Knoll International Inc (US) and S. Hille and Co Ltd were involved
through Hille's UK subsidiary, Form Furniture. Both groups are
mainly in the business of designing high quality furniture. Knoll had
granted Hille-Form exclusive manufacturing and distribution rights
to UK and Ireland for its various 'programmes' — most of which
were created by internationally famous designers and protected by
trademarks, copyrights and so on. Hille-Form was not allowed to
sell in the rest of the EEC. The exclusive licence agreement was in
effect terminated by the Commission, on the grounds that the
products were not new enough to justify exclusivity, nor was the
investment involved sufficiently high to restrict the copyrights in
that way. This case was settled following preliminary investigations.

Termination of refusal to sell

Another 1983 case involved both Polaroid Nederland and Polaroid
UK. The former was approached by a small Dutch firm (SSI
Europe) for a large order of instant film. Polaroid Nederland refused
to supply on the grounds that the quantity supplied was far in excess
of that required for either the Dutch or European market. The UK
company was also asked to supply but, anxious to know the destination of the shipment, it too requested information. Although the sale
to SSI Europe was again abandoned while this abuse of dominant
position was under formal investigation, this type of case defines the
boundary conditions for many others.

Pricing policy in the motor vehicle industry

For a number of years this has been a major source of contention,
with the Commission's attention being frequently drawn to significant differences in prices net of tax for motor vehicles as between
one member state and another. Table 6.2 shows that these became
more pronounced in the early 1980s. By 1982 prices before tax in

Table 6.2: Motor vehicle before tax prices in the European Community in three engine capacity categories

Year	Country	UK	D	F	I	NL	B	L	IRL	DK
					(UK index = 100 for each year)					
1975	a	100	97.2	102.3	100.7	91.1	86.4	87.3	93.4	85.9
	b	100	101.6	102.6	108.9	97.7	94.3	96.5	95.7	89.2
	c	100	94.5	99.0	100.6	91.5	89.9	90.2	90.2	84.3
	d	(100)	(97.8)	(101.3)	(103.4)	(93.4)	(90.2)	(91.3)	(93.1)	(86.4)
1980	a	100	81.0	79.0	85.0	69.0	65.0	72.0	75.0	58.0
	b	100	83.0	81.0	92.0	78.0	75.0	79.0	84.0	66.0
	c	100	78.0	81.0	84.0	77.0	72.0	70.0	87.0	70.0
	d	(100)	(80.7)	(80.3)	(87.0)	(74.7)	(70.7)	(73.7)	(82.0)	(64.7)
1981	a	100	68.3	69.7		65.0	63.7	64.5	87.5	50.0
	b	100	72.1	76.3		68.0	67.8	66.9	80.7	54.3
	c	100	75.6	69.1		63.7	64.2	62.2	81.6	55.7
	d	(100)	(72.0)	(71.7)		(65.6)	(65.2)	(64.5)	(83.3)	(53.3)
1982	a	100	71.5	70.0	72.0	68.5	60.0	58.0	93.0	48.0
	b	100	78.4	74.4	78.2	73.9	58.2	65.7	90.0	57.1
	c	100	75.3	72.9	81.3	73.3	65.9	64.6	97.0	·59.9
	d	(100)	(75.1)	(72.4)	(77.2)	(71.9)	(61.4)	(62.8)	(93.3)	(55.0)

Notes: a < 1,000 cc; b 1,000 to 1,500; c > 1,500 cc. d = average.
Source: European Economic Communities (1983), *Twelfth report on competition policy*, Brussels, Table 9, p. 178: for 1975 and 1980, Eurostat survey; for 1980 and 1982, BEUC survey, Commission calculations. The prices in national currencies were converted into ECU. The sample used comprises some 15 models in their standard version for each country, without any adjustment for the different equipment supplied as standard.

the UK were almost double those in Denmark. Table 6.2 does not take differences in purchasing power parities into account, which would for example have worsened the 1980 differential between the UK and West Germany (108 to 70, instead of 100 to 80.7). There are many variables which could explain these price differences. These include exchange rates and inflation, differences in purchasing power, in consumer preferences, in extras within models, tax systems, price control arrangements, transport and distribution costs and so on. In the EEC view [34] none of these can adequately explain the scale of the differentials in the table, and they regard the UK situation as an example of partitioning of the European market. One element of the price differences lies in the existence of British Leyland as a high cost producer. The other key dimension in the picture is the behaviour of the major multinational car producers in the UK market. Ford has recently been the usual price leader, with GM taking the initiative on occasion. Thus rises in the value of sterling did not in fact result in a decline in car import prices in the UK in the early 1980s. Parallel imports were limited both by technical factors (principally the supply of right-hand drive vehicles) and by dissuasive practices by European manufacturers, including refusal to sell, aligning continental right-hand drive cars to UK prices, very long delivery dates and so on. The EEC has acted on a number of these practices as observed earlier, while continuing pressure from the UK consumer associations has increased the flow of parallel imports.

The matter is by no means settled. It is complicated by the integration of production systems within Europe, an area in which, as was noted previously, Ford, Vauxhall and Peugeot/Talbot have led. The application of European sourcing policies involving 'tied imports' constitutes diminished grounds for the UK price differentials. A recent House of Lords Committee[35] on this topic therefore welcomed EEC proposals to investigate any price differentials exceeding twelve per cent between member countries while at the same time recognising that manufacturers are expected to use all their ingenuity to avoid any new EEC rules.

Other aspects

EEC anti-trust initiatives do not always have a restraining effect on multinationals in UK or elsewhere. A number of publicly declared cases attest to this. Among permitted forms of cooperation in the last five years has been the continuation of joint R & D agreements across national boundaries. Equally several mergers involving multinational investment were approved in the face of allegations of abusing a dominant position, including the 28 per cent equity purchase in Eagle Star (Holdings) Ltd of the UK by the German-based Allsanz Versicherung AG.

Labour laws

Since the mid-1970s developments in this policy area have caused widespread concern in most multinational companies in Europe simply because they are based on the proposition that employees should have a greater involvement in the conduct of a company's activities. The EEC's labour law programme has two principal dimensions, namely that concerned with employment protection and that with employee consultation. The former emphasis was expressed in two EEC directives respectively aligning the laws of member states on company responsibilities in the event of mass dismissals (February 1975) and employee rights in cases of changes in company ownership or control (February 1977). However by the mid-1980s neither of these directives was fully implemented into national laws, although both required that companies envisaging redundancies or acquisitions should have prior consultations with workforce representatives with a view to these affecting final managerial decisions. These measures were designed to ensure that MNEs face a minimum standard of law in Europe and thus do not select sites in the EEC on the basis of legislative differentials. Implementation procedures on both these measures have been markedly slow within the UK, the acquired rights directive in particular requiring a new legal departure for the UK. The UK did introduce the necessary legislation to incorporate the 1975 directive, in the form of Sections 99 to 107 of the Employment Protection Act, which came into force in March 1976. These sections did in fact go well beyond the basic requirements laid down in the directive, probably because the Labour government of the day were sympathetic to its aims.

Whereas the establishment of minimum protection standards for local European workforces of MNEs is controversial but acceptable, the creation of entirely new information and consultation rights which are ultimately aimed at headquarters management, is quite a different matter. Into this latter category fall the Fifth Directive on worker participation (initiative in 1972) and the highly contentious Vredeling initiative on employee information and consultation in multinational companies (in the latest draft domestic enterprises may also be included) which dates from 1980.[36] It is particularly in the Vredeling context that the irreconcilable concerns of the company and trade unions come together. The one defending the essential independence and flexibility of strategic management, the other demanding the rights to be consulted in such processes. The Vredeling proposal is directed to the multinational undertaking as a single legal entity, thereby removing the potential differential dispensing of information as required by national law and exposing the company on many employment-sensitive issues.

It is not the purpose of this section to appraise these proposals in detail, but rather to consider UK attitudes towards them in that they act as indicators of what the inward investor might expect in the UK in the late 1980s. The UK government's consultative document on both proposals issued in November 1983 made it clear that it had profound reservations about them. In particular the view is expressed that such legislation would contribute nothing to the establishment of a common market, but would rather increase employers' costs and damage the competitive position of industry in the Community. Further it was argued that 'the effects in the UK would be particularly damaging because of the inappropriateness of such legislation to the general structure of industrial relations in this country and because of the UK's relatively high share of the Community's inward investment.'[37] Given the strength of opposition to these proposals from Government and business interests in the UK it seems almost certain that the UK will attempt to block the implementation of both of them. The whole issue is further complicated by the inconsistencies between the two proposals, emanating as they did from two separate Commission directorates. Even after many amendments the Fifth Directive and Vredeling would, for example, currently require different attitudes to secret information, different time scales of reporting on the company's financial position and considerable legal wrangles over the definition of 'parent undertaking', 'administrative organ' and so on. In addition there are a number of implementation problems peculiar to the UK situation according to bodies such as the Engineering Employers' Federation. They argue that multi-unionism and the absence of single industry-based unions, together with the more adversarial attitudes towards collective bargaining and industrial relations, make it very difficult to achieve harmonisation through a superstructure of common obligations which do not fit into the cultural foundations of all member states.

Turning to the future, it is probable that the UK will continue to oppose both measures. Vredeling can only be approved if all the members of the Council of Ministers vote in favour of it; any one country's opposition is enough to veto it. While the Fifth Directive can be approved without unanimity (with a 'qualified majority'), it is probable that further drafting will continue until the late 1980s and in the process be toned down considerably before approval is sought from the Council of Ministers.

Corporate responsibilities

It will perhaps be clear from the comments above that the Fifth Directive acts as a link between the EEC efforts to legislate for a greater managerial focus on issues of concern to employees, while at the same time creating an organ of control over executive decisions. So worker participation and the proposed two-tier board system are designed to link EEC company and labour law. These measures again have a special impact in the UK (and France) in that they require adjustments in the single board structure, in contrast to the supervisory board system prevailing in Germany, Denmark and the Netherlands.

Other proposals in this area are more directly designed for multinational business. In particular the objective of the draft Ninth Directive aims to 'unlimit' the liability of the parent for the subsidiary. Such measures reflect a growing European (and OECD) concern that there is an inadequate level of responsibility imposed by national laws on a parent company in its dealings with its affiliates. Business interests are hostile to any such proposals on the grounds that they offend the very basis of capital investment, namely limited liability and detract from the flexibility to manage the MNE as a single, unified entity. Again this proposal is at an early preliminary stage with little prospect of its early application, if ever.

Now adopted by member states, the Seventh Directive on group accounts, represents a further move to reform the financial account-ability of multinational companies in Europe. Its principal impact will probably be on companies headquartered in Europe, as well as on non-European firms whose requirements on consolidated accounts offend its various clauses. The major requirement is a worldwide consolidation for any multinational corporation with significant operations in the EEC. Publicly-held US multinationals already have to meet similar requirements as laid down by the Securities and Exchange Commission, and so would be little affected. The contrary is, however, true for privately-held US companies and the growing number of Japanese firms in Europe. On a similar vein the EEC has, since a 'mutual assistance directive' of 1977, been endeavouring to increase the flow of information between the tax authorities of the member states in order to stop the artificial transfer of profits within corporate groups. As to whether this will prove to be the precursor of an EEC transfer pricing code, only time will tell. But it does again signal EEC intentions.

Control of state aids

Community action to coordinate regional financial incentives dates from 1971. It was initially concerned with distinguishing between central and peripheral areas, in order to limit national discretion in aid schemes in central regions and reduce competitive bidding. Although not specifically directed towards international investment, the aid ceilings which have emerged under Articles 92–94 are perhaps the most important EEC constraint on inward investment attraction. One of the benchmark cases in 1980 was that concerning the Dutch government and the US tobacco multinational Philip Morris, while later that year a judgement was given by the court against the Belgian government over aid to an Exxon refinery. It is to be expected that the most intensive aid scrutiny will initially be directed to the most attractive international locations or to the areas in most direct competition with each other. An illustration of the latter emerged in the UK in 1983 when the Commission opened an Article 93(2) procedure against training aids of £10 million which were proposed for a Hyster plant in Scotland. To date such instances are relatively unusual, although all aid packages negotiated by member countries are subject to EEC approval. In the light of the evidence of Chapters 3 and 4, further constraints in this area could pose serious problems within some of the UK regions, especially with new investment packages.

In the context of this discussion of UK policy measures and directions, most of the EEC 'measures' and proposals (excluding anti-trust) are a backcloth to MNE operations. In general the UK is out of step with much of the EEC in terms of the pace of implementation, but change will come. The UK will not in effect be able to retain a protected status in view of its own high stakes in inward investment. More fundamentally, the UK has not been in sympathy with all the more radical measures considered above. In the likely event of some of them being rejected at EEC level it is improbable that they would feature within UK legislation unless under a Labour government.

OECD POLICY AND INWARD INVESTMENT IN THE UK

The OECD Guidelines, adopted in 1976 as a voluntary code, are in sharp contrast to the emerging EEC legislative framework.[38] They fall into that interesting category of 'soft law', namely a series of 'politically-agreed guidelines for behaviour which cannot be directly legally enforced but cannot either be legitimately infringed'. For the business concerned, such constraints are open-ended, with a price for contravention being measured in negative public relations, weakening negotiating positions and so on. The predominant impact area of the OECD Guidelines has undoubtedly been industrial relations. This is in part due to the fact that the international trade union movement (in the form of the Trade Union Advisory Committee to the OECD — TUAC) has used the guideline on employment and industrial relations as its principal lever to influence managerial decisions — especially in Europe. Such has been the effect of these pressures that it paved the way for the Vredeling initiative, which seeks much stronger mandatory information and consultation rights for trade unions in MNEs. Outwith industrial relations, these guidelines recommend behavioural norms in disclosure of information, competition, financing, taxation, science and technology.

The publicity generated by some of the cases has been considerable and should not be underestimated in the role that they have played in stimulating interest in EEC legislation. By 1984 over two dozen cases had been cited by unions at OECD intergovernmental level as instances where MNEs had broken the spirit or letter of the guidelines. Many others were raised via 'national contact points' set up in 1979. Not all of these cases have been upheld by governments. But the detailing of practices has in itself considerably raised the visibility of MNE issues, even although the OECD Committee on International Investments and Multinational Enterprises (IME) does not act as a judiciary.

Again, the UK has not been the subject of particular focus for reference cases. It is, however, enlightening to consider some examples involving inward investors. In the case of Black and Decker, the General and Municipal Workers Union (through TUAC) alleged a lack of management cooperation in promoting the unionisation of employees in its UK subsidiary and that the company had refused to grant recognition to unions. The OECD did not uphold this view, arguing rather that the MNE was not required to encourage unionisation actively, but that it should ensure the freedom of choice for its employees to organise or not as they saw fit. In a subsequent case, that of Citibank in the UK, the OECD made it clear that management should not discourage employees from unionising. The charge against Citibank by NUBE (the UK National Union of Bank Employees) and FIET (the International Federation of Employees and Technicians) was that the company conducted a worldwide anti-union policy, avoiding their recognition and actively encouraging managers to create an environment where they were unnecessary.

The OECD Guidelines are subject to review in the light of experience. The first review of 1979 led to the setting up of the national contact points referred to above. Such arrangements within national governments were designed to promote the guidelines, collect data on national experience with them and provide a framework for unions and managements to discuss operational problems. Here individual governmental attitudes are again a key determinant of practice. In the UK the contact point is within the Department of Industry, which appears to have taken a very low profile, mainly delivering union complaints and returning managerial reactions. It is highly questionable whether this style of operation falls within the spirit of the guidelines, although there is little general evidence that the contact points were really used to resolve conflicts in other OECD countries. The one exception is perhaps the US, where the Advisory Committee on International Investment, Technology and Development of the Department of State, has been quite active in monitoring the behaviour of foreign MNEs in the US — mainly as regards trade union recognition.

The second review of these guidelines was published in 1986.[39] There has been a tendency for the OECD interest to shift from the exercise of control over MNEs to the encouragement of international investment on equitable terms, especially relative to the changing balance of direct investment as between the US and Europe. Another important pressure towards change lies in the general trade union disappointment with both the substance and the differential application of the guidelines by national governments. The vast majority of issues pursued against individual MNEs have been the product of politically active trade unions in Northern Europe, with over 50 per cent of the complaints being directed towards subsidiaries of the US companies. This series of pressures might well combine with EEC interests to produce a less selective application of the guidelines in the late 1980s, with corporate disclosures, transfer pricing and parental responsibility all emerging more strongly. In any event, the UK government is very unlikely to pioneer the more extensive application of these measures and once again the inward investor could well remain sheltered under the canopy of British self-interest.

CONCLUDING REMARKS

The preceding paragraphs have served to emphasise the variety of objectives which underlie the different strands of UK policy. The enhancement of industrial efficiency, employment, technology transfer and, implicitly, the improvement of competitiveness are all part of the mix and as such feature in benefit/cost assessments. The special features of the British case in the reconciliation of corporate and governmental objectives have also been drawn out. At one level they might be regarded as constraints, given the scale and diversity of British outward investment; while at another, they provide an opportunity, given the level of intra-MNE trade.

Taken as a whole, UK policy is firmly based on the presumption of net national benefit accruing from the foreign sector. As such it is predominantly centred on investment attraction and the maintenance of a favourable environment which would enable the UK to continue to compete with other European countries as an investment location on at least equal terms. How then is the effectiveness of UK policy to be judged? As was hinted in the introduction to the chapter, there are perhaps two distinct levels at which that question has to be addressed. The first is at the aggregate and national level. Measured in terms of employment, investment stock, contribution to structural change in industry and so on, UK policy can be deemed to have been effective. Of course, there are many other factors outwith government policy which account for the role which the UK plays in inward investment.

The second level at which effectiveness is to be judged is both more problematic and more contentious. Not everyone would wish to look for a more specific accrual of net benefit at regional, sectoral or corporate level. Nor would they wish to associate a contribution to long run competitiveness with the foreign-owned sector. The approach taken in this study lies in these directions and views them as complementary to the seeking of aggregate benefit. There is some evidence in this chapter to suggest that these components of UK policy have been growing in recent years and that they have affected particular sectors and investment from particular sources. Hence the earlier styling of the UK policy position as one of bounded prejudice; namely actively and occasionally calculated, but generally benign.

However, what has happened to date falls a long way short of the related points made in the conclusions of earlier chapters, to say nothing of the future agenda emerging ·from Chapter 1. On the positive side, for example, the shaping of the terms and conditions of technology transfer in the oil sector is related to the enhancement of competitive indigenous capacity; and it has been suggested that policy towards pharmaceuticals has had a positive effect on the competitiveness of UK firms. Again the emergence of performance requirements in particular cases is primarily motivated by employment and balance of trade concerns, although such action has some spin off in the improvement of competitive indigenous subcontracting to raise local content. But it is difficult to argue that these policies have been driven by objectives directly related to the enhancement of competitiveness or that there is any planned link between inward investment policy and improving the competitiveness of British-owned industry. To pursue such a link would inevitably involve a more studied approach to the role of foreign investment in individual situations, rather than the implementation of blanket regulations on performance and behaviour. It would, moreover, only be achieved within the framework of an active industrial policy.

These concluding comments have both handed out some plaudits for the past and some pointers for the future. To follow the latter requires a rather different approach to foreign investment and one which is based on a different set of expectations. It is to the exploration of these and an assessment of their realism that the brief final chapter is devoted.

NOTES

1. See for example Carter, C. (ed.) (1981), *Industrial policy and innovation*, Heinemann, London; and Imberg, O. and Northcott, J. (1981), *Industrial policy and investment decisions*, Policy Studies Institute, London

2. One major reason for the 1981 rescue of ICL was that the government was locked into ICL products for much of its own data processing. Rescue and subsequent innovation support has probably been a cheaper option than wholesale change of data processing systems

3. Hodges, M. (1974), *Multinational corporations and national government*, Saxon House, London

4. First report of the Committee on Welsh Affairs (1980), *The role of the Welsh Office and associated bodies in developing employment opportunities in Wales*, HC 731-I, HMSO, London; and Second report from the Committee on Scottish Affairs (1980), *Inward investment*, HC 769-I, HMSO, London

5. Invest in Britain Bureau (1983), *Annual report*, London

6. For a detailed consideration of the operation of LIS see Young, S. (1984), 'The foreign-owned manufacturing sector', Chapter 4 in Hood, N. and Young, S. (eds), *Industry, policy and the Scottish economy*, Edinburgh University Press

7. Wilks, S. (1984), *Industrial policy and the motor industry*, Manchester University Press, p. 261

8. Steuer, M.D., *et al.* (1973), *The impact of foreign direct investment on the United Kingdom*, HMSO, London

9. Bain, A.D., Ashcroft, B.K., Love, J.H. and J. Scouller (1987), *The economic effects of the inward acquisition of Scottish manufacturing companies, 1965–80*, Industry Department for Scotland, Edinburgh

10. Monopolies and Mergers Commission (1976), *Euro-Canadian Shipholdings Ltd and Furness, Withy and Company Ltd and Manchester Lines*, HC 639, HMSO, London

11. Monopolies and Mergers Commission (1980), *Hiram Walker — Gooderham and Worts Ltd and the Highland Distillers Company Ltd*, HC 743, HMSO, London

12. Monopolies and Mergers Commission (1981), *Enserch Corporation and Davy Corporation Limited: a report on the proposed merger*, Cmnd. 8360, HMSO, London, September

13. *The Economist*, 10 April 1984

14. See for example, Bracewell-Milnes, B. (1980), *The economics of international tax avoidance*, Kluwer, Netherlands, pp. 98–101.

15. Among the contentious consultative documents emerging from the UK Board of Inland Revenue on this topic see, *Company residence and tax havens and the corporate sector* (January 1981); *International tax avoidance* (November 1981); *Taxation of international business* (December 1982); *Draft clauses and schedules relating to controlled foreign companies* (October 1983)

16. See Johns, R.A. (1982), 'The British Isles offshore finance centres', *National Westminster Bank quarterly review*, November

17. International Management and Engineering Group of Britain Ltd (1972), *Study of the potential benefits to British industry from offshore oil and gas developments*, HMSO, London

18. The definitions and figures themselves have been the subject of continual controversy. For a critical view see, for example, Mackay, G.A. (1984), 'The oil and oil-related sector', in Hood, N. and Young, S. (eds), *Industry, policy and the Scottish economy*, Edinburgh University Press

19. Monopolies and Mergers Commission (1973), *A report on the supply of Chlordiazepoxide and Diazepam*, HC 197, HMSO, London

20. 'Profits on prescription', *The Economist*, 11 August 1984

21. Points made in Brech, M. and Sharp, M. (1984), *Inward investment: policy options for the UK*, Chatham House papers 21, Routledge and Kegan Paul, London, p. 49

22. A view reflected in Cooper, M.H. (1975), *European pharmaceutical prices 1964–74*, Croom Helm, London

23. Chemicals EDC, (1972), *International price competition*, HMSO, London

24. For a further consideration of the issues see Reekie, W.D. and

Weber, M.H. (1979), *Profits, politics and drugs*, Macmillan, London

25. Lake, A.W. (1976), *Foreign competition and the UK pharmaceutical industry*, NBER working paper 155, National Bureau of Economic Research, Washington, D.C.

26. *The Financial Times*, 6 December 1977

27. Sinclair, S.W. (1978), *Trade adjustment problems to the British radio industry*, Overseas Development Institute, London

28. 'Hitachi was chased away', *The Economist*, 10 December 1977

29. 'Nissan shifts gear', *The Economist*, 29 October 1983

30. Maxcy, G. (1981), *The multinational motor industry*, Croom Helm, London

31. Jones, D.T. (1985), *The import threat to the UK car industry*, Science Policy Research Unit, University of Sussex was used as a source for this section

32. For a useful consideration of the evolution of EEC policies towards multinationals see Robinson, J. (1983), *Multinationals and political control*, Gower Press, London, Part 2

33. For a summary of the applications of competition policy to all types of multinational corporations, see European Economic Communities (1982), *Eleventh report on competition policy*, Brussels, pp. 37–9

34. As considered in the European Economic Communities (1983), *Twelfth report on competition policy*, Brussels, pp. 177–82

35. House of Lords Select Committee on the European Communities (1984), *The distribution, servicing and pricing of motor vehicles*, HMSO, London, August

36. For an extended consideration of these proposals see Blanpain R. *et al.* (1983), *The Vredeling proposal, information and consultation of employees in multinational enterprises*, Kluwer, Netherlands

37. Ibid., p. 56.

38. Organisation for Economic Cooperation and Development (1976), *International investment and multinational enterprises*, Paris

39. OECD (1984), *International investment and multinational enterprises: the 1984 review of the 1976 declaration and decisions*, Paris, July

7

Conclusions and Future Directions

This final chapter has the role of providing a summary and conclusions to *Foreign multinationals and the British economy*, as well as giving some pointers to policy and UK competitiveness in the future. Figure 7.1 provides an overview of the principal thrusts of the book. At its simplest, being concerned with impact and policy, the book has had as its touchstone the 'impact zone' shown in the figure and observed in the introduction to Chapter 6. The basic premise has been that corporate strategy and government policy are closely intertwined and not always compatibly so. As the diagram suggests, some of the chapters, notably 1, 2 and 5 have been concerned with a series of inputs into the MNE decision processes and a resultant range of outcomes. Many of the former have served to remind both corporations and governments that, dynamic though this sector is, it is not immune from dramatic change, restructuring, loss of competitiveness and so on. On the other side, the outcomes, as Chapter 2 indicated, present the UK with both threats and opportunities through new forms of investment and investment from new sources. In this regard it is particularly important to interpret the implications of Chapter 5 for the UK, pointing as they do to more integrated MNE strategies and less country allegiance as such. The signals here are not unequivocal. On the one hand, there is growing cost pressure for higher levels of local supply, through 'just in time' and associated procedures, the net effect of which would be to place a new premium on sound local infrastructure. On the other hand, shortening product cycles and reduced project cost recovery periods enhance mobility in some high technology projects.

The issues at the interface 'impact zone' are seen in Figure 7.1 to arise in two distinct contexts throughout the book. The one dimension concerns the micro and policy aspects of competitiveness and

Figure 7.1: Overview of foreign multinationals and the British economy

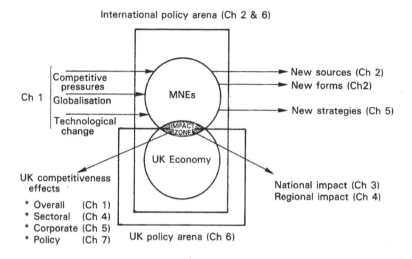

its associated effects in Chapter 1; the other emerges at the more macro level of national (Chapter 3) and regional impact (Chapter 4). As the contents of these chapters have made clear, there are well defined variables interacting within the impact zone, even although there are many outstanding data problems associated with their measurement. Moreover, as the nature of MNE processes and activities changes under the pressure of the new inputs, so the impact zone changes in shape and complexity. As the figure suggests, policy measures attempt whenever possible to encompass these new issues, but Chapter 6 has shown how difficult it is to address many of them in the UK context, and in effect policy steers a route through this zone, making no claim to being truly comprehensive.

Moving from the general to the specific, most of the remainder of this chapter takes Figure 7.1 as a basis for summarising the findings of this book both as regards impact and policy. For the purposes of discussion, three dimensions are highlighted: firstly, the UK as a host to international investment; secondly, the impact of inward investment at national and regional levels, highlighting the crucial aspect of competitiveness; and thirdly, multinationals, the global issues and the UK.

THE UK AS HOST TO INTERNATIONAL INVESTMENT

Leaving aside for the moment the question of benefit accruing from multinational operations, a number of findings emerge which are relevant to the flow of international investment into the UK:

The UK has been losing its predominant position within Europe as a location for inward investment both from the USA and Japan; and Continental European MNE interest is mainly outside Europe

Within an arena in which a long-run slowdown in international investment flows is apparent, competition for this investment is continuing to increase, the gradual enlargement of the EEC being one factor among many in this. Cuts in regional aid in Britain recently have not helped the British competitive position

The Pacific Rim countries (both Japan and the NICs) seem likely to offer major investment opportunities for the rest of this century, reflecting the changing balance of technological leadership. The UK has less of an historical advantage in this region

The investment from the Pacific Rim into sectors in which American subsidiaries and domestic firms are already present, and into potentially over-capacity sectors, raises a range of additional issues of an impact nature

The growth in the 'new forms' of international investment — joint ventures, licensing agreements, management contracts, etc. — is to date mostly apparent in international business activity in developing countries.

Despite the above, changes are taking place, especially in hi-tech sectors, affecting Britain also. These include internationalisation at an earlier stage in the corporate life cycle, smaller average project size, and greater uncertainty about subsidiary growth prospects when these hi-tech MNEs locate abroad (because research breakthroughs fail to materialise, markets develop more slowly than anticipated, spiralling costs create funding problems, etc.) So the risks as well as the rewards are high, meaning that inward investment attraction becomes in part a venture capital funding exercise. There is, furthermore, a tendency, in some sectors at least, to work in corporate families, effectively networking and sharing risks; this is often associated with activity where technological development costs are high, and in such cases the sharing is invariably between MNEs themselves.

Inward and outward investment flows cannot be disassociated from one another. The same disadvantageous locational factors reducing some of the former attractions of the UK as a host, may be stimulating the internationalisation of British companies. If the allegations of job exports linked to outward investment are valid, then the economy will become increasingly reliant on the inward investors.

What is apparent from the above is that more radical changes are occurring in the international investment environment at the present time than have been experienced for 40 years. Examples include the emergence of Japanese car, electronics and machinery MNEs; the overseas expansion through joint ventures and technical cooperation agreements of South Korean firms, including the carmakers Hyundai, Daewoo, Kia and Dong-A; the exhortations from within the economy for Singaporean firms to prepare for multinationality; Spanish entry into the EEC and with it the liberalisation of its rules on foreign investment; strong competition among American states for companies', including foreign MNEs', R & D laboratories, etc. Within this melting pot, there is still room for optimism from a UK perspective. For example, surveys of US electronics firms consistently show UK regions such as Scotland topping the list of desirable European sites for investment. And generally, the balance of evidence points to there being more opportunity than threat to the UK, provided the necessary operational adjustments are made in policy. As Chapter 6 revealed, the major focus of UK inward investment policy has been attraction. Although inherent tensions were revealed between the Invest in Britain Bureau and the territorial agencies, the UK's promotional effort stands comparison with its competitors. Moreover, there are signs of effective responses to the challenges highlighted, in terms of targeting by sector, sub-sector, company and project, with the tracking and monitoring of companies in the development process, flexible support packages for inward investment — what may be described as a merchant banking approach to constructing competitive packages, and linked to the latter, public and private sector collaboration.

Perhaps even more could be done in terms of technology tracking, to enable UK agencies to invest in the development of foreign companies in their pre-internationalisation stage; while risky and controversial, the odds of the UK obtaining the subsequent international investments of such companies will be that much greater. A fairly immediate priority, in addition, must be to increase attraction efforts in the Pacific Basin. Longer term, if the growth in new

244

forms of international business activity extends into developed countries, there will be a requirement for attraction agencies to operate across the whole spectrum of technology transfer and market exploitation methods rather than focus solely on inward investment. Equally, these trends place greater dependence on indigenous company boards and management teams and less on government attraction agencies. To maintain UK competitiveness for all types of international investment, finally, continued attention needs to be paid to the quality of the infrastructure in place in this country.

IMPACT OF INWARD INVESTMENT AT NATIONAL AND REGIONAL LEVELS

The purpose of this section is to draw together the discussion in Chapters 3 and 4 concerning the impact of foreign direct investment on the United Kingdom. The broad conclusion for the country as a whole was that the balance of evidence was continuing to point towards net benefit, albeit with much more variability than was the case when earlier studies were undertaken. Turning to individual components of impact, a number of observations may be made:

From a market structure viewpoint the conclusion was, as expected, that MNEs have assisted in the UK's economic restructuring. This is of considerable significance in an economy whose major problem has been and probably remains (witness the fight to save declining heavy industries in the regions) the slow pace of restructuring in response to technical change. The converse of this conclusion is, of course, equally valid, namely that multinationals have made the UK economy more vulnerable to fluctuations in international demand and supply conditions

Despite the above, the composition of the direct capital inflow into the UK has been moving towards less technology-intensive sectors, with foreign MNEs in the more technology-intensive industries expanding abroad much faster than in the UK

There are still considerable uncertainties about the impact of foreign acquisitions on the British economy, and this is certainly an area where policies need to be clarified. Is it necessary to change the onus of proof so far as inward acquisitions are concerned?

Subsidiary R & D has an important contribution to make in the

245

technology performance of the economy. Britain has not declined as a centre for multinational R & D; but the indicators reveal that the foreign share of overall UK R & D has been, if anything, falling, and R & D/sales and employment ratios for foreign subsidiaries have been growing much more rapidly in Germany than in Britain

Inward investment is generally considered to have had beneficial effects on the UK's trade performance and the balance of payments, and will continue to do so while the inward capital stake is growing. The Select Committee on Overseas Trade highlighted the deterioration in the UK balance of payments position attributable to electronics and automobiles, sectors with a substantial foreign presence, and this is likely to remain as a cause for concern; while the dependence of British exports on a small number of multinationals may be equally problematic

Within a general environment in which technological innovation is having major job replacing effects, few criticisms can be levelled at the foreign sector as regards employment performance. And transfers of innovative foreign personnel and labour utilisation practices could have positive demonstration effects on domestic firms

It is, in fact, in the crucial area of linkage and spillover effects that the major disappointments are evident. Principally on the basis of weak linkages and very limited spillovers, Chapter 4 on 'Foreign multinationals in the UK assisted areas' concluded that MNEs have not and will not cure deficiencies in the competitiveness of the regions. The regional economies can in some ways be regarded as classical dual economies, with the hi-tech MNE subsidiaries somehow cocooned, like the antiseptic work environs of their electronics factories, from the real problems of the assisted areas.

What is portrayed, therefore, is a foreign sector in Britain which outperforms indigenous industry and, therefore, makes a positive and welcome contribution to the economic well being of the country, particularly in a structural sense. Comparisons with parent operations and perhaps with foreign subsidiary activities in some other European countries may not be quite so favourable; and foreign industry in Britain has only had very limited effects in improving the competitiveness of the economy as a whole. The two points are linked, and derive from the micro and software deficiencies of the economy as illustrated in Figure 1.2. It is the case that the strategies established by parent MNEs will influence both the relative position of British subsidiaries within corporate networks and linkages with, for example, the indigenous supply industries in Britain. However, British management and labour performance, in turn a function of the deep-rooted socio-economic factors of attitudes, culture, education, etc. will also affect both the performance of foreign subsidiaries in the UK and the ability of British suppliers to sell to the multinationals. The challenge is to replace this 'vicious circle' by a 'virtuous circle', in which the presence of dynamic international companies in the economy helps to foster an entrepreneurial culture through supply etc. linkages and through the spin off of managers into new business starts; in which such activity evokes new responses from the financial sector by raising the demand for venture and development capital; and through which the UK's competitive position within the international economy is improved.

What precisely could be done to break into and reverse the circular sequence? Increasing the interaction between the foreign-owned and indigenous sectors by policy measures is difficult, some might say impossible, given EEC and OECD constraints and the likelihood of adverse effects on British overseas investment and trade relationships in general. Governmental pressure has been used to try to expand local content in the consumer electronics and automobile sectors. However, in relation to the latter, 1987 signs of a revival in foreign carmakers activities in Britain were as much to do with currency relationships, and the strength of the DM against the £, as government and media moans. So while it may be possible to sustain the UK as a welcoming host nation for international business activity in whatever form, it will be much more difficult to capitalise fully on the specific benefits which could accrue from such activity. Certainly it is possible to conceive of industrial strategy and labour market policies as pursued effectively in other countries which could impact upon the problem areas discussed here, but these would not be specific to the multinational sector.

MULTINATIONALS — THE GLOBAL ISSUES AND THE UK

Before discussing policy questions any further, it is advisable to move to the final and key theme concerning the interaction between multinationals, globalisation and the United Kingdom. It was indicated at the start of this book that the globalisation and technology imperatives represented agendas for the future, with their full impact likely to be felt only in the last years of the twentieth century. While this is true, multinational strategic change was shown in Chapter 5 to be a major variable influencing MNE impact in the UK through the 1970s and 1980s also. Many American MNEs which set up their first European manufacturing facilities in the 1950s and 1960s have gone through a series of strategic changes in the direction of European integration, although their responses to the new challenges posed by global competition are not yet obvious. Newer entrants, including the Japanese, still appear in the main to be directing their operations towards supplying the European market as a whole; although there are instances where companies have taken the decision not to duplicate all of their manufacturing investments in different continents, implying single or dual sourcing of certain components/products for world markets. And there are (isolated) cases of MNEs which have moved in the direction of divisional responsibilities for subsidiaries in host countries such as the UK.

The strategy perspective provides an important means of distinguishing between MNEs in terms of their impact on the UK economy. Although there is virtually no research evidence on the subject, Figures 5.3 and 5.4 highlighted some of the 'strategy types' likely to be present in the multinational sector and their impact in relation to employment, the balance of trade, technology transfer and entrepreneurial capacity. The conclusion was that what were termed Miniature Replicas and Rationalised Manufacturers were predominant in Britain, deriving from strategic reorientation among the established MNEs and the early stage of development of recent entrants. The latter group possess some desirable characteristics, such as integrating the British affiliate into the multinational's global corporate system, but generally the direct benefits associated with these operations were considered to be quite limited and/or indirect effects were negligible. The balance of argument was seen to favour another group — Strategic Independent affiliates with World Product Mandates. As far as can be ascertained there are few foreign subsidiaries in the UK in this category at present. Their characteristics include subsidiary autonomy with overall responsibility for all aspects of R & D, manufacturing and international marketing; and the presumption would be of strong linkages into the domestic sector and, with the presence of a range of managerial decision-making functions, greater possibilities for entrepreneurial spin offs.

In an era in which the development of internationally- or globally-focused corporate strategies is becoming ever more critical to gain and sustain international competitiveness, increasing attention will inevitably be paid to strategy formulation and implementation at the level of the foreign affiliate too. On reflection it is apparent that much of the earlier discussion concerning centralisation and autonomy, the existence of 'branch plants' in the assisted areas, the presence or absence of R & D, etc. can be encompassed within the subsidiary strategy theme. The next question is whether UK policy can help in encouraging or requiring 'desirable strategies'. Every inward investment authority knows precisely the direction in which it would like to see MNE affiliates develop, with higher status decision-making functions, expanded local content, more R & D and so on. The attitude to date has been that few of these can be negotiated on other than a project-by-project basis and only by using very selective incentives. Even then projects can change in shape dramatically in the early years of their operation. Once again, moreover, the constraints placed upon the UK as a member of the European Community emerge. And in any event internationalisation and globalisation are processes which pose policy problems for any one nation state. If a policy approach directed in some way towards subsidiary strategies is rejected as impracticable or undesirable, the alternative must be in the maintenance of the UK environment as one within which parts of international corporate networks can grow and develop, with adjustment assistance to ease the domestic problems associated with global restructuring.

Before concluding on this, there is merit in reviewing the policy debates which have taken place in Canada on the subject. As Chapter 5 indicated, this is virtually the only country where serious attention has been given to the attraction of world product mandates. In December 1983, the federal government in Canada announced that as part of an aggressive trade drive, the establishment of world product mandates for foreign affiliates would be encouraged through competition policy and direct funding.[1] Policy advice and action on WPMs has come from a variety of government departments and agencies, including:

The Department of Supply and Services, which advocated the use of the federal government's $6 billion annual purchasing requirements as a lever to encourage WPMs

The Foreign Investment Review Agency (FIRA — now defunct), which tried to obtain undertakings regarding exclusive export rights for Canadian subsidiaries or exclusive responsibility for R & D and manufacturing of specific product lines

The Department of Regional Industrial Expansion which

supported the use of duty remission schemes, loan guarantees and
industrial assistance programmes to obtain WPMs

The Government of Ontario, which considered using a preferential purchasing policy to require WPMs.

These various measures did lead to a number of WPMs in product
areas such as speciality chemicals, pneumatic timing relays, sealing
compounds, equipment and software for monitoring industrial
processes, and helicopter engines. Other WPMs reported at foreign
affiliate level in Canada have included small gas turbines, inertial
navigation systms, temperature control systems and an orbital
sander.[2] Serious problems have been encountered, nevertheless,
and not only in terms of the obvious cost to the public treasury.
Complaints of discrimination by the private sector in Canada, the
fear of adverse reactions by the international business community
outside Canada and bilateral tensions with the US represented
further constraints; in the context of the latter, the US brought a
formal complaint before the GATT in 1982 and also raised the issue
with the OECD in relation to the principle of 'national treatment'.
In any event the interventionist policy approaches in Canada effectively ended in September 1984 when the Progressive Conservative
Party of Canada came into power.

It is apparent that the negative constraints existing in Canada
appear in much sharper focus in Britain. What is concerning is that
these questions have not been considered to any extent in the UK.
From a policy perspective, this chapter has shown that the closer one
gets to corporate strategy and corporate behaviour the weaker is the
UK inward investment policy response. The piecemeal approaches
to increasing local content, etc. still do not conceive of UK
subsidiaries as part of multinational corporate systems.

Clearly there would be merit in an extensive policy debate in
Britain directed towards multinationals and competitiveness, but a
few initial thoughts may be in order. Leaving aside the possibilities
of coordinated action at EEC level, of integrated, sectorally-based
industrial policies, and of significantly increasing expenditures on
industrial assistance (which, at least as far as regional policy goes,
is substantially inward investment assistance), there are still various
options open. For example, assistance packages could be made even
more selective, against certain types of impact such as subsidiary
roles or subsidiary R & D. The limited evidence on the latter subject
has suggested that 'negative inducements' (e.g. permission to invest
or sell in a country is only given against an undertaking to establish

250

an R & D unit) are more effective than incentives, but the latter could be considered.[3] At present assistance schemes are job-related and do not face in the direction of competitiveness. Once again greater selectivity could involve linking incentives to the quality of jobs.

The most problematic issues concern relationships between the foreign and indigenous sectors. Although formal local content conditions would contravene GATT rules, the Japanese seem prepared to accept 'undertakings' and it might be possible to develop this into some type of local content policy. Other options might focus on the methods of using international firms as vehicles for promoting indigenous industry, e.g. MNEs running training courses for potential suppliers, seconding managers into supply industries, etc. Within an increasingly integrated and interdependent world economy, the challenge thereafter is to encourage and prepare these indigenous supply companies to internationalise themselves.

CONCLUSIONS

The overall conclusion of this book is that foreign multinationals never have been and never will be anything other than a modest palliative for the British economy. Certainly their impact on UK competitiveness has been limited. Of course, with the world moving even closer to the reality of the 'global village', the interdependencies between Britain and the multinationals (foreign and UK) can only grow. For that reason and for the reason of continuing structuring defects in the economy, there is no option but to continue to compete vigorously and professionally for inward investment and whatever other international business forms evolve to complement or supplement this in years to come. But Britain's competitive weaknesses will not be solved by multinationals. Policy measures may be implemented to improve linkages and spillovers and other aspects of impact as indicated above, and MNEs may indeed comply with such policies, even to the extent of allocating world product mandates to their foreign affiliates in Britain, where there is a coincidence with their global strategies. Once again, however, the benefits for competitiveness can only be small. It is tempting, indeed, to go so far as to argue that by disguising underlying weaknesses in the British economy, MNEs have in fact delayed the necessary efforts to improve competitiveness in indigenous companies.

251

NOTES

1. Sarna, A.J. (1986), 'Direction of policy on world product mandates', in Etemad, H. and Dulude, L.G. (eds), *Managing the multinational subsidiary*, Croom Helm, London

2. Rugman, A.M. and Bennett, J. (1982), 'Technology transfer and world product mandating in Canada', *Columbia Journal of World Business*, 17(4), pp. 58–62.

3. Behrman, J.N. and Fischer, W.A. (1980), *Overseas R & D activities of transnational companies*, Oelgeschlager, Gunn and Hain, Cambridge, Massachusetts

Bibliography

Abernathy, W.J., Clark, K.B., and Kantrow, A.M. (1981), 'The new industrial competition', *Harvard Business Review*, September–October

Aharoni, Y. (1966), *The foreign investment decision process*, Harvard Business School Division of Research, Cambridge, Massachusetts

Allied Irish Bank (1981), *Report on attitudes of overseas companies towards investment in Ireland*, Dublin

Amin, A. and Goddard, J.B. (1986), *Technological change, industrial restructuring and regional development*, Allen and Unwin, London

Ashcroft, B.K. and Ingham, K.P.D. (1982), 'The comparative impact of regional policy on foreign and indigenous firm movement', *Regional Studies*, 16, pp. 81–100

Bain, A.D., Ashcroft, B.K., Love, J.H. and Scouller, J. (1987), *The economic effects of the inward acquisition of Scottish manufacturing companies, 1965 to 1980*, HMSO, Edinburgh

Behrman, J.N. and Fischer, W.A. (1980), *Overseas R & D activities of transnational companies*, Oelgeschlager, Gunn and Hain, Cambridge, Massachussetts

Black, J. and Dunning, J.H. (eds) (1982), *International capital movements*, Macmillan, London

Blackburn, A. (1978), 'Multinational enterprises and regional development: a comment', *Regional Studies*, 12, pp. 125–7

Blackwell, N. (1982), 'How to market technology', *Management Today*, December

Blanpain, R. *et al.* (1983), *The Vredeling proposal, information and consultation of employees in multinational enterprises*, Kluwer, Netherlands

Booz, Allen and Hamilton (1979), *The electronics industry in Scotland: a proposed strategy*, Scottish Development Agency, Glasgow

Bos, H.C., Sanders, M. and Secchi, C. (1974), *Private foreign investment in developing countries*, D. Reidel, Dordrecht

Bracewell-Milnes, B. (1980), *The economics of international tax avoidance*, Kluwer, Netherlands

Brech, M. and Sharp, M. (1984), *Inward investment: policy options for the United Kingdom*, Chatham House papers 21, Routledge and Kegan Paul, London

Buckley, P.J., Berkova, Z. and Newbould, G.D. (1983), *Direct investment in the United Kingdom by smaller European firms*, Macmillan, London

———— and Davies, H. (1979), *The place of licensing in the theory and practice of foreign operations*, University of reading discussion papers in international investment and business studies 47, November

———— and Enderwick, P. (1985), *The industrial relations practices of foreign-owned firms in Britain*, Macmillan, London

Carter, C. (ed.) (1981), *Industrial policy and innovation*, Heinemann, London

253

M. Casson (ed.) (1983), *The growth of international business*, George Allen and Unwin, London

Caves, R.E. and Krause, L.B. (1980), *Britain's economic performance*, Brookings Institute, Washington, D.C.

Chemicals EDC (1972), *International price competition*, HMSO, London

Cooper, M.H. (1975), *European pharmaceutical prices 1964–74*, Croom Helm, London

Crum, R.E. and Gudgin, G. (1977), *Non-production activities in UK manufacturing industry*, Commission of the European Communities, Brussels

Department of Trade and Industry (1978), 'Direct exporters and credit terms of exports in 1976', *Trade and Industry*, 32(3), 31 July

—— (1983), *Regional industrial policy: some economic issues*, DTI, London

Doz, Y. (1986), *Strategic management in multinational companies*, Pergamon Press, Oxford

Draper, P., Hood, N., Smith, J. and Stewart, W.S. (1987), *Scottish financial sector*, Edinburgh University Press

Dunning, J.H. (1958), *American investment in British manufacturing industry*, Allen and Unwin, London

—— (1974), 'The future of the multinational enterprise', *Lloyds Bank Review*, 113, July, pp. 15–32

—— (1976), *US industry in Britain*, EAG business research study, Wilton House, London

—— (1979), 'The UK's international investment position in the mid-1970s', *Lloyds Bank Review*, 132, April

—— (1981), *International production and the multinational enterprise*, Allen and Unwin, London

—— (1985), *Multinational enterprises, economic structure and international competitiveness*, John Wiley, Chichester

—— (1985), *US and Japanese manufacturing affiliates in the UK: some similarities and contrasts*, University of Reading discussion papers in international investment and business studies, 90, October

—— (1986), *Japanese participation in British industry*, Croom Helm, London

—— and Cantwell, J.A. (1982), *Joint ventures and non-equity foreign investment by British firms with particular reference to developing countries: an exploratory study*, University of Reading discussion papers in international investment and business studies 68, November

—— and Norman, G. (1979), *Factors influencing the location of offices of multinational enterprises*, LOB research paper 8, Economists Advisory Group Ltd, London, October

Elder, D.W. (1981), *Scottish banking in the light of oil*, MBA dissertation, University of Strathclyde

Etemad, H. and Dulude, L.S. (eds) (1986), *Managing the multinational subsidiary*, Croom Helm, London

European Economic Communities (1983), *Twelfth report on competition policy*, Brussels

254

First report of the Committee on Welsh Affairs (1980), *The role of the Welsh Office and associated bodies in developing employment opportunities in Wales*, HC 731-I, HMSO, London

Fishwick, F. (1982), *Multinational companies and economic concentration in Europe*, Gower, Aldershot

Fitzpatrick, J. (1982), 'Foreign investment in Ireland in the 1980s', *Multinational Business*, 4

Franko, L.G. (1978), 'Multinationals: the end of US dominance', *Harvard Business Review*, November–December, pp. 93–101

Gaffikin, F. and Nickson, A. (1983), *Job crisis and the multinationals: deindustrialisation in the West Midlands*, Russell Press, Nottingham

Guisinger, S.E. and Associates (1985), *Investment incentives and performance requirements*, Praeger, New York

Hamill, J. (1983), 'The labour relations practices of foreign-owned firms in the UK', *Employee Relations*, 5(1)

—— (1984), 'Multinational corporations and industrial relations in the UK', *Employee Relations*, 6(5)

—— (1985), *The internationalisation of British companies: a survey of research and developments*, Strathclyde International Business Unit working paper 85/8, University of Strathclyde

—— (1985), *Multinational Enterprises and the UK's Trade Performance: 1978–83*, Strathclyde International Business Unit Working Paper 85/4, University of Stratchclyde.

—— (1986), *Foreign multinationals: labour and industrial relations effects*, paper presented at an IRM/SIBU conference on 'Scotland and the multinationals', Glasgow, 18 September

Hamilton, G. (1983), 'International codes of conduct for multinationals', *Multinational Business* 3, pp. 1–10

Harrison, R.T. (1982), 'Assisted industry, employment stability and industrial decline: some evidence from Northern Ireland', *Regional Studies*, 16(4), pp. 267–85

Haug, P., Hood, N. and Young, S. (1983), 'R & D intensity in the affiliates of US-owned electronics companies manufacturing in Scotland', *Regional Studies*, 17(6), p. 383–92

Holland, S. (1976), *Capital versus the regions*, Macmillan, London

Hoare, A.G. (1978), 'Industrial linkages and the dual economy: the case of Northern Ireland', *Regional Studies*, 12(2), pp. 167–80

Hodges, M. (1974), *Multinational corporations and national government*, Saxon House, London

Hood, N. and Valhne, J.-E. (eds) (1988), *Strategies in global competition*, Croom Helm, London

—— and Young, S. (1976), 'US investment in Scotland: aspects of the branch factory syndrome', *Scottish Journal of Political Economy*, 23(3), pp. 279–94.

—— and Young, S. (1982), *Multinationals in retreat: the Scottish experience*, Edinburgh University Press

—— and Young, S. (1983), *Multinational investment strategies in the British Isles: a study of MNEs in the assisted areas and in the Republic of Ireland*, HMSO, London

———— and Young, S. (1984), *Industry, policy and the Scottish economy*, Edinburgh University Press

House of Lords Select Committee on the European Communities (1984), *The distribution, servicing and pricing of motor vehicles*, HMSO, London, August

———— (1985), *Report from the Select Committee on Overseas Trade*, 238–I, Session 1984–5, HMSO, London, 30 July

Imberg, O. and Northcott, J. (1981), *Industrial policy and investment decisions*, Policy Studies Institute, London

Incomes Data Services (1980), 'Staff status', *IDS study 227*, October

Incomes Data Services (1984), 'Employee communications', *IDS study 318*, July

Industry Department for Scotland (1983), 'Employment performance of overseas-owned manufacturing units opening in Scotland, 1954–77', *Statistical Bulletin*, No. A1.1, May

———— (1984), *Overseas ownership in Scottish manufacturing industry*, briefing note 2, Edinburgh, March

———— (1986), 'The electronics industry in Scotland', *Statistical Bulletin*, No. C1.1, January

———— (1986), 'Employment in the electronics industry 1975–85', *Statistical Bulletin*, No.C2.1, September

International Management and Engineering Group of Britain Ltd (1972), *Study of the potential benefits to British industry from offshore oil and gas developments*, HMSO, London

Jelinek, M. and Golhar, J.D. (1983), 'The interface between strategy and manufacturing technology', *Columbia Journal of World Business*, spring, pp. 26–36

Jenkins, M. (1981), *British industry and the North Sea*, Macmillan, London

Johns, R.A. (1982), 'The British Isles offshore finance centres', *National Westminster Bank quarterly review*, November

Johnson, S.B. (1984), 'Comparing R & D strategies of Japanese and US firms, *Sloan Management Review*, 25(3), pp. 25–34

Jones, D.T. (1985), *The import threat to the UK car industry*, Science Policy Research Unit, University of Sussex

Jones, J. (1986), 'An examination of the thinking behind government regional policy in the UK since 1945', *Regional Studies*, 20(3), pp. 261–6

Killick, T. (1982), 'Employment in foreign-owned manufacturing plants', *British Business*, 26 November

———— (1983), 'Manufacturing plant openings, 1976–80: analysis of transfer and branches', *British Business*, 17 June

Lake, A.W. (1976), *Foreign competition and the UK pharmaceutical industry*, NBER working paper 155, National Bureau of Economic Research, Washington, D.C.

Lall, S. (1984), 'Transnational and the Third World: changing perceptions', *National Westminster Bank Quarterly Review*, May, pp. 2–16

———— and Streeten, P. (1977), *Foreign investment, transnationals and developing countries*, Macmillan, London

Leigh, R. and North, D.J. (1978), 'Regional aspects of acquisition activity in British manufacturing industry', *Regional studies*, 12(2), pp. 227–45

Lloyd, P.E. and Shutt, J. (1983), *Recession and restructuring in the North West region: the policy implications of recent events*, discussion paper 13, North West Industry Research Unit, University of Manchester

McCalman, J. (1986), *What's wrong with Scottish electronics firms? Local sourcing by foreign electronic companies in Scotland*, working paper 2, Department of Management Studies, University of Glasgow, June

McGreevy, T.E. and Thomson, A.W.J. (1983), 'Regional policy and company investment behaviour', *Regional Studies*, 17(5), pp. 347–58

McInnes, J. and Sproul, A. (1987), 'Electronics employment in Scotland', *Fraser of Allander Quarterly Economic Commentary*, 12(3), pp. 77–82

Macharzina, K. and Staehle, W.H. (eds) (1986), *European approaches to international management*, Walter de Gruyter, Berlin

Manpower Services Commission (1984), *Closure at Linwood: a follow-up survey of redundant workers*, MSC, Edinburgh, April

Mascarenhas, B. (1986), 'International strategies of non-dominant firms', *Journal of International Business Studies*, spring, pp. 1–25

Maxcy, G. (1981), *The multinational motor industry*, Croom Helm, London

Monopolies and Mergers Commission (1973), *A report on the supply of Chlordiazepoxide and Diazepam*, HC 197, HMSO, London

——— (1976), *Euro-Canadian Shipholdings Ltd and Furness, Withy and Company Ltd and Manchester Lines*, HC 639, HMSO, London

——— (1980), *Hiram Walker — Gooderham and Worts Ltd and the Highland Distillers Company Ltd*, HC 743, HMSO, London

——— (1981), *Enserch Corporation and Davy Corporation Limited: a report on the proposed merger*, Cmnd. 8360, HMSO, London, September

Morgan, K. and Sayer, A. (1983), *The international electronics industry and regional development in Britain*, working paper 34, Urban and Regional Studies, University of Sussex, September

National Economic Development Council (1982), *Direct inward investment*, Memorandum by the Secretary of State for Industry to the NEDC, NEDC (82) 7, January

——— (1983), *The Department of Industry's strategic aims*, NEDC, London

——— (1985), *British industrial performance: a comparative survey over recent years*, London

Oakey, R.P. (1983), *Research and development cycles, investment cycles and regional development*, CURDS discussion paper 48, Centre for Urban and Regional Development Studies, University of Newcastle

——— (1984), *High technology small firms: regional development in Britain and the USA*, F. Pinter, London

O'Loughlin, B. and O'Farrell, P.N. (1980), 'Foreign direct investment in Ireland: empirical evidence and theoretical implications', *Economic and Social Review*, 11, pp. 115–85

Oman, C. (1984), *New forms of international investment in developing countries*, OECD, Paris

——— (1986), 'Changing international investment strategies in the North-South context', *The CTC Reporter*, 22, autumn

Organisation for Economic Cooperation and Development (1976), *International investment and multinational enterprises*, Paris

—— (1981), *Recent international direct investment trends*, Paris

—— (1984), *International investment and multinational enterprises: the 1984 review of the 1976 declaration and decisions*, Paris, July

Panić, M. and Joyce, P.L. (1980), 'UK manufacturing industry: international integration and trade performance', *Bank of England Quarterly Bulletin*, March

Parsons, G.L. (1983), 'Information technology: a new competitive weapon', *Sloan Management Review*, 25(1), pp. 3–13

Pelling, H. (1956), *America and the British left: from Bright to Bevan*, Adam and Charles Black, London

Porter, M.E. (1986), 'Changing patterns of international competition', *California Management Review*, 28(2), pp. 9–39

—— (1987), *Competition in global industries*, Harvard Business School Press, Boston, Massachusetts

Pratten, C.F. (1976), *Labour productivity differentials within international companies*, occasional paper 50, Department of Applied Economics, University of Cambridge

Reekie, W.D. and Weber, M.H. (1979), *Profits, politics and drugs*, Macmillan, London

Robinson, J. (1983), *Multinationals and political control*, Gower Press, London

Ronstadt, R. (1977), *Research and development abroad by US multinationals*, Praeger, New York

Rugman, A.M. and Bennett, J. (1982), 'Technology transfer and world product mandating in Canada', *Columbia Journal of World Business*, 17(4), pp. 58–62

Sauvant, K.P. (1986), 'Services, TDF and the Code', *The CTC Reporter*, 22, autumn

Sawers, D. (1986), 'The experience of German and Japanese subsidiaries in Britain', *Journal of General Management*, 12(1), autumn, pp. 5–21

Sayer, A. and Morgan, K. (1984), *The electronics industry and regional development in Britain*, paper presented at an ESRC/CURDS workshop, University of Newcastle upon Tyne, March

Science Council of Canada (1980), *Multinationals and industrial strategy: the role of world product mandates*, Ottowa, September

Scottish Development Agency (1980), *The international offshore oil and gas market*, Aberdeen

—— (1982), *The Scottish electronics subcontracting and components supply industries*, SDA, Glasgow, May

—— (1986), *Electronics Scotland*, Newsletter of the Electronics Division of the SDA, Glasgow

Second report from the Committee on Scottish Affairs (1980), *Inward investment*, HC 769-I, HMSO, London

Secretary of State for Trade and Industry (1983), *Regional industrial development*, Cmnd. 9111, HMSO, London, December

Shepherd, D., Silberston, A. and Strange, R. (1985), *British manufacturing investment overseas*, Methuen, London

Sinclair, S.W. (1978), *Trade adjustment problems to the British radio industry*, Overseas Development Institute, London

Smith, I.J. (1979), 'The effect of external takeovers on employment change in the northern region between 1963 and 1973', *Regional Studies*, 13(5), pp. 421–37

——— (1980), *Some aspects of direct inward investment in the United Kingdom, with particular reference to the northern region*, discussion paper 31, Centre for Urban and Regional Development Studies, University of Newcastle upon Tyne, March

——— (1982), 'Some implications of inward investment through takeover activity', *Northern Economic Review*, February, pp. 1–5

——— (1985–6), 'Takeovers, rationalisation and the northern region economy', *Northern Economic Review*, winter, pp. 30–8

Steuer, M.D., Abell, P., Gennard, J., Perlman, M., Rees, R., Scott, B., and Wallis, K. (1973), *The impact of foreign direct investment on the United Kingdom*, HMSO, London

Stewart, J.C. (1976), 'Linkages and foreign direct investment', *Regional Studies*, 10(2), pp. 245–58

Stopford, J.M. (1979), *Employment effects of multinational enterprises in the United Kingdom*, working paper 5, International Labour Office, Geneva

——— and Dunning, J.H. (1983), *Multinationals: company performance and global trends*, Macmillan, London

——— and Turner, L. (1985), *Britain and the multinationals*, John Wiley, Chichester

Tebbit, N. (1983), 'Industrial relations in the next two decades: government objectives', *Employee Relations*, 5(1)

Telesis Consultancy Group (1982), *A review of industrial policy*, National Economic and Social Council, Dublin

Trevor, M. (1983), 'Does Japanese management work in Britain?', *Journal of General Management*, 8(4), pp. 28–43

Turner, L. (1987), *Industrial collaboration with Japan*, Chatham House papers 34, Routledge and Kegan Paul, London

United Nations Centre on Transnational Corporations (1983), *Transnational corporations in world development, third survey*, New York

United Nations Economic and Social Council (1974), *The impact of multinational corporations on the development process and on international relations: report of the Group of Eminent Persons*, New York

UN CTC (1983), *Salient features and trends in foreign direct investment*, New York

US Congress, Joint Economic Committee (1982), *Location of high technology firms and regional economic development*, US Government Printing Office, Washington, D.C.

US Department of Commerce (1981), *The use of investment incentives and performance requirements by foreign governments*, Washington, D.C., October

Van Nieuwkerk, M. and Sparling, R.P. (1985), *The Netherlands international direct investment position*, Martinus Nijhoff, Dordrecht

Vernon, R. and Davidson, W.H. (1979), *Foreign production of technology-intensive products by US-based multinational enterprises*, a study funded by the National Science Foundation, Boston, Massachusetts, 15 January, mimeo

Webber, D., Rhodes, M., Richardson, J.J. and Moon, J. (1986),

'Information technology and economic recovery in Western Europe: the role of the British, French and West German governments', *Policy Sciences*, September

White, R.E. and Poynter, T.A. (1984), 'Strategies for foreign-owned subsidiaries in Canada', *Business Quarterly*, summer

Wilks, S. (1984), *Industrial policy and the motor industry*, Manchester University Press

Yannopoulos, G.N. and Dunning, J.H. (1976), 'Multinational enterprises and regional development: an exploratory paper', *Regional Studies*, 10, pp. 389–99

Young, S. (1987), 'Business strategy and the internationalization of business: recent approaches', *Managerial and Decision Economics*, 8, pp. 31–46

—— and Hood, N. (1976), 'The geographical expansion of US firms in Western Europe: some survey evidence', *Journal of Common Market Studies*, 14(3), pp. 223–39

Young, S. and Hood, N. (1977), *Chrysler UK: a corporation in transition*, Praeger, New York

—— and Hood, N. (1980), 'The strategies of US multinationals in Europe: a host country perspective', *Multinational Business*, 2

——, Hood, N. and Hamill, J. (1985), *Decision-making in foreign-owned multinational subsidiaries in the United Kingdom*, working paper no. 35, International Labour Office, Geneva

Index

For Product Safety Concerns and Information please contact our EU representative GPSR@taylorandfrancis.com Taylor & Francis Verlag GmbH, Kaufingerstraße 24, 80331 München, Germany

Printed and bound by CPI Group (UK) Ltd, Croydon, CR0 4YY
01/05/2025
01858437-0003